The Spirit of Jesus Unleashed on the Church

The Spirit of Jesus Unleashed on the Church

Acts of the Early Christians in a Changing Culture

RON CLARK

CASCADE *Books* · Eugene, Oregon

THE SPIRIT OF JESUS UNLEASHED ON THE CHURCH
Acts of the Early Christians in a Changing Culture

Copyright © 2016 Ron Clark. All rights reserved. Except for brief quotations in critical publications or reviews, no part of this book may be reproduced in any manner without prior written permission from the publisher. Write: Permissions, Wipf and Stock Publishers, 199 W. 8th Ave., Suite 3, Eugene, OR 97401.

Cascade Books
An Imprint of Wipf and Stock Publishers
199 W. 8th Ave., Suite 3
Eugene, OR 97401

www.wipfandstock.com

ISBN 13: 978-1-62564-891-4

Cataloging-in-Publication data:

Clark, Ron.

The Spirit of Jesus unleashed on the church : acts of the early Christians in a changing culture / Ron Clark.

viii + 196 p.; 23 cm—Includes bibliographical references and index.

ISBN 13: 978-1-62564-891-4

1. Bible, Acts. 2. Bible, Acts Criticism, interpretation, etc. 3. Practical theology. I. Title.

BS2625 .C55 2016

Manufactured in the USA.

TABLE OF CONTENTS

Acknowledgements | vii
1. How Did We Get Here? | 1

SHOULD WE STAY OR SHOULD WE GO?

2. Acts and Jesus Unleashed (Acts 1) | 19
3. The Spirit Comes (Acts 2) | 31
4. Resistance to the Spirit (Acts 3–5) | 43
5. Resisting the Spirit: Community Resistance (Acts 6–9) | 60
6. Resistance from Within (Acts 10–12) | 76

AN EMPIRE SENT BY THE SPIRIT

7. The Second Wave Begins (Acts 13–14) | 89
8. A Council on Foreign Relations Meets (Acts 15) | 105
9. Witnessing in Greece (Acts 16–18) | 118
10. Witnessing in Asia (Acts 19–20) | 140

ENDURING RESISTANCE FOR THE SAKE OF THE EMPIRE

11. On to the Promised Land? (Acts 21–26) | 155
12. Paul Goes to Rome (Acts 27–28) | 167
13. The Spirit Unleashed in the Church Today | 176

Bibliography | 181
Subject Index | 189
Scripture Index | 191

ACKNOWLEDGEMENTS

THIS BOOK IS THE third in a series concerning the restoration of Israel, reconciliation with God, and the acceptance of those on the margins of society. In *The God of Second Chances: Finding Hope in the Prophets of Exile,* I suggested that the prophets were God's messengers who lived in exile and painted an alternate vision for those captives in other countries. They spoke on behalf of God in that they confronted the corrupt leaders of their day and offered forgiveness and grace to those distanced by their sin, shame, and guilt. These men were models for the church today in that we too are called to represent a loving and relational God. We are also called to paint an alternative view of the world for those continuing to suffer shame, humiliation, sin, and fear.

In *Jesus Unleashed: Luke's Gospel for Emerging Christians,* this same God was seen living and teaching among us. Once again those in power marginalized and oppressed other vulnerable people, creating a "social exile." Jesus not only confronted those abusing their power but he offered forgiveness, hope, and acceptance to the "vulnerable ones." Today we continue to be challenged by a Lucan social justice Savior who was criticized by leaders for associating with sinners. He was also the same Lord who claimed, "If anyone is ashamed of me and my words, so will the Son of Man [Jesus] be ashamed when he comes in the Father's glory with his holy angels" (Luke 9:26). We must paint an alternative view of the world as well as live it in the midst of those marginalized by our society.

Finally in *The Spirit of Jesus Unleashed on the Church: Acts of the Early Christians in a Changing Culture,* I maintain that Luke continued his narrative with the themes of restoration, freedom to the captives, and an empire of relationship, holiness, and peace. This trilogy is an attempt to not only discuss God as Father, Son, and Spirit but God as relational; manifested through the prophets, Jesus, the Spirit, and the early Christian leaders.

ACKNOWLEDGEMENTS

Today many speak of "waiting" for the direction of the Spirit. However, Luke reminds us that the Spirit has already come—therefore we must go, led by this same Spirit. It is my prayer that we as a movement will again be a *move*ment rather than an *establish*ment.

I am thankful for Lori, who has been my wife, partner in ministry, best friend, and confidant since 1987. This book is not only a reflection of her support and love, but one that shows her heart for people as she has both challenged me and encouraged me to remember that people matter to God, therefore they must matter to me. To my sons Nathan, Hunter, Caleb, and daughter-in-law Nyla: thank you for your love and support as well. Thank you for pretending to be interested in my writing and helping me to finish this massive project. May we all understand the unity and peace that the Holy Spirit can provide by forgiving two people's past who later marry and raise a family to radiate that same compassion and love of Jesus.

To my church family at Agape Church of Christ who listened to the sermons on Acts in 2013 and offered feedback: I thank you for this journey and your willingness to live out the message of Jesus. To the many Christians who support Agape, our outreach to the marginalized, and our various ministries and internships, we thank you for your generosity. May we together witness to the movement of the Holy Spirit. To my colleagues and graduate students and George Fox Evangelical Seminary: I have learned much from you. I am excited to see the new churches planted, dissertations published, and opportunities for scholarly collaboration that is flowing from the Spirit in our relationship. I have learned much from you and hope that you are as encouraged as I am in the witness of the power of the resurrected Lord. May we all know true unity and shalom in the Spirit of Jesus.

Thank you to Kairos Church Planting, Park Plaza Church of Christ, and Wipf and Stock Publishing for all your encouragement to blend ministry, academics, and theology in these three volumes. To those men and women in the mission field: thank you for going and showing us that Christianity has always had those who fully embrace the book of Acts as Scripture, a plan for ministry, and guidance. May we in America learn from your courage, faith, and willingness to be "bound by the Spirit."

Ron Clark
Agape Church of Christ
2015

1

HOW DID WE GET HERE?

Those who wait in Yahweh will renew their strength. (Isa 40:31)

I QUICKLY STEPPED ON to one of the light-rail cars that run throughout Portland, called MAX. I was in a hurry to connect with one of our outreach groups working on the other side of the downtown area. Each week we gather at the Pioneer Courthouse Square Starbucks for our meeting, study, and prayer. After that we break into teams and visit with many of the homeless camps that include some of our people at Agape. We visit them and make sure that they are safe and had supplies. This is a convenient method of tracking the groups and offering help to those wanting to leave the streets. It is also a convenient way to make sure that the young females in the groups are safe and have access to health and hygiene care.

I had gone out alone to check on a camp and after finishing, walking a couple miles to meet one of our teams. I ran to catch the MAX and quickly hopped aboard as the doors closed. I found an empty section of the train with one person sitting by himself, surrounded by eight vacant seats. I was surprised that this usually crowded car had so many empty seats, as I sat across from the man and began to read. After a minute I realized why the seats were empty. He, like many people in a crowded city, must not have had access to a toilet and it was obvious that he had had an accident. However, I stayed in my seat and read. Having lived in rural Missouri and worked in a livestock company I have smelled some of the worst odors one can imagine. I felt it might also be rude to make a scene, as I was sure he was not pleased with his circumstances.

"Are you reading a book on geology?" he asked. I looked up, smiled, and closed my book, responding, "Close, it's a boring book about archaeology." "I'm sorry to bother you," he said, "you can go back to reading—I won't talk to you anymore." "It's OK," I responded, "do you like geology?"

I have learned, through the Spirit, that when God puts someone in our path, it is our responsibility to listen and explore how the Spirit is working with them. I believe that Jesus is already active in people's lives and is simply waiting for us to catch up. Sometimes I have to take out the earphones, close the book, or put away the iPhone so that I can listen to them.

He told me his name was Mike, and talked about geology, his schooling, and trying to find a job. His group home was nice and he had a loving family. Mike asked me what I did and why I read my book. After a few minutes a young man boarded the train, sat near me, turned up his nose (while looking at me), and then played with his phone. Mike asked him what type of phone he had and the two began to chat.

After a few minutes of conversation he told Mike and I, "I have a medical marijuana card, since I can't work cause of my back injury. I don't use all of it. You guys want any?" He told us that he had more than enough each month and was willing to share. He mentioned that Oregon needed to legalize marijuana since people like him have injuries. "Does it work?" I asked. "What do you mean?" he said. "Pain, does it take away the pain?" I responded. "I dunno," he said, "but it keeps my friends happy." We all laughed.

He and Mike talked about marijuana laws and we discussed the music we liked, as well as restaurants in Portland. It was quiet in our own isolated unit on the crowded train. As the young man stood up at his stop he shook our hands, thanked us, and let us know he had some pot if we needed it, then left. Mike smiled and loudly said, "Nice guy!" About that time a middle-aged man boarded the train, stepped to our area, crinkled his nose, looked at me, and then sat down. He had just finished work and was headed home.

"Cool shirt," Mike loudly exclaimed, "where did you get that?" The man looked up and raised his voice, "Look man, I just got off work—I don't wanna talk, I just want to sit here and be left alone." We were silent. Everyone on the train seemed silent. Awkwardly silent! At the next stop Mike stood up, gave me a fist bump, and left. I looked at the man next to me and smiled. His eyes were tired, but he said, "I'm not being rude, I just don't want to talk. I mean, I know the guy has issues but I'm tired, I want to be left alone. Do you understand?" I knew he was not telling me to leave him alone, yet he felt guilty and wanted to explain why he responded harshly. He may have also felt uncomfortable with the awkward silence that he created on the MAX. I think he truly wanted to care, but he probably was tired, or had a bad day, or didn't want to talk to a man who smelled like human waste. I think that he felt genuine shame for his response and maybe wanted validation.

"It's OK," I said, "we're all tired. Sometimes we don't want to talk." He nodded his head yes. I got off at the next stop. He was hanging his head. I felt bad for all three of my rider friends. One was smelly and lonely, another was high and lonely, and the other was tired and lonely. All three were lonely, and yet Jesus offers relationship. How? That's not the question. Not all who were lonely isolated themselves. Two formed a relationship or at least a conversation while one prevented one from occurring. If Jesus involves relationship then shouldn't we be working to reconcile people to God and each other? The question is, "Are we willing to offer what he offers?"

What is interesting to me is that a pot salesman and a man struggling with hygiene were more accepting of people, including me, than the "working man." I understand we are tired, and I understand that sometimes we want privacy. I have many times wanted to say to people, "please go away" or "I'm doing something—can you stop talking to me?" Fortunately I have not, yet. It's probably the Spirit that reminds me that I have been bought with a price and have a responsibility to honor that price. I also understand that odors can offend us. Even more, I understand that as a Christian (especially an evangelist) I have an obligation to engage people, listen to them, and realize that in public I must be obedient to the Spirit's leading. When the Spirit is unleashed in our world, something that we continually pray for, we have to accept where it leads and who is led to us. Even more, we have to be willing to follow to where the Spirit leads, even if we are intimidated by or uncomfortable with the people at the end of that road. It is not about waiting for Jesus. It is not about Jesus coming to us. It is about following him and going where we are sent.

What I don't understand is how we can cut people off, ignore them, or believe that obedience to the gospel allows some of us to mistreat other humans, who, like us, are made in the image of the Almighty Creator. Over the years I have heard people suggest that we must, like Jesus said to the apostles, "wait for the Spirit" (Acts 1:4). This waiting becomes a time to be alone, isolate, or separate from the hustle and bustle of the streets. We need to be "left alone." This waiting is viewed as our reflection and preparation for a future ministry for Christ. We somehow believe that we should wait until we know what to do. Then we step on the MAX, take a whiff of the air, and ask to be left alone. Interestingly the air we smell tells us what we are to do. We are reminded when we are with people that Jesus has already given us a mission, yet many times we retreat because we want to be left alone to wait and wonder what the Spirit has for us. Or maybe we don't like the mission so we opt for a different assignment that we can accept.

Jesus had told his followers to remain in Jerusalem until the Holy Spirit was given to them. However, the instructions did not end with that command. The charge continued, "But when the Holy Spirit comes upon you, you will receive power and will be my witnesses in Jerusalem, all Judea, Samaria, and to the end of the earth" (Acts 1:8).[1]

WAITING FOR THE LORD

The concept of "waiting" was common in the prophets. The people of God struggled to obey Yahweh and cleave exclusively to their Lord. Throughout the Hebrew Scriptures Israel wavered back and forth between serving Yahweh or the gods of the other nations that seemed more powerful. They struggled to trust that their God would protect and save them and often turned to cultures with mighty armies for help. In turning to these nations they were influenced to live like them and worship the gods that they worshipped. Israelite history was filled with their unfaithfulness, neglect, and abandonment of Yahweh. Israel had become the unfaithful spouse that cheated on their marriage vows, violated the trust that once existed, and abused the partner who offered love, acceptance, forgiveness, and safety. Like an uncaring spouse, Israel flaunted its affairs. Like an arrogant wife Israel offered love to others rather than the one who was devoted and loyal to the marriage.

In addition to this Israel became insensitive, uncaring, and cruel to those in their family. Economic oppression, social injustice, murder, extortion, and abuse were common in the household of God. While Yahweh offered hope and security, the people in positions of power exploited the poor, oppressed the weak, abused the vulnerable, and led the people to turn from their true God. Like an older brother who molests his siblings or introduces

---

1. All Scripture quotations are my translation of *Biblica Hebraica* and *Novum Testamentum Graece*.

them to pornography at a young age, Israel violated trust among its people. Like an aunt who terrorizes her nieces and nephews, Israel oppressed those who sought help from its leaders. Like a cousin who steals from his relatives, some of the Jewish leaders extorted those who were helpless. Israel was accused by God of not only cheating on its Maker but bringing unjust suffering to people in the family.

After centuries of confrontation, repentance, forgiveness, and injustice the prophets were exhausted, as was God's patience. Yahweh had one option left: a divorce (Jer 3:6–10; Isa 54:7; Zech 11:10–11). In the case of the northern kingdom of Israel the Assyrians delivered the divorce papers, kidnapped the people, transported many to their hometown, and repopulated the capital city of Samaria with other Gentiles (2 Kings 17:7–40). The southern kingdom, Judah, saw this disaster—but unfortunately, a century later, did not learn its lesson. The Babylonian army was sent by Yahweh, the hurt spouse, to deliver the news of the breakup, leveled Jerusalem's walls and temple, slaughtered thousands of Jews (faithful and unfaithful), and transported the best and brightest to their capital, leaving the poor to live among the ruins (2 Chr 36:15–21). Yahweh's spouse had crossed the line and now God's honor was a priority. All the world stood in awe as the neighborhood gathered to witness the hurt woman screaming at her husband, throwing his belongings out the window, while he stood in handcuffs, reeling from a hangover, and smelling like other women. It was over and he knew it. No matter how loud he yelled, cried, or begged, the windows were shut, the doors locked, and the relationship over. Amidst the snickering and shock of the neighbors the handcuffed spouse was shoved into a police car and taken to jail.

Yahweh had only wanted loyalty, faithfulness, and devotion. The prophet Jeremiah, like so many other messengers of God, had repeatedly been warning that the Creator simply wanted respect. "When I brought your forefathers out of Egypt and spoke to them, I did not just give them commands about burnt offerings and sacrifices, I gave them this command: Obey [listen to] me, and I will be your God and you will be my people. Walk in all the ways I command you, so that it will be good for you" (Jer 7:22–23). The Hebrew word for "obey" means "listen." Yahweh desired respect, honor, and loyalty. God had given them everything they needed; it was the least they could do. The prophet then said, "But they did not listen [obey] or pay attention. They followed the desires of their evil hearts. They went backward rather than forward. From the time your ancestors left

Egypt until now, constantly I sent you my servants the prophets. But they did not listen or pay attention to me. They were stiff-necked and were worse than their ancestors" (Jer 7:24–26).

Israel struggled for centuries to be faithful to God. Why? The prophet shared with us Yahweh's explanation. The people of God were stubborn, stiff-necked, and had evil hearts. While not everyone disobeyed God, there were leaders among the people who closed their ears to God's voice. They made a choice, they ignored the truth, and they followed someone else. They violated their promise, their covenant, and their vows. While in captivity the prophets reminded the people of God that *they* had made this choice, *they* had walked away from God, therefore *they* were unfaithful. Even Ezekiel confronted those who blamed God for their punishment, "You say, 'The way of Yahweh is not right.' Listen [obey], house of Israel: My way is unjust? Your ways are wrong!" (Ezek 18:25, 29). The people of Judah not only had violated their marriage vows, they had blamed the faithful spouse for not forgiving them and taking them home. However, Yahweh had drawn the line and demanded respect, loyalty, and love.

Yet while in captivity faithful men and women rose up, were devoted to God, displayed courage in the face of foreign oppression, and called the nation to repentance. Leaders such as Daniel, Esther, Nehemiah, Joshua, Mordecai, Ezra, and the prophets Jeremiah, Ezekiel, Haggai, Habbakkuk, Zechariah, Zephaniah, Malachi, Joel, and Obadiah confronted sinful leaders but overwhelmingly offered hope to a nation struggling to believe. While these men and women lived in the ruins of Jerusalem or among the captives in Babylon, Isaiah, Micah, Jonah, Nahum, Amos, and Hosea called the people of Israel to hope, even while under Assyrian colonization. Ordinary people became heroes by the Spirit of Yahweh—faith, courage, and submission to God.

While in captivity or under threat of colonization the people were told to wait and hope.

> Those who wait/hope in Yahweh will renew their strength. (Isa 40:31)

> You must return /repent to your God; practice faithfulness and justice, and wait for your God always. (Hos 12:7)

> As for me, I watch for Yahweh, I rest in God my Savior; my God will hear me. (Mic 7:7)

> Build houses, settle down, plant gardens, and eat the fruit. Marry and have sons and daughters; find wives for your sons and give your daughters in marriage, so that they too may have children. Grow in number while you are there; do not decrease. Seek the peace of the city to which I have carried you into exile. Pray to Yahweh for it, because if it has peace, you too will be at peace. (Jer 29:5–8)

The people of Israel and Judah were told to wait, hope, and live in their foreign home. Those who were faithful listened and served their community, led their people in a foreign land, and honored God through their obedience and repentance. Those surviving in Judah tried to remain faithful among the ruins. Those who had fled to Egypt also continued to serve God and follow Torah in their small communities. Then, at the end of seventy years, God led the people home to Jerusalem. A voice crying in the wilderness prepared the way for Yahweh to lead the nation from the east to Jerusalem (Isa 40:3). The people traveled hundreds of miles to their city to rebuild, restore, and reignite their nation, faith, and relationship with Yahweh. They struggled through the guilt, shame, and resistance in their relationship with their God. How could Yahweh forgive us? Why would God want us? How can we move past this desolate relationship? The land was cursed, creation suffered, people had died, and there was too much bad history. God had consistently said that "this people has always been stiff-necked." Was there any hope of Yahweh's forgiveness, healing, or even love?

The prophets both proclaimed and wrote down the messages of Yahweh. Even though the land had been destroyed Yahweh was willing to create a "new heavens and new earth," in order to take back the divorced spouse (Isa 65:17–25). Yahweh would write the law on their hearts and help them be devoted so that they could be faithful (Jer 31:31; 33:38). The prophets Haggai and Zechariah claimed that God would wipe the slate clean and start over (Hag 2:19; Zech 3:9). It was clear that in order for this to work, Yahweh would have to shoulder the burden of reconciliation, forgiveness, and reestablishing the relationship. Judah was not to be passive in this covenant, and still needed to obey; things had not changed that much. However, God was willing to offer the hand of peace, love, and relationship to a people struggling to repent and forgive themselves.

The Lord Cometh

Almost five centuries later the people of Judah found themselves in a similar situation. Jerusalem had been the center of national attention as Greece, Syria, Egypt, and finally Rome exploited the city to advance their own interests. The land of the Jews had tremendous value and if an outpost existed in these cities one could keep an eye on Egypt. Egypt, however, needed an outpost in Judah in order to keep an eye on everyone else. Wars were fought in Jerusalem. Jews were murdered, kings were enthroned and dethroned, mercenaries were given free reign at times, and God's temple was both honored and desecrated. Men and women shed their blood to be loyal to Yahweh and the Torah. The city struggled to survive while leaders once again sought help from outside sources. Eventually Rome conquered the nation and colonized the surrounding areas. Galilee, the northern section of Judeah, also enjoyed times of economic prosperity, religious freedom, and new building projects.[2]

However, the people of God found ways to survive. Corrupt religious leaders realized that political favor was more appealing than loyalty to Yahweh. Submission to the Romans, while painful, provided a sense of peace, economic support, and local control. Rome found that exploiting other nations offered a benefit to the capital city, while under the guise of peace to all nations. The outer regions of Galilee resisted the Jewish ruling classes and were populated with many non-Jewish residents.[3] The nation once again became unfaithful to its God and oppressed its family. Poverty, extortion, and marginalization of vulnerable groups was common even though it was not supported by the religious teachings of the Jewish nation. "Sinner" became a term developed by the Pharisees, leaders of the religious community, which was used to label, segregate, and oppress people who did not fit into their societal mold.

> It is the Pharisees who introduced the term "sinners," using it as a label. In the hands of the Pharisees, "sinners" demarcate those who associate with toll collectors as persons living outside the faithfulness of God. By means of vituperative apposition, then, toll collectors are dismissed, along with sinners, as possible friends; from the Pharisaic perspective, they are outside the boundaries, beyond the margins. In Lukan parlance, though, toll collectors and

---

2. Aviam, "People, Land, Economy," 11; McCullough, "City and Village in Lower Galilee," 71.

3. Aviam, "People, Land, Economy," 12, 43.

sinners would be included among "the poor," those to whom Jesus has been sent to proclaim good news. [4]

Instead of returning to Yahweh these corrupt religious leaders had enabled the Roman Empire to exploit, oppress, and marginalize vulnerable people in their own communities.

Instead of God sending an army, God decided to visit the seat of religious injustice personally. The prophet, John the Baptizer, became the voice crying in the wilderness (Luke 3:4–6). Luke also added another characteristic to John's ministry which was found in Malachi 3:1. "I will send my messenger ahead of you who will prepare your way . . ." (Luke 7:27). John was not only preparing the way for the Lord to return from captivity, he was preparing the way for Yahweh to visit and judge the people of God. While Luke shared with the audience that Jesus came to free the captives (Luke 4:16–19) he also came to visit the city of Jerusalem, the temple, and confront the corrupt leaders of his day (Luke 19:45–48). In the Hebrew Bible God's visitation was called the Day of Yahweh. It was a time of judgment. The nation of Judah was in social exile, rather than geographical exile. When Jesus "visited" Jerusalem he came to free social captives and confront the corrupt religious leaders. He came to remove the chains that bound the marginalized and oppose those who had extorted them. The Day of Jesus was a time not to destroy Jerusalem but to free its outcasts.

However, Jesus' journey ended at Jerusalem, the home of God. When he came home, he was rejected. In the Hebrew Scriptures God was pierced, detested, rejected, scorned, abused, and wounded by unfaithful Israel (Zech 11:8; 12:10). Some had done to Jesus what they had done to Yahweh, the prophets, and other faithful leaders (Luke 20:9–19). God was rejected, despised, and murdered when Jesus was betrayed, denied, and crucified (Luke 22:53). The one who came from the wilderness/East to free the captives had met his death in his own home. The place where Yahweh was to be worshipped had become a gang hideout (Luke 19:46). As a homeowner who rents to ungrateful and destructive tenants returns to see their house, so Jesus returned to see how things were going with the tenant leaders. As the ungrateful renters tear up the owner's house and investment, form a methamphetamine laboratory, and terrorize their neighbors, so the corrupt leaders of Jerusalem oppressed people in the temple (Yahweh's house). In this case the renter tried to take action, but the tenants turned on the one who offered them a home, safety, and put hard work into creating a

4. Adams, *The Sinner in Luke*, xi.

beautiful house. Before the eviction notice was served the tenants killed the owner, who only wanted to protect this investment. The restoration of the Empire of Yahweh had taken a different twist. There could be no waiting, no hope, and no future. The plan did not occur as it had in the past. Or so they thought.

Three days later God did a miracle. Jesus came back to life and appeared to his followers. The owner returned to rescue the neighbors and post the eviction notice. Luke's first story ended with a resurrected Savior who taught, commissioned, and promised something for the disciples. The story seemed to end with a unique twist and left more questions than answers. "In the Persian period, dreams of exiles returning to the Promised Land and rebuilding the Jerusalem temple began to be fulfilled; but in the minds of many Israelites the prophetic vision was never fully realized in the Second Temple era."[5]

- What about the restoration from captivity?
- What will Yahweh do now?
- Are humans going to carry out this mission?
- Will the mission be led by prophets and men and women who have been faithful?
- Will the temple need to be rebuilt?

WAITING FOR THE SPIRIT

The answers lie in the Holy Spirit. In the prophets Yahweh promised to pour out the Spirit on the people (Joel 2:28–32; Isa 42:1; Jer 31:6; Mic 3:8; Zech 12:10), to write on their hearts, and lead the faithful home. The driving force behind the next wave of restoration would be this Spirit, not humans. Jesus even told the apostles "I am going to send you what my Father has promised; but stay in the city until you have been clothed with power from above," (Luke 24:48–49). The apostles were to wait for the Spirit as it would complete the story. Restoration would happen through this Spirit. The captives would be freed by this Spirit. The temple would be rebuilt by this Spirit. The empire would be restored through this Spirit. The Spirit would give them courage, strength, and wisdom to be witnesses of the resurrection of Jesus.

5. Spencer, *Journeying Through Acts*, 36.

Not only would this Spirit be the driving force behind restoration, it would lead Jesus' disciples to witness his glory and honor. This Spirit would live within and without to honor Jesus through the mouths and actions of the disciples. This Spirit would be an unseen force, but in the life of the disciples it would be a known presence, a valued truth, and produced observable behavior. This is why the Apostle Paul suggested that God's people are both "led by" and "controlled by" the Spirit (Rom 8:6–11). The Spirit acted within the disciples to lead the restoration of Israel and the people to a relationship with God. There was no waiting, for that time had passed.

In Acts the Holy Spirit was given to these faithful men and women who "waited," (Acts 2). Once the Spirit came upon them they had power and witness. This power and witness to Jesus' resurrection completed the story of the restoration of Israel. One of the disciples asked Jesus if he was going to restore the empire to Israel (Acts 1:6). Jesus' response was that they were to wait for God. However, once the Spirit was given, the task would be theirs. There would be no need to wait, the Spirit had come and they were to "go."

RESTORATION TODAY

At the beginning of the twenty-first century it has become clear to clergy, theologians, and Christians that Christianity in North America is not only declining, but experiencing tremendous change.[6] Tickle suggested that we are experiencing the historical "rummage sale" that all religions have observed every 500 years.[7] Scholars and sociologists have been prophetically preaching that we in America have become apathetic, materialistic, and consumer driven. American churches have been accused of no longer focusing on the mission of the Spirit, but on the mission of successful businesses.[8] Authors such as Kinnaman, Kimbal, and Woodward have written that many young people are leaving Christianity and not returning.[9] With the baby boomer generation we saw a return to the stable views of the church. With the millennials and busters, we have continued to wait for

---

6. Woodward, *Creating a Missional Culture*, 29.

7. Tickle, *The Great Emergence*, 17–18.

8. Johnson, *Prophetic Jesus*, 125.

9. Kimball, *They Like Jesus But Not the Church*, 79–89; Kinnaman, *You Lost Me*, 11; Woodward, *Creating a Missional Culture*, 29, 65.

their return.[10] Martin Luther King Jr. once wrote that this would happen if the church did not embrace social justice issues.

> The judgment of God is upon the church as never before. If today's church does not recapture the sacrificial spirit of the early church, it will lose its authenticity, forfeit the loyalty of millions, and be dismissed as an irrelevant social club with no meaning for the twentieth century. Every day I meet young people whose disappointment with the church has turned into outright disgust.[11]

Authors today continue to suggest that not only have young people left the church, but those of us who remained behind have not led them as the Spirit has called us. We have also failed to create an environment where young people can feel safe and struggle through faith issues. "The need among young adults in this generation, however, has reached an acute level of spiritual crisis. Continued failure to prayerfully and proactively gather local communities of Christ's disciples to invest relationally in the spiritual journeys of young adults will ultimately have catastrophic spiritual consequences."[12]

Globally, Christianity is exploding in countries where Christians are not only persecuted, but live in deep poverty. Young men and women are being led through new and innovative methods of church in third world countries, Europe, and areas that have been resistant to Christianity.[13] Churches began to meet in bars, abandoned buildings, homes, and other "nonreligious settings." Fortunately these methods have affected North American church plantings. A fresh wave of the Spirit has been moving in new locations of their communities. Churches meet in schools, auditoriums, movie theaters, bars, pubs, homes, and many other locations that are unlike "church." As Tickle suggested, during the "Great Emergence" the church experienced three shifts. First, *a new and more vital form of religion emerges.* Second, *the dominant form is reconstituted as a less ossified expression of its former self.* Finally, *the gospel spreads abroad in a greater way due to the emergence of the new form and reconstitution of the older.*[14] The

---

10. Gibbs, *Churchmorph*, 77–80; Gibbs and Bolger, *Emerging Churches*, 21–23.

11. King Jr., *Why We Can't Wait*, 93.

12. Dunn and Sundene, *Shaping the Journey of Emerging Adults*, 19; Kinnaman, *You Lost Me*, 11.

13. Bolger, "Introduction," xxxvi–lii.; Frost and Hirsch, *The Shaping of Things to Come*, 115–17.

14. Tickle, *The Great Emergence*, 16–17.

Spirit works both by leading a new expression of the church, and helping to reform the older expression. This is restoration.

The disciples were only told to wait until the Spirit came upon them, then they were to go, witness, and proclaim that Jesus was the new Caesar. The Spirit would lead new people to experience and bear fruit in new and imaginative ways. People confined by fear to their own city and belief system would travel to other cultures, speak new languages, and develop cross-cultural relationships through this Spirit. Others would return to their homes and practice of faith with a greater appreciation for a God who not only set them free, but desired to set others free as well. The Empire of God would once again be on the move, led by the power and love of the Holy Spirit. Things would change, beliefs would not be the same, and people would be given new life. As John the Baptist paved the way for the coming of the Lord to Palestine, the church would pave the way for the coming of Jesus into Asia, Syria, Egypt, Europe, and Rome. As the Holy Spirit descended on Jesus in baptism, it would also rest upon a small group of believers who would baptize others and proclaim Jesus in their own languages. Synagogues that were outposts for Yahweh would have the opportunity to revive, see the conversion of Gentiles, and understand the prophets in a new light. That is, if they were willing.

Modern Captivities

In *Jesus Unleashed* I made the distinction between the Jewish exile (geographical captivity) and occupied Palestine (social captivity). While the Jewish nation, during Babylonian exile, was kidnapped and transported to a culture vastly different than theirs, they found a way to be faithful and serve Yahweh. During the time of Jesus, even though the Jewish nation was overpowered and politically oppressed by the Romans, those in power found a way to marginalize and oppress others who were dependent on their leadership, spiritual wisdom, and protection. Those who had resources withheld from those who needed them. They, as victims of Roman oppression, oppressed their brothers and sisters. They knew the pain of isolation, but continued to isolate and captivate others.

The Spirit led the church into this type of world. The apostles' presence first among the Jewish community offered a chance for them to experience God's promises and blessings through Jesus the Messiah. However, when they realized that this was also a call to reach out to the Gentiles (their oppressors) tensions mounted. As Jesus developed friendships and relationships with those labeled and marginalized by the corrupt religious leaders (sinners and tax collectors), so the church began to grow exponentially among the Gentiles, women, widows, the poor, as well as religious leaders in the community. The message of the church was not to wait for salvation, but to go and follow the Spirit, who, like Jesus/God, preferred to be among the captives, marginalized, and outcasts.

Today the mission is similar. Christians are not called to wait, they are called to go. We know what Jesus wants and feel the prompting of the Spirit, however our struggle is not in *understanding* but *accepting* or *resisting* the responsibility given to us.

> The task of the members of faith communities is to be "witnesses" to Jesus. This means more than simply telling one's personal story or faith or transformation, as important as that may be. To be Christ's witnesses is to bring forward into our own time and place the truth of the gospel. Just as Matthew, Mark, Luke, and John each took the words, teachings, deeds, life, death, and resurrection of Jesus and brought it to bear in their particular time and their communities, so the church's essential calling and task is to bear witness to what God has done and is doing in Jesus, to this outpouring of grace and healing, to this victory over the myriad powers of death at work in the world and in us—to witness to the power of Jesus to heal all that distorts, disfigures, and diminishes God's dream for life.[15]

In November 2005 I was sitting in Starbucks meeting with Dr. Stan Granberg from Kairos Church Planting. Stan and I were friends and had taught at Cascade College together, worked in ministry, and collaborated on a few ministry events in the Portland area. Stan is a good man who spent decades in Kenya establishing churches and was always open to listening and praying for those of us in ministry who struggled. Stan and his wife Gena had recently begun Kairos Church Planting as an effort to help ministers in churches of Christ replicate new churches, as was being done nationally on many levels.

I had begun to share my frustration with Stan as a minister in a large church trying to reach out to lost and marginalized people with the gospel of Jesus. Things weren't going well as I realized that being prophetic meant that I was not skilled at dealing with the politics of a large church, working

---

15. Robinson and Wall, *Called to Be Church*, 43.

with leaders who I had lost respect for, and trying to motivate them to set an example for our people in outreach and community involvement. Stan listened and provided a sympathetic ear. Finally, after lamenting for thirty minutes and stating that my only options seemed to be moving back to the South and preaching at a large church, Stan changed the tone of the meeting. He looked at me and said, "You need to plant a new church. We have been praying for key leaders to help this movement take off, and you are one of them. We also need strong leadership to form pillar churches that will become Antioch congregations and birth new churches." There it was, he had said it. Maybe he had just blurted it out, or he was called by the Spirit to tell me.

I am ashamed to write that my response was to laugh and say, "Sure, Lori won't go for that." "Why don't you pray about it and ask her?" He replied. I talked with him about Kairos, how *they* were doing, and expressed appreciation for all *they* were doing, since I believed it was not something I was called to do. However when I went home and jokingly shared this with Lori, she said, "He's right—we need to do this." Our oldest son was in junior high and said he thought it was a great idea as well. So the long journey began.

I read books concerning church planting, the state of churches in America, reaching this generation, and others on church growth. Most of what was being written confirmed what we had observed in people, churches, and church leaders. We had been so immersed in our culture and community that we had begun to feel that churches, Christians, and Christian leaders were not connecting with those outside the buildings. Through time we attended Kairos' Discovery Lab to determine if we had the giftedness and calling for this. During the week we spent at Delano Bay, Washington in February 2006 there were record low temperatures, the power went out for two days, our two little boys were both vomiting and dealing with a stomach virus, and I felt that this was a sign from God. However Lori kept saying we would be fine and things returned to normal. We were given the "green light" to church plant after that Discovery Lab.

With only a vision to plant a church in downtown Portland I resigned my position as a minister the week before Easter 2006. We had not completed our next level, Strategy Lab, to determine how to plant a new church, nor did we have funding for this new church. We knew how to do ministry, how to work with small and large churches, and how to lead people to

Christ. When I look back on that situation I remember that we were not worried. We believed that God would provide.

Within two weeks of our resignation a large church in Tulsa, Oklahoma called looking to support a church planter in the Northwest. They provided all of our salary, startup costs, and even boosted my ministerial salary. God truly provided for us and along the way established partnerships, relationships, and support for our outreach, and for our supporters. It has been a testimony for us that vision, courage, and faith are key components for being led by the Spirit. Our supporting church in Tulsa, Kairos Church Planting, and our new people at Agape have always been people who not only model faithfulness for us, but help us to trust and believe that Jesus can fulfill the vision if we are willing to step out on faith.

Jesus gives us, the church, the same promise that he did 2,000 years ago. "You will receive power when the Holy Spirit comes upon you . . . ." Therefore the promise is for us. Assuming we want it! Assuming we are willing to take out the earphones, close the book, and put away the iPhone so that we might listen to the person next to us.

SHOULD WE STAY OR SHOULD WE GO?

2

ACTS AND JESUS UNLEASHED

They will be my people and I will be their God. (Jer 32:38)

IN MY PAST BOOK, *Jesus Unleashed: Luke's Gospel for Emerging Christians*, I suggested that Luke's narrative was written as an attempt to present the story of Jesus as an epic novel or story of the beginnings of a new empire.[1] Luke, like many other ancient authors, would have been trained to write by imitating classical works such as those by Homer, Virgil, and others. "Prose authors imitated the *Odyssey* more frequently than any other book of the ancient world. It was supplemented, parodied, burlesqued, dramatized, prosified, and transformed to secure an array of un-Homeric values."[2] Ancient schools exposed students to these works and encouraged them to become familiar with their styles, plots, narratives, and themes.[3] Students were also taught to adapt their work using common literary devices for the author's intent and purpose.[4] Luke indicated that his Gospel was narrative (Luke 1:3), suggesting that he had been exposed to an advanced education. He was also writing to prove that Christianity was a legitimate religion.[5]

---

1. Clark, *Jesus Unleashed*, 25–26; Bonz, *The Past as Legacy*, 93; Malina and Pilch, *Social-Science Commentary*, 7;

2. MacDonald, *The Homeric Epics*, 5.

3. Bonz, *The Past as Legacy*, 17–21; MacDonald, *The Homeric Epics*, 6; Parsons, "Luke and the Progymnasmata," 40; Johnson, *The Acts of the Apostles*, 53.

4. Brawley, *Luke-Acts and the Jews*, 53; Tyson, "From History to Rhetoric and Back," 41.

5. Pickett, "Luke and Empire," 5; Marshall, *Luke*, 22; Johnson, *Prophetic Jesus*, 4; and

Luke also used some of the common devices in Luke and Acts to highlight the history of the movement and the rise of this new empire.[6] He used speeches, journey, summaries of narrative, and parallels with characters which were common ancient rhetorical devices used by this author.[7]

CAPTIVITY AND RESTORATION OF THE EMPIRE

Luke also relied heavily on themes that were common not only in the prophets of Israel, but the captivity, return from exile, and restoration of the nation of Judah. His heavy emphasis on *repentance* suggested that the people of God needed to turn back to Yahweh and each other for restoration. When the early Christians proclaimed the message of Jesus, repentance became a major theme and requirement for salvation as well as the receiving of the Spirit (Luke 3:3; Acts 2:38; 3:19; 17:30).[8] Repentance preceded baptism and forgiveness, suggesting that an individual seeking relationship with God must first address sin.

The *Holy Spirit* was also a common phrase and theme in both Luke and Acts (Luke 1:35, 41, 67; 2:26–27; 3:16, 21–22; 41, 14, 18; 11:13; 24:40–48; Acts 1:2, 4–5, 8,15; 2:2–4, 17, 18, 33, 38; 4:25, 31; 5:3, 9, 32; 6:5, 10; 7:51, 54; 8:15–19, 29, 39; 9:17; 10:19, 38, 44–47; 11:12, 15, 24, 28; 13:1, 4, 52; 20:22, 23, 28; 21:11; 27:25). The Holy Spirit was not only a sign of relationship and salvation in the prophets (Joel 2:28–29; Isa 42:1; Jer 31:26; Mic 3:8; Zech 12:10) but in Luke/Acts the Spirit was a witness that God sought relationship with people (Acts 2; Luke 11:13).[9] In Acts specifically the Spirit empowered the believers to preach, witness, prophesy, and communicate the message of Jesus cross-culturally (Acts 2:1–20).[10] It also gave credibility to the movement.[11]

Spencer, *Journeying Through Acts*, 14.

6. Smith and Tyson, *Acts and Christian Beginnings*, 1–2.

7. Johnson, *The Acts of the Apostles*, 9–10; Longenecker, *Jesus On the Edge and God in the Gap*, 50, 60; Thompson, *The Acts of the Risen Lord Jesus*, 90–92; MacDonald, *The Homeric Epics*, 4–5; and Dawsey, *Peter's Last Sermon*, 9.

8. Shepherd, *The Narrative Function of the Holy Spirit*, 20.

9. Ibid., 17.

10. Haya-Prats, *Empowered Believers*, 47, 110; Burke, "The Holy Spirit as the Controlling Dynamic in Paul's Role as Missionary to the Thessalonians," 144–45.

11. Shepherd, *The Narrative Function of the Holy Spirit*, 2; Pickett, "Luke and Empire," 45.

The use of the *prophetic texts* concerning the restoration of Israel were also common themes in Luke's narratives. Jesus was compared to the suffering servant (Isa 40–55) or seen as the one who led the people to salvation and embraced the sins of the nation (Luke 4:16–19; Acts 8:26–36). The servant was also applied to the people of God who brought the message of hope to Zion and promoted the inclusion of the Gentiles who would give glory to Yahweh (Acts 13:47–48; Isa 49:6). The exilic prophetic texts were quoted to support the renewal of God's people as a church, community, and spiritual temple (Acts 15:16–18; Amos 9:11).

The establishment of *social justice*, inclusion of the Gentiles, and healing of the marginalized were characteristics of restoration language. Luke's indication that the body of believers shared with the poor, healed the sick, gave sight to the blind, and offered financial relief from the Gentiles to the Jews was meant to prove that the early Christian community was the restored nation of Israel. In response to the disciple's question to Jesus (Acts 1:6) Luke indicated to the reader that the empire was *being restored* as the disciples were led by the Spirit.[12]

Finally, the emphasis on *resurrection* continued the theme of restoration. In the book of Acts Jesus' crucifixion was referred to only three times.[13] It is surprisingly absent from the major speeches of Peter and Paul, however, the early Christians were focused on the resurrection, rather than the death of Christ. In Ezekiel the resurrection of the "valley of dry bones" was a symbol of the new hope and life that the nation would one day receive from the power of God (Ezek 37:1–14). The pouring out of the Spirit, new life of the Spirit, and a new heart were all symbols in the prophets of the new hope of the resurrection of God's people (Ezek 37:14; Joel 2:28–32).

Luke's narrative of Jesus seemed to be written against the backdrop of the return from captivity. The captivity symbolized the punishment for the sins of Israel and their return represented forgiveness and God's desire to establish relationship with humans. In the Gospel of Luke Jesus was the God who visited the nation and became the "friend of sinners and tax collectors" (Luke 5:29–31; 7:34).

The Holy Spirit working in the early church became this vehicle for restoration. While the Spirit was the driving force the church fulfilled the role of the prophets. The prophets brought the message of God to a people needing hope, confrontation, and support. They did this through the Holy

---

12. Malina and Pilch, *Social-Science Commentary*, 21.
13. Borgman, *The Way According to Luke*, 251.

Spirit and Word of God. The Spirit also intervened at times to "jump-start" the Christian ministry. "Acts sees the salvific action of Christ continually actualized in communities. The communication of the Spirit to the disciples is not, therefore, a total substitute for Christ, but rather the transfer of his prophetic mission."[14] In Acts the early Christians likewise brought the message of God to a people on the margins of society needing hope, confrontation, and support.

LUKE'S AUDIENCE

Scholar Patricia Walters' classic work, as well as the work from the *Acts Seminar Report*, make a strong case against Luke as the author of Acts.[15] Their points are well taken and well defended. While there is not enough space to discuss this work here, truth and honesty demand that we take their work seriously. However, there is a growing body of evidence that also suggests that Luke could have written Acts and this evidence also demands honesty. Unfortunately this book is focused on ministry and Acts and is not designed to explore the academic discussion of the author. Both sides have strong arguments but I will admit to leaning toward the belief that Luke did write Acts and will take this position throughout the book. However, I am aware of the disagreement with this view and will be open with the evidence as we move forward.

In both Luke 1:1–4 and Acts 1:1–4 the author suggests that the audience who read this work was part of the upper-class members of society.[16]

> In my first writing, Theophilus, I worked concerning all the things Jesus began to do and teach until the day when he was taken up, in the presence of his apostles. He had chosen them through the Holy Spirit and gave commands/instructions, presenting many proofs that he was alive after his suffering. He appeared for forty days and spoke concerning the Empire of God (Acts 1:1–4).

First, in Luke's earlier introduction, Theophilus was labeled "most excellent," a term used for upper-class Romans, members of the equestrian unit,

---

14. Haya-Prats, *Empowered Believers*, 47, 72.

15. Walters, *The Assumed Authorial Unity of Luke and Acts*; Smith and Tyson, *Acts and Christian Beginnings*, 1–4.

16. Clark, *Jesus Unleashed*, 29.

and possibly an official (Luke 1:3).[17] The term was used later in Acts for Governor Felix (Acts 23:26). Theophilus may have funded Luke's writing or been a wealthy host providing for Luke's personal expenses. Second, the house where Jesus preached, and the paralytic was placed, had tile roofs and a special outside walkway (Luke 5:17–26). While Mark's gospel used the normal flat-style roof found in Capernaum, Luke used a wealthier style home, suggesting that his audience may have been on a coastal town or near Rome and less familiar with Capernaum houses. Luke is also unique as a writer in that he mentions the poor, widows, Gentiles, Samaritans, and sinners more than the other writers combined. It is thought that Luke's audience was Gentile, indicating that his story was an attempt to reach out to them, as marginalized by their communities.

Finally, Luke seemed to attempt to defend the resurrection of Jesus. He mentioned throughout Acts that Jesus and the Spirit offered proof and evidence that he rose and sent out the Christian community. This new empire was, like the many authors of ancient fiction, ordained by God/the gods and received constant intervention by divine powers, known in Acts as the Holy Spirit. For Luke, Acts was not the "Acts of the Holy Spirit" alone but the "Acts of the Holy Spirit through the Church." The new Empire of Jesus was restored by the Spirit and led to proclaim Jesus throughout the Roman world as a testimony to his resurrection.

Acts and Lukan Themes

In this book we will assume that Luke was the author of both Luke and Acts, and that he was the one closely associated with the Apostle Paul. He left us hints in this second work that he had met and accompanied the Apostle Paul and that his team responded to a call into Macedonia. Before reaching the Greek city of Troas Luke referred to the team as *"Paul and his companions . . ."* (Acts 16:9), and then later, "From Troas *we* put out to sea . . ." (Acts 16:11). It has been suggested that Paul met Luke while at Troas and invited him to join his team. If this is the same Luke Paul mentioned who was a physician (Col 4:14) then he would have been wise to add a medic to his team, since he experienced many violent attacks. A temple of Asklepius existed at Troas, which was the temple of healing and a place physicians

---

17. Robinson and Wall, *Called to Be Church*, 19; Moxnes, "Patron-Client Relations," 267.

would have frequented.[18] Their libraries gave access to research, something Luke indicated he had done (Luke 1:1–2). Luke's mention of dogs licking Lazarus's sores was also commonly practiced at the Asklepions. Luke also suggested that Philippi (the city he and Paul's team visited and the site of a major medical school) was "a leading city" (Acts 16:12), a sign that he was proud of the city and that it was possibly a place where he had lived. Physicians who had education were viewed a little higher socially than other artisans.[19] While Luke's gospel was a report and narrative of events he had only heard about, he suggested that much of Acts involved events he was familiar with. He claimed to be an eyewitness, traveling companion, and active member of the growth of this new movement.

My understanding of both books is that they are not just a narrative of the life of Jesus, but the history of the founding of a new empire. As Virgil, highly influenced by Homer and other writers, seemed to write the *Aeneid* as a history of the foundation of Rome, Luke also may have written both volumes to express the founding of a new empire. Early schools encouraged their students to modify or "better write" through telling their story in a similar manner.[20] Luke seems to have been a highly trained writer who, through research, delivered a history of a new nation, empire, and movement called Christianity. He also saw his writings as a "better writing of the story."

Questions have been presented concerning the unity of both books. While Luke's gospel ended with a summary of the disciples meeting Jesus and returning to the temple, Acts began with a fuller explanation of Jesus' promise of the Spirit and mission for the church. In both accounts Luke began with a prologue to Theophilus, the recipient of the letter. In both accounts Luke suggested that his narratives had a purpose, to convince the community of the truth and safety of this new empire. For Luke, both letters began as narrative events of this new movement.

Speculation has been presented that Acts ended with a desire to begin a third volume (one either not completed or one that is missing).[21] The abrupt ending of the book with Paul living at Rome in an apartment un-

---

18. Conway, *Behold the Man*, 137; Shepherd, *The Narrative Function of the Holy Spirit*, 14.

19. Harland, *Associations, Synagogues, and Congregations*, 42

20. MacDonald, *The Homeric Epics*, 6.

21. Puskas, *The Conclusion of Luke-Acts*, 16–32; Cassidy, "Paul's Proclamation of *Lord Jesus as a Chained Prisoner in Rome*," 143.

der house arrest, showing hospitality to Jews and Gentiles, and preaching boldly and without resistance, seems to suggest to scholars that Luke had in mind a third volume that discussed the persecution and death of Paul. It does seem odd that a man whose life and ministry was filled with suffering and persecution would end peacefully at the capital of the world. Luke even seemed to ignore the suffering that the early Christians would later face, as he ended the book suggesting that Paul lived out his days in his own apartment in peace.

However, Luke and Acts were not biographies but narratives of the birth and growth of an empire. First, *this empire was in captivity and became a movement that continued to bring glory to God.* As the Hebrew Bible ended with the Jews returning to Jerusalem and the call to rebuild, so Acts ended with the realities that this new empire had possibilities (2 Chr 36:23). As the Hebrew Bible offered stories of individuals who were faithful during captivity and ended their life in peace, so Luke's second book described disciples and apostles who lived faithfully, suffered, and finished their years in peace. Second, *the goal of the Jews in captivity was to return to their homeland and become a light to Gentiles* (Isa 60). The goal of Jesus, in Luke's narrative, was not only to free the captives (Luke 4:16–19), but to return to Jerusalem, die, and then send the apostles to the Gentiles (Luke 9:44; 24:45–49). Rome was the end of the journey, the return from captivity, and the fulfilling of the presentation of the Gentiles to Zion.[22]

When Will the Empire Come?

> When he was eating with them, he gave them this command: "Do not leave Jerusalem. Wait for the gift my Father promised. You have heard me speak about. John baptized with water, but in a few days you will be baptized with the Holy Spirit." Then they gathered with him and asked him, "Lord, are you at this time going to restore the kingdom to Israel?" He said to them: "It is not time for you to know the times or dates the Father has set by his own authority. But you will receive power when the Holy Spirit comes on you; and you will be my witnesses in Jerusalem, and in all Judea and Samaria, and to the ends of the earth."
>
> After he said this, he was taken up before their eyes, and a cloud hid him from view. They were gazing into the sky as he was going, when suddenly two men dressed in white stood beside

---

22. Kim, "Paul as Eschatological Herald," 16.

them. "Men of Galilee," they said, "why do you stand here looking into the sky? This same Jesus, who has been taken from you to heaven, will come back in the same way you have observed him go into heaven." (Acts 1:4–11)

Luke continued the theme of the restoration of Israel by placing this question, from the mouth of one of the disciples, at the beginning of this second book. While Luke's gospel left hints of this restoration through the prediction of John to Zechariah (Luke 1:16–71); the Davidic promise to Mary (1:32–33); and Simeon's and Anna's desire for the consolation and redemption of God's people (2:25, 38), Acts is much more direct. The last time that Jesus ate with the larger group of disciples, commonly known as the Last Supper, he had promised that he would again eat with them after the empire had come (Luke 22:18). As they all ate together one of them asked, "Lord are you at this time restoring the Empire to Israel?" This was a valid question. The question asked by the disciple was in the present tense, suggesting ongoing restoration. The disciples were not only wondering if the empire had come, but if or when it was coming to Israel. Jesus had promised after the resurrection that there would be a restoration. However, he promised them not only the power of the Spirit (a sign of restoration) but also that God would still be in control of the event.

For Jesus the lesson concerned their conviction of the resurrection, hence Luke's use of a word for proof that was meant to convince skeptical people or confirm one's authority.[23] The disciples would become an active part of an ongoing restoration of spiritual Israel. They were to be mobile witnesses and carry the message to the end of the earth. Once convinced of the resurrection the disciples would have a responsibility to also prove to the world that Jesus was not only Lord, but the risen Son of God.

As Jesus was offering his call to be his witnesses, he was taken up into the sky in front of them. Their intent gaze (1:10) is suggested by Malina and Pilch to represent a trance, as they witnessed Jesus' ascension.[24] While in this transitory state, the messengers told them that they no longer needed to stare into the sky. While many religious groups spend time searching the sky for details, the Christian church was called to focus on the earth. The disciples were to wait for the Holy Spirit and power, but this did not mean that they stared into the sky to wait for someone to rescue them. Instead, the disciples would know when Jesus returned. He would return as Yahweh

---

23. Robinson and Wall, *Called to Be Church*, 31.
24. Malina and Pilch, *Social-Science Commentary*, 23.

returned—on the clouds in judgment. However, disciples must be active on earth fulfilling the mission to witness to Jesus and offer proof of the resurrection.

THE REPLACEMENT

I have heard many discussions concerning Judas, why he betrayed Jesus, and his motives for being different as a follower, failure, and eventually one who took his life. Some believe he was an unfortunate target of a Bible prophecy that chose him to betray Jesus. Others suggest that he had a choice to be different but chose to rebel and stab his friend in the back, even though his friend was the Messiah. We struggle not with his choices, but with his role as unfaithful man offering a two-faced friendship. The Gospel writers, after the fact, shed light that Judas was not a moral individual. John wrote that Judas was a thief (John 12:6). He also suggested that when Jesus was washing their feet, Satan entered Judas' twice, indicating that Judas kept an open heart toward evil (John 13:2, 27). While the Gospels record Judas hanging himself, Acts revealed that Judas was wicked and a guide for those arresting Jesus. The money he received for betraying his friend was used to buy a field, where Judas hung himself. Papias, a disciple of the Apostle John, wrote that he hung for days and his body decayed and became swollen.[25] Acts indicated that he fell into the field and his body burst open (likely his body separated from the head as it was decaying and burst on the field). The story is graphically disgusting but similar to the death of Herod (Acts 12), who also died in a horrible fashion.

The Bible doesn't always tell us the psychology of those who do evil. It is not concerned with the motives or understanding one's entire mental health concerning their evil actions. It simply tells us that people who do evil eventually receive their reward. As therapist George Simon suggested, there are bad people who do hurtful things to others. They are "individuals who know well the difference between right and wrong and understand what most others might regard as appropriate and responsible conduct, but who knowingly and purposely adopt an approach to life and dealing with others that is adverse, inconsiderate, and reckless. Such individuals frequently, and often deliberately, bring pain into the lives of those with whom they come into contact."[26] Judas had betrayed his friend even though

25. Apollinarius, *The Fragments of Papias*, 18.
26. Simon, *The Judas Syndrome*, 2.

he had a chance to change. He was wicked and received the punishment that he deserved.

> In those days Peter stood up among the believers, a crowd numbering about a hundred and twenty. He said, "Brothers [and sisters], the Scripture had to be fulfilled in which the Holy Spirit spoke through David concerning Judas, who was a guide for those who arrested Jesus. He was of our number and shared in our ministry."
> ... Peter said, "It is written in the Book of Psalms, May his place be deserted; let there be no one to dwell in it, and, May another take his oversight. It is necessary to choose one of the men who have been with us the whole time the Lord Jesus was living among us, beginning from John's baptism to the time when Jesus was taken up from us. For one of these must become a witness with us of his resurrection (Acts 1:15–22).

The church had gathered in a rented room, possibly the one where they had shared the Passover and where Mary, John Mark's mother (John Mark was the author of the Gospel of Mark, cousin of Barnabas, and member of the first mission team sent out from Antioch [Luke 22:12; Acts 12:12]), lived. This home became a base for the Jerusalem ministry, located in the area close to the Mount of Olives. It is believed to have been one of the houses in the wealthy quadrant of Jerusalem. Here homes were large enough to accommodate 120 people.[27] Luke's narrative emphasized the completeness of the Jewish faith by the addition of a twelfth apostle. There was no time to grieve or mourn over the loss of one who betrayed his community. Someone must replace Judas and help the church fulfill its mission. Matthias was chosen from two who had been with Jesus from the baptism of John to the resurrection. It is interesting that in order to be an apostle and fulfill the mission of Jesus, one had to be present for the three years that Jesus was teaching.

Preparing to Restore the Empire of Jesus

Jesus had not only proven to his disciples that he rose from the dead, he hung out with them, ate with them, and taught them concerning his mission. Imagine the conversations about his suffering, experiences, and the occasional asking for forgiveness for not believing and for abandoning him at the cross. Imagine the anger and frustration over Judas's betrayal. Even

---

27. Gehring, *House Church and Mission*, 65, 68.

more, imagine the sadness to again be told that Jesus was leaving. They had spent time with their friend, but he was leaving because he had promised the Holy Spirit as a gift, partner, and helper. Yet it would not be the same. They may have experienced grief and sadness on losing their friend, but also joy knowing that the mission would continue. The healings, casting out of demons, confrontations with corrupt leaders, teaching, preaching, feeding, and miracles would continue—only this time it would be through them. Jesus would not be the only witness to the Father, they would also carry that role. The Spirit would help them be a testimony to the power and love of God. The empire would be restored (or restoring) and they were part of the vision.

More questions would have come to them.

- "How can simple Galileans take on the educated elite that dominate societies?"
- "How can those of us with such a simple language bring a message to Greeks, Romans, and other cultures?"
- "How can those of us who cannot read learn the Torah so quickly?"
- "What will we do for money, work, or supporting our families?"
- "How can we forgive those like Judas, who will raise their heel against us?" (Psalm 69:25)

These were all valid questions. They were asked out of fearful but practical thoughts. These were the questions that ministers, interns, missionaries, and other Christian leaders ask themselves, their families, and others before they enter ministry. Ministry is a beast—when you ride it you fall. Some ride longer than others but all of us fall off the bull. We fall not only because we make mistakes but because the bull is difficult to ride. Ministry is a restoration of lives, people, and communities. Some long to be included. Others refuse to be inclusive. Some desire grace while others refuse to hand out forgiveness. Some seek change while others resist it. Some despise sin and want to remove it from their lives. Others embrace it and have been corrupted by it.

The Spirit empowers Christians to proclaim, witness, and offer restoration with God. The Spirit sought open hearts and desired to heal, forgive, and transform open lives. All of these take work. Yet the Spirit equipped the church to be the resource on the front lines of battle to offer this hope and restoration. Some of us stand gazing at the risen Lord wondering when he will return. Others carry the shame of betrayal and hide in a field bought with wicked money. Still others have become comfortable with the good life and see no need to follow a Messiah who was crucified and asks us to join him.

Shannon came to church one Sunday. He was released from prison the Tuesday before. He was told by someone that he would be accepted at our congregation. He read one of our tracts and told me, "I need to be baptized."

I met Shannon and we studied some passages of Scripture, prayed, and visited. He was struggling to remain sober. Years as a sergeant in Desert Storm and months in jail had convinced him that he needed to change his life. Baptism was something he wanted. "I just want to get on with it and do whatever God tells me to do."

He was soon baptized in our "holy horse trough." When I submerged Shannon he stayed under water for well over half a minute. Everyone laughed. Some of our people said he was enjoying this transformation. A few seconds later he emerged out of the water celebrating, hugged me tight, and everyone in the room clapped and cheered.

It's been tough for Shannon. We have walked the road of making amends/repentance, sobriety, finding housing, work, and relationships. He baptized a friend and brings others to church with him. It's been hard but for Shannon restoration is sweet. He felt clean, like he had a new chance and a relationship with Jesus. He was and is eager to change his life and validate others who may have been hurt by him. He is one who waited outside for the Empire of Jesus and now enjoys his place in it. This is why the church needs to be missional/incarnational. We are called to take a message of reconciliation and restoration to those struggling in our world. Most of these individuals will not "join a church," but will need to be engaged and "joined" while in their community. This mission and engagement is a sign of a restored empire. As Woodward once wrote: "Creating a missional culture helps the church live out her calling to be a sign of the kingdom, pointing people to the reality beyond what we can see, a foretaste of the kingdom where we grow to love one another as Christ loves us, and an instrument in the hands of God to bring more of heaven to earth in concrete ways."[28]

Restoration is sweet. Do we rejoice in that restoration as well? Have we desired that restoration in our lives and the lives of others?

---

28. Woodward, *Creating a Missional Culture*, 29.

3

THE SPIRIT COMES

After this I will pour out my Spirit on all people. (Joel 2:28)

THE PEOPLE OF JUDEA had been waiting, hoping, and preparing for the restoration of the Empire of God. For decades they may have heard that God's people would be redeemed from Roman occupation. In Galilee, where many, including the disciples, had lived, the economy was experiencing changes and thriving at a newer level than in Jerusalem.[1] Smaller businesses were beginning to grow and people were trading within their communities.[2] While James and John's father Zebedee owned more than one boat and employed a hired servant, it seems that they had a co-op fishing business with Peter and Andrew (Mark 1:19–20). When Jesus called Peter and Andrew to follow him, they were casting a simple shoreline net, indicating that the boat Peter owned may have been his only resource or one rented from Zebedee (Mark 1:16–17; Luke 5:3). All four of these fishermen would have despised Matthew the tax collector, who would have had a good income whether or not he was honest. Judas may have been part of the terrorist group "Sicari" as evidenced by Judas "I–s–cariot." Simon the Zealot was also believed to be part of a rebel group in Galilee. All of the apostles and their families would have desired a change to their economy, a better lifestyle, and greater connection to God. However, like those in most

---

1. Fiensy, "Assessing the Economy of Galilee," 169.

2. Aviam, "People, Land, Economy, and Belief," 27; McCullough, "City and Village in Lower Galilee," 49.

struggling societies, they may have had less concern with their relationship to God than their social status.

Jesus had changed their view of reality. In Luke's gospel the disciples and crowds had journeyed with Jesus only to see him killed at Jerusalem. Luke's "journey" motif was a metaphor for Jesus' ministry similar to that used by classical Greek authors (Luke 9:51–53, 57; 10:38; 13:31–33; 17:11; 19:28).[3] In the classical journey the hero killed the marginalized people (monsters) he met on the trip. In Luke's journey the hero healed, saved, and called those marginalized people he met. The resurrection was a reminder that while people have neglected, rejected, and turned against God for centuries, God still wins. Even more it was a reminder that those who hoped and believed would find redemption through this resurrection. The disciples had come to realize that restoration and the Empire of God had little to do with Herod's empire-wide reforms, Caesar's offer of peace, or the religious leaders' outward belief system. The empire that Jesus sought featured peace/shalom, which involved the redistribution of resources, social justice, love, and compassion. They had been preparing for three years to proclaim this message, and Jesus had told them to wait. As they gathered in a second-story room something remarkable happened to begin this restoration.

> When the day of Pentecost came, they were in one location. A sound like the blowing wind came from heaven and filled the house where they were sitting. They saw tongues of fire that separated and came to rest on each one. All of them were filled with the Holy Spirit and began to speak in other languages as the Spirit enabled them. . . . Amazed and perplexed, they asked one another, "What does this mean?" Some, however, made fun of them and said, "They are drunk!" (Acts 2:1–4, 12–13)

Pentecost was an important day for the Jewish nation. First, *pente* meant "fifty," which referred to the fiftieth day after the Passover. The Passover was the celebration of God's leading the nation of Israel out of Egypt and delivering them from a cruel and oppressive leader (Pharaoh). The Passover was celebrated yearly and was one of the most important events among the Jews. This festival was a celebration of redemption, freedom, and the power of God. On the fiftieth day (seven weeks plus one day after the Sabbath [Saturday]) the Festival of Weeks began during the summer harvest. This festival had two important components.

---

3. Longenecker, *Jesus on the Edge and God in the Gap*, 50.

First, *the celebration of the harvest was a time to give the best and first-fruits to Yahweh* (Exod 23:16). Second, *the Jewish communities that lived near the Dead Sea celebrated this as the delivering of the Torah to Israel.* The book of Jubilees indicated that the Torah was to be read in the seventy languages of the people (Jub 1:1–26).[4] The overseer of the congregation would read the giving of the Torah in all of the languages of the community (CD 14:8–10; 13:8–12; 1 QS 1:20–21). Pentecost was viewed as a divine event and was overshadowed by the Spirit. The emphasis of this holiday involved God's global blessings through the Spirit, the Torah, and the harvest. The Jews from many sects would have viewed this proclamation of Yahweh in multiple languages as a fulfillment and restoration of their nation.

It is no surprise that the Holy Spirit's first major action at Pentecost was to empower the early Christians to share God's greatness in diverse languages. Luke was emphasizing that Jesus' empire, like that of the Romans, was to rule the world. However, this reign would be done not through a common language, but multiple languages. Those who had come to celebrate Pentecost were from Persia/Mesopotamia, Rome, Africa, Greece, Arabia, Egypt, Judea, and other nations. While all nations may have spoken Greek, many would have spoken Aramaic. Few would have spoken Latin or the various dialects of each culture, yet Luke wrote that the apostles not only spoke in the world languages, but in each native dialect. His list (or table) of nations was also a common theme in epic stories, suggesting that the Holy Spirit and the gospel conquered the world.[5]

The message of the Spirit concerning the restoration of God's empire was expressed in many ways. First, *this Pentecost experience indicated that God desired and prepared the church to be global.* The Holy Spirit empowers the church to proclaim the message of Jesus worldwide. If the thrust of the Holy Spirit is preaching, prophesying, and witnessing the resurrection, then Luke's focus was on the global nature of that ministry. Any church not open to those of other languages will not be able to operate by the power of the Spirit.

A second point to this event was that *the Holy Spirit was designed to remove the barriers that prevent the spread of the Empire of Jesus.* A natural response of the Galilean apostles, who knew two or three languages, would be that they could not take the gospel past Samaria, due to the language barrier. They were not bold, educated, or skilled at speaking. Yet the Spirit

---

4. Chilton, "Festivals and Holy Days," 374.
5. Bonz, *The Past as Legacy*, 101.

filled this community to the point where even the religious leaders were amazed at their skill and courage (Acts 4:13–14). The Holy Spirit's focus was to make the resurrection of Jesus become known *throughout the world*.[6] As the prophets shared that Yahweh's desire was to have this holy name known throughout the world, it would happen through the restoration and reconciliation of Israel in the return from captivity.

> After this I will pour out my Spirit on all people. Your sons and daughters will prophesy, your old men will dream dreams, your young men will see visions. In those days I will pour out my Spirit on my male and female servants. I will show wonders in the heavens and on the earth, blood, fire, and smoke. The sun will be turned to darkness and the moon to blood before the coming of the great and terrible day of Yahweh. Everyone who calls on the name of Yahweh will be saved . . . . (Joel 2:28–32)

Third, *the experience was a witness to Joel's prophecy concerning the return from Babylonian captivity and the renewal and restoration of God's people through the Spirit*. Peter quoted Joel 2:28–32, paralleling both the Greek and Hebrew texts with the exception that Peter changed the prophet's text from "In those days . . ." to "In the last days . . .". For Peter and the early Christians the pouring out of the Spirit and restoration of God's people through the resurrection of Jesus was a sign that the church was the renewal of a people. The coming of the empire would be ushered in through the power of the Spirit and the preparation of the Gospel to be carried worldwide. The restoration and rebuilding of Jerusalem and the temple was the result of the pouring out of the Spirit, the new heavens and new earth, the glory of God, and the shining of Zion's light to the Gentiles. Likewise, the Pentecost event in Acts 2 signaled the restoration and rebuilding of the people of God.

> Then Peter standing with the Eleven, raised his voice and proclaimed to the crowd: "Fellow Judeans and all of you who live in Jerusalem, let me explain this to you; listen carefully to what I say. You are assuming that these people are drunk. It's only nine in the morning! No. This is what was spoken by the prophet Joel . . . . Everyone who calls on the name of the Lord will be saved (Acts 2:14–16, 21).

Peter quoted the Joel prophecy and offered hope to the nation under Roman occupation. As in the days when Judah returned from Babylonian captivity, the people would have had dreams instead of nightmares, young

---

6. Haya-Prats, *Empowered Believers*, 34.

men and women would have had the courage and knowledge to speak for God, adults would have had hope and vision, and slaves would become part of the restored people. The signs and wonders in the constellations was written and spoken through apocalyptic language, a highly descriptive language of vision for an oral audience. The Pentecost event was a great day of Yahweh. It, like the return from captivity, was an earthshaking event. For God to take back rebellious Israel, after it broke the covenant, required a cosmological transition (Isa 54:6; Jer 3:8–12). The new heavens and new earth was necessary to provide a safe place to repair the broken relationship between Yahweh's people and their God. While Judah may have not realized it, their God was performing a miracle in order to receive them back from exile. Likewise, after the crucifixion of Jesus, who was God in the flesh, a miracle had to happen to repair the broken relationship. For Peter, this event was a divine intervention of the Spirit and God's extension of hope, forgiveness, and reconciliation through the church.

An interesting point in this text is the response of "some people." While there were those witnessing the outpouring of the Spirit among the early Christians who heard and understood the languages of these Spirit-filled Christians, there were a few who thought that the speakers were drunk (Acts 2:13). Their reason for thinking this was not based on the apostles' behavior or actions. I remember as a young man occasionally hearing preachers address this text while talking about the Holy Spirit. They would stagger and share that the people thought the apostles were drunk. They would then mention that when one is filled with the Spirit non-spiritual people believe they are intoxicated.

However, this was not the point in Luke's story. The hearers assumed the speakers were drunk because they didn't understand what they were saying. Those who understand more than one language know when people speak another dialect and, even though they did not understand the words, they recognized that it was another language. Those who only know one language, and/or refuse to learn another, typically don't understand when someone is speaking another dialect. This seems to be the case in Acts 2:13. In a multicultural world who would choose to be monolingual?

Among the Judahite religious leaders there were those who spoke Hebrew and believed it was the only language that God had called them to speak. While they might have been aware of Aramaic, Greek, and Latin, their belief system would not allow them to embrace these languages and other cultures. There were rabbis who believed that the common Aramaic and Greek versions of their Bible (called the Targum and Septuagint) were corrupted, evil, and not worth reading.[7] They perpetuated the resistance to other translations of Torah. The comment concerning drunkenness is less a critique of the apostles and more an explanation of the hearers' hard-heartedness. These individuals may have been strict Hebraic Jews and would have believed that learning Greek and its culture was unacceptable to Yahweh. Some from this group of people became antagonistic toward the Spirit's leading for the Empire of Jesus. These were the ones who were at the center of the circumcision, foreign synagogue, temple, and law of Moses discussions with Paul. These were also the ones who prevented and resisted the Spirit from going global and drawing in people from other cultures, lifestyles, and ethnicities. They later persecuted Paul and his mission teams. The corruption and fear from many of the leaders manifested itself through stricter observance of the Torah, collaborating with government authorities, and trying to control associations within their community. Outsiders typically presented a threat and were either expelled or labeled as deviant.[8] From the beginnings of the church in Acts, resistance existed.

> "Let all Israel be assured of this: God has made Jesus, whom you crucified, Lord and Messiah/Christ." Hearing this, they were cut to the heart and said to Peter and the other apostles, "Brothers, what shall we do?" Peter replied, "Repent and be baptized, every one of you, in the name of Jesus Christ for the forgiveness of your sins. You will receive the gift of the Holy Spirit. The promise is for you, your children, and all who are far off—all whom the Lord our God calls." . . . Those who received his message were baptized, and about three thousand were added to their number that day. They devoted themselves to the apostles' teaching, to fellowship, to the breaking of bread, and to prayer. Everyone was filled with awe at the many wonders and signs performed by the apostles. All the believers were together and had everything in common. They sold property and possessions to give to anyone who had need. Every day they continued to meet together in the temple courts. They broke bread in their homes and ate together with glad and sincere hearts, praising God and enjoying the favor of all the people. The Lord added to their number daily those who were being saved (Acts 2:36–47).

7. Dawsey, *Peter's Last Sermon*, 9.

8. Malina and Neyrey, "Conflict in Luke-Acts," 104–8; Johnson, *Prophetic Jesus*, 145; Lee, "Pilate and the Crucifixion of Jesus in Luke-Acts," 94–95; and Saldarini, *Pharisees, Scribes, and Sadducees in Palestinian Society*, 6, 9.

There were men and women who embraced the new vision of the Spirit. The crucifixion of Jesus became a stumbling block/offense to some. Jesus' teaching that the Messiah was to suffer and be rejected was not what they were looking for from the anointed leader. While the crowds may have joined the corrupt religious leaders and persuaded Pilate to crucify Jesus, they now had to reinvestigate their actions based on the global manifestation of the Spirit and fulfillment of Joel. Peter's words hurt them emotionally. They may have known what they had done was wrong, and tried to live with it for fifty days. However, seeing God's power and hearing Peter's impassioned plea convicted them. They were guilty and knew it. They, like the people in Babylonian captivity, needed a fresh start. Here was their chance.

When they asked Peter for advice he called them to transform their lives. He did not ask them to pray a prayer, accept Jesus into their lives, or to only confess their sins. He called them to make a bold choice. They needed to repent and be baptized (immersed in water) as John had preached earlier (Luke 3:1–5). For any Jew the call to repent and be immersed in water signified two things. First, *it meant that they were being cleansed from past sin and defilement*. Second, *it meant that they were preparing to meet their God*. As John preached a baptism of repentance for the forgiveness of sins in the wilderness (signifying the restoration of God's people), so Peter and the early Christians preached a simple baptism, but one that was in the name of Jesus. Any Jewish man or woman performing this act was stating that Jesus was Yahweh, Lord, and their God. They were pledging allegiance to him. It was a bold and courageous decision.

Throughout history the Christian church has practiced this event. Before infants were included in this action and before it became a "sacred rite" baptism was simply a bold and courageous action. Peter claimed that it was an appeal to God for a clear conscience (1 Pet 3:21). Paul wrote that it was the spiritual dying and resurrecting with Jesus (Rom 6:1–6; Col 2:11–12). He also wrote that it was "putting on Christ" (Gal 3:25–27), the bathtub of rebirth (Titus 3:5), and the point where people's past sins/behaviors were washed away (1 Cor 6:11).

Over the many years of teaching and baptizing people I have found that it has become a difficult decision. As Johnson suggested, baptism is risk in that not only are one's sins forgiven, but one must decide to live a life of holiness to Jesus and be willing to forgive the sins of others as well.[9] Baptism is that point where many people hesitate in their relationship

---

9. Johnson, *Prophetic Jesus*, 92–93.

with Jesus. It has always been easy to have people state their belief, confess Jesus as Lord, or accept him in their life through a prayer. However, I have found that when we show people the Bible and ask them to take the step of baptism there is a hesitance in some while others willingly take the "plunge." The hesitance suggests that this, in human minds, demands commitment, courage, and conviction. It is the bold decision to die to our old life and leave a permanent image in one's mind that they are transferring from life to death. Everett Ferguson, in his classic book on baptism in the ancient church, claimed that the Christians saw baptism as a saving act that brought them from darkness into the Empire of Jesus. "The New Testament and early Christian literature are virtually unanimous in ascribing a saving significance to baptism. If anything the early church exaggerated this aspect of baptism's significance. John 3:5 was taken outside its context in the Fourth Gospel and given in absolute sense. Only a few (fringe) heretics of the ancient church tried to dehydrate the new birth. The main variation among mainstream Christian authors was in how strongly different individuals affirmed the necessity for baptism. Baptism, however, was not seen as a human work but as God's work, and the salvation in baptism was premised on the saving effect of Christ's death on the cross and his victorious resurrection."[10] For Peter, baptism was the call to commitment.

When Moses descended from Mt. Sinai with the Torah tablets he heard the people partying and worshipping a golden calf (Exod 32:4). He smashed the tablets and sent the Levites to massacre the disobedient living among the congregation. Three thousand people died that day. When the new Empire of Jesus came from heaven in the outpouring of the Holy Spirit, three thousand people died to sin and were born again (Acts 2:41). Luke shared that this large number took the bold step of faith and were baptized, creating a restored community added to Jesus' church. In response they became a community of hope, reconciliation, and holiness.

First, *they followed the new Torah, which was the apostles' teaching.* The apostles, uneducated Galileans, were now teaching and guiding people, as Jesus had done previously. They had followed Jesus for three years and now were leading others closer to God. Second, *they were devoted to fellowship.* The Jewish Christians had become ethnically diverse as a community and embraced diversity, as opposed to the synagogues, which were ethnically distinct (Acts 6:9–10). They shared meals and spent time in prayer. Finally, *they took care of each other's needs.* While there would have been many Jews

---

10. Ferguson, *Baptism in the Early Church*, 854.

from other countries visiting Jerusalem for Pentecost, the early Christians shared with them and in many cases opened their homes. The apostles developed their ministry through family/home visitation and teaching in the temple courts. This 3,000-plus-member congregation (not including children) would have struggled to find one location to worship together, but the apostles accommodated the people by going where they could meet. Luke indicated that the Spirit transformed a people who had been culturally different and isolated into a community that embraced diversity, compassion, and hospitality. According to Luke, God added to their number as the church began to grow.

PATTERNS OF DISCIPLESHIP

Acts 1—2 was the preparation for the new ministry in Jesus' empire. In Luke 1—2 the author of this narrative introduced the characters and themes of his stories. Restoration, the presence and power of the Holy Spirit, repentance, reconciliation, social justice, sharing meals, hospitality in the home, the journey, and a new empire were themes in his narrative.[11] Luke 2 ended with Jesus at the temple, later returning home and growing in wisdom and physical build with God and people. Likewise Acts 1—2 concluded with the apostles teaching in the temple and helping their home communities grow. The disciples also grew in wisdom and size with God and people. Acts continued, as in Luke's earlier gospel, with the preaching and witness for Jesus through those ordained by God to proclaim repentance and baptism.

Acts 1—2 has introduced the reader to these themes that were prevalent in Luke. First, *the repentance/restoration of the nation was the hope of God's people* (1:6). While in occupied Palestine people hoped for renewal and revival from God because Rome and the corrupt Jewish elite were not producing that empire. Second, *the Spirit was the vehicle for this restoration and global witness to Yahweh in Jesus*. Finally, *when the people responded to God's plea for reconciliation through Jesus, a vibrant community not only grew but practiced this reconciliation and redistribution in the community*. This community responded through repentance, economic justice, hospitality in the home, sharing meals, removing socioeconomic barriers among their community, and proclaiming Jesus as the new emperor.

Today the church has a similar opportunity. With the emphasis on church growth, church planting, and outreach one thing continues to

11. Clark, *Jesus Unleashed*, 38–40.

remain—we are failing to engage our communities. In some ways we have focused on Peter's sermon or recording numbers of conversions, rather than the reconciliation of the Spirit. In addition to this we find ourselves similar to the people with old wineskins who refuse to learn a language other than English. "Those people are drunk and talking about something I don't understand." Churches that operate out of fear or high anxiety enact a higher level of control in order to "get results" from their people. In addition to this delegating and releasing people to be led by the Spirit and do ministry is difficult. While change becomes "scary" it is a key component to being led by the Holy Spirit (and assuming others are also led by the same Spirit).[12] Instead of repenting that we failed to learn about others we assume everyone should learn our ways, speak our language, and follow our circumcision rites. Unfortunately this will be the downfall of our churches. When the Spirit moves the church to speak the languages of others, those who refuse to learn will be left behind.

While preaching in a larger church in Portland we began an English as a Second Language (ESL) ministry. Since Portland is a very ethnically diverse city, many of our people wanted to reach out to immigrant families seeking to learn English since their children were able to learn in school. As the ministry grew we began to have families visit our church. In addition to this the church was the headquarters for a mission organization that taught English and the Bible on every continent. We decided to have a Missions Sunday to celebrate the call to world evangelism, our outreach in the community, our ESL ministry, and the truth that the Spirit is ethnically diverse. It was an exciting day. The Scriptures were read in over fifteen languages, mostly by our members, and a few from the guests whom we had invited to our assembly.

Immediately that week I had received a call from an older couple whom our family loved dearly. They had moved to Portland from the southern United States and had concerns about Sunday. While visiting they claimed, "Those people need to learn English and speak English. That's why they came here." While I wanted to tell them we were teaching them English I decided to focus on Jesus instead. "Surely you don't believe God only speaks English?" I said. "No," they said, "we're not talking about God—we're talking about those people." I realized what they were saying then asked, "So, how are we going to teach people who don't speak English? How are we going to bring the gospel to people of other ethnicities here in

---

12. Johnson, *Prophetic Jesus*, 128; Stark, *What Americans Really Believe*, 36.

Portland?" "I don't know," the woman sadly said. While I never saw this couple as a problem or confrontational they reminded me of the people in Jerusalem who possibly reacted out of fear. Fear that the way was being diluted by other languages. Fear that the language of God was more diverse than they could understand. Fear that change was coming faster than they could comprehend. Fear that the world was becoming so diverse that they felt overwhelmed. However, when the Spirit leads we have no option but to follow and embrace the changes driven by the divine Spirit.

The Spirit, however, offers vibrant life to the church. Whether the church is small, medium-sized, large, new plant, or an established part of the community, the Spirit empowers God's people to dream, have a vision, and view salvation and a relationship with Jesus as a cosmic event. We have the opportunity to understand our faith as a time to reconcile with Jesus and others. Our homes, our food, our money, and our worship become something we share. We find ourselves redistributing our resources into the community and the lives of others. We learn their languages, invite them into our homes, and eat our food together. We pray with them, meet with them, and worship with them. God desires unity and reconciliation and it comes through the Spirit.

A year after my conversation with the couple from the South I was going to visit one of the Kosovar families in our ESL ministry. Our ministry practiced a house-to-house method where teachers adopted a family and taught them. Typically this happened over a meal that was a powerful bonding moment for teacher and student. Our Kosovar family had been driven from their country when the Serbian dictator, Milan Milosovic, had begun his brutal slaughter of Muslim Kosovarians and driven many from their homes. The Ramas were one of these families. I had returned that week from Albania and was eager to share some of what I learned with the Ramas as they also spoke Albanian. Elas met me at the door and gave me the customary kiss-and-hug greeting. As I slipped off my shoes he motioned that I could keep them on, something they would say to let us know we were guests and were exempt from removing our shoes. However I put them by the other shoes and motioned that I was going to keep them off. Then I replied in Albanian "Une jame shqiptar" (I am Albanian). Elas laughed loudly, hugged me, and said, "Maybe—we shall see. Come and sit down." Acceptance is important in cultures and while speaking the languages doesn't equal inclusion, it is the first step. Jesus knew that Christians must take that first step in order for the gospel to find acceptance.

We're not drunk.

We are just witnessing that what God promised, through the prophets, will be done.

Will you join us?

4

RESISTANCE TO THE SPIRIT

"Return [repent] to me," declares Yahweh Almighty, "and I will return [repent] to you." (Zech 1:2)

MANY YEARS AGO I was a younger preacher at a small church in Bonne Terre, Missouri. After three years of youth ministry and six months of marriage, Lori and I moved to this small rural area outside of St. Louis to work with an older church. The people were wonderful and the elderly couples loved us like their own children. I learned much from many of the men and found that the church grew quickly as we became active in our community. This was also a unique church as the congregation was less conservative than many of the southern Missouri Churches of Christ. We were engaged in the community and partnered with many other churches to reach out to the working poor, single mothers, and children in many of the poverty-stricken neighborhoods.

One Sunday a middle-aged man visited our congregation. Everyone made him feel welcome and visited with him, yet he seemed a little distanced from people. He had been living in Bonne Terre for six months and hadn't found a church home. Later that week I visited his apartment to thank him for coming and see if he needed anything. We visited about church, where he was raised, and if he had a spiritual background. He sat for a minute looking at the floor, and then said to me, "I've heard about your church. I was raised in the Churches of Christ and my parents have warned me about some of your church's teachings." I nodded my head, having heard this before, and asked what it was that gave him a problem. He couldn't quite name anything but mentioned that his parents said he should be cautious. I asked him how many other churches he had visited in the town, and what he thought about them. He admitted he hadn't gone to church since he moved to Bonne Terre. Then he said, "You know, I have found it is better to not go to church than to go to the wrong church." I responded, "So, since the Bible tells us to go to church on Sunday, and Satan would rather us not—you're telling me it's better to do what Satan wants than what God told you to do? If you at least went to church wouldn't you be at least trying to obey God?" I was young, did not have the best filter, and typically had little patience. However, he just huffed at me and said, "Well, you know what I mean." We visited a while longer and I prayed with him. I never saw him again. I did leave wondering how someone could feel that disobedience, in any form, was an acceptable form of discipleship.

RECONCILED COMMUNITIES

After the Spirit empowered the early Christians to fulfill the ministry of Jesus, the new movement manifested the fruits of reconciled communities that were living in God's shalom. As the early church began to grow, the new Christians formed a tremendous community by crossing cultural, economic, and social boundaries. In addition to this those with wealth began to redistribute resources to those in need. For Luke, this was not only a sign of the power of the Spirit, it was a reflection of Jesus' ministry. Shalom/peace and economic justice was idealized through the forgiveness of debts, relief to the poor, and sharing of resources among the marginalized.[1] The uniting of Jews from various ethnic backgrounds also signaled the restoration of a new diverse people.[2]

The city of Jerusalem, while under the oppression of the Roman government, had become fragmented and contributed to the marginalization of groups among them. For Luke, the center of the world was not Jerusalem but Rome. He mentioned Jerusalem and Rome more than other Christian authors, sixty-two times as compared to twelve for all the others.[3] Luke also used the Greek name for Jerusalem twenty-seven times as opposed to twenty-six by the other writers combined. Luke's gospel suggested that

    1. Levine, *The Misunderstood Jew*, 49–50; Grottanelli, *Kings and Prophets*, 127; Lee, "Pilate and the Crucifixion of Jesus in Luke-Acts," 90.
    2. Miller, "Paul and His Ethnicity," 38.
    3. Bachmann, "Jerusalem and Rome in Luke-Acts," 61–62; 67.

the corrupt religious leaders of the Jewish community had labeled as sinners those who were not part of their class. In Luke's gospel he referred to the groups as "tax collectors and others," while the religious leaders labeled them "tax collectors and sinners." These individuals comprised the poor, artisans, those who worked unclean or despised trades, slaves, and women.[4] While a small percentage of individuals could read and write and became part of the educated and elite classes, the majority of individuals comprised the marginalized classes.[5] In Acts, however, this "sinner" title disappeared, suggesting that the church was reaching those on the margins rather than labeling them.[6]

The Spirit had anointed Jesus to "proclaim freedom to the captives" (Luke 4:16–19). For Luke this not only happened during Jesus' day, but continued to happen in the early church as it practiced his ministry. Acts 2 ended with a sign that reconciliation was occurring within the new community both socially and economically. Acts 3 began with a healing story that seemed familiar to those Jesus performed in the Gospels.

Peter and John, as did Jesus, continued the pattern of attending the temple to pray and fulfill the role of faithful Jewish males. The temple was still a major location for Luke's theology. Even as Rome became the new focus of Christian ministry Luke continued to refer to Jerusalem throughout Acts.[7] The stories in Acts will continue to loop through Jerusalem as the movement journeys farther and farther from this city center.[8] While at the temple the apostles healed a crippled man who was at the entrance to the court of women (Acts 3:2). This gate, called Beautiful, was the location where people placed him every day, hoping to receive money (alms). As with many handicapped individuals in the ancient world, he depended solely on the mercy and gifts of strangers. The text also explained that "he was carried and placed . . ." suggesting that he, like the poor man, Lazarus, and the paralyzed man in the Gospels had to be carried by family or friends (Acts 3:2; Luke 5:18–19; 16:19–31). The text also suggested that he expected money from these two apostles, indicating that when he saw them they were no different than any other temple attendee, and their reputation had not become known. Following the way of Jesus, Peter touched the man and

---

4. Adams, *The Sinner in Luke*, 89; Clark, *Jesus Unleashed*, 28.
5. Clark, *The Better Way*, xviii–xx.
6. Adams, *The Sinner in Luke*, xv.
7. Bachmann, "Jerusalem and Rome in Luke-Acts," 69–71.
8. Johnson, *Prophetic Jesus*, 20.

lifted him to his feet. The man not only stood, he jumped up, walked, and praised God. The crowd was rightly amazed because this adult male had been crippled from birth, suggesting that his legs, feet, and ankles would have been extremely small and thin. However this miracle, like the miracles of Jesus, amazed the crowd.

Ancient writers typically used appearances and physical disabilities to suggest to the reader one were evil or deservingly cursed. However, for Luke, those with physical maladies became the locations for the glory of God and the Christian followers.[9] The thought of a crippled man with soft, weak ankles jumping and praising God was not only a testimony to Jesus' power, but a reminder that people who didn't "fit" in their society were viewed as outcasts and those on the social margins of life. As always this gave the Christian leaders the opportunity to preach Jesus. Peter asked why the crowd was surprised, which was a good question considering that they were at the temple, the house of Yahweh.

> The God of Abraham, Isaac, Jacob, and our fathers, has glorified his servant Jesus. You handed him over to be killed, and you disowned him before Pilate even though he had wanted to release him. You abandoned the Holy Righteous One and asked that a murderer be forgiven. You killed the author of life, but God raised him from the dead. We are witnesses of this. By faith in the name of Jesus, this man whom you see and know was strengthened. It is Jesus' name and the faith that has completely healed him, as you can all see. Now, brothers and sisters, I know that you acted in ignorance, as did your leaders. But this is how God fulfilled what he had foretold through all the prophets, saying that his Messiah would suffer. Repent, then, and turn to God, so that your sins may be wiped out, that times of refreshing may come from the Lord, and that he may send the Messiah, who has been appointed for you—even Jesus. Heaven must receive him until the time comes for God to restore everything, as he promised long ago through his holy prophets.... You are heirs of the prophets and of the covenant God made with your fathers. He said to Abraham, "Through your offspring all peoples on earth will be blessed." When God raised up his servant, he sent him first to you to bless you by turning each of you from your wicked ways. (Acts 3:13–18, 25–26)

---

9. Parsons, *Body and Character in Luke and Acts*, 15.

The Joy of Repentance

The focus of the message was not the crucifixion. For Peter and John the focus was the incarnation and resurrection. Peter shared with the crowd the reasons why Jesus came to earth. First, *Jesus came so that they would have an opportunity to repent of their sins and change their behavior as a nation.* Second, *Jesus came so that through their repentance they could receive forgiveness of sins and be refreshed.* Finally *Peter suggested that Jesus must remain in heaven until the time to restore the empire, something that they were looking forward to receiving.* Peter was not simply calling the people to repent; he was offering them a new perspective of the God of Israel. He was also reminding them that the incarnation was God's will, which included the rejection, suffering, and resurrection of Jesus.

First, repentance *is typically a good term.* Many might believe it is negative. This may be because we have heard angry preachers, parents, or other Christians speaking of the evils of our world and that we must repent in order to avoid the impending doom from God. While this might be our common experience, repentance in the Bible offers hope and a new chance. At Agape many of our people have experienced recovery from various addictions. Making amends is a common term used by recovery groups that requires the recovering addict to repent or validate those they have hurt, wronged, or cut off while in their addiction. Tremendous healing happens during this time. Men and women do what adults should do by validating and apologizing those they have hurt. Many who suffered feel better and appreciate hearing that they have been wronged. Those who make amends share with us that they return with either repentance, forgiveness, or a renewed relationship. When it is over, both parties typically feel a sense of peace, joy, and love. Relationship is restored. Repentance is an *opportunity* to change one's life and restore relationships.

Peter suggested that Jesus was sent to call people to repentance and that they could heal, be renewed, and reestablish their relationship with God. In addition to this Peter stated that this was a blessing (Acts 3:26). Repentance was not condemnation or threat. It is an opportunity to heal a wounded, broken, or tumultuous relationship by making amends with the one or ones we have hurt. Some in the crowd would have remembered yelling "Crucify him" to Pilate during the Passover festival. Peter preached the truth: "Pilate wanted to let Jesus go, but you forced his hand." Peter reminded them again that they killed and disowned Jesus, the Holy One sent from God.

Second, Yahweh desires and deserves our repentance. God was the hurt spouse pursuing the guilty party who had left and stayed isolated because of shame. While Yahweh did not allow Israel to continue to abuse and degrade the covenant, God held out hope of forgiveness. God would be the one to forgive and offer hope if that is what was needed to reconcile the relationship. Israel was still expected to be faithful and make amends, but to those overcome with shame, it took someone to first offer the hand of hope and forgiveness. Yahweh, through the prophets, pursued Israel and offered this hope. Peter indicated that Jesus was this offer of hope, forgiveness, and love. This was the incarnation. This was what it meant for Jesus to save his people. For a people steeped in shame, guilt, sin, and oppression, repentance was a way out. It was something they needed to do and something that God desired.

Finally, repentance states that Jesus is the way. This does not mean that Christians have a one-way ticket to heaven, or that our ways are better than other beliefs, religions, or philosophies. We have had enough skeletons in our historical closets to prove that we are no different than any other religion. However, it does mean that Jesus showed us how to repent, how to change our lives, and is God's offer of a relationship. Instead of arguing whether we have the correct religion we simply need to repent of our sins and develop a relationship with God. We must make amends to our community and live in harmony with it. It causes us to be people of relationship, not hypocrisy or judgment. Repentance helps us practice reconciliation and redistribution. We repent because God/Jesus deserves to hear, "I'm sorry I hurt you and I will change my ways." Repentance is "a mournful and joyless piety driven by sin-consciousness and guilt, and means conversion or . . . turning."[10] Jesus is our path to being in a relationship and partnership with God. We practice Christ's love, reconciliation, and community on this earth because he becomes our model of life. Jesus as the way means that he is the model of reconciliation and his life and actions are what God wants us to do. I find that few people would argue with Jesus' life. Whether they follow him or not, they at least know that his way is one that provides hope for humanity. It is one that truly reflects the compassion of Yahweh. It also reflects harmony in relationships.

---

10. Johnson, *Prophetic Jesus*, 91.

THE RESISTANCE

While the crowds were celebrating the lame man's healing, the religious leaders arrived on the scene. It is hard to get a sense of who these men were by only reading the Gospels. In the Gospels we may understand these men as corrupt and hypocritical leaders and view their practices as controlling and oppressive. In some cases this was true, however there were other leaders who were honest and God-fearing men. Joseph of Arimathea, Zechariah the priest, Gamaliel, and Nicodemus represent the men who loved Yahweh with their hearts (Luke 1:5–8; 23:51; John 3:1–3). As the book of Acts progressed many Jewish leaders became Christian, including the Pharisee Saul of Tarsus (Acts 4:4; 6:7; 9:1–19). The Pharisees, Sadducees, and others should not all be viewed as fake, false, or dysfunctional as a religion. The Torah was still Yahweh's ethical code and many of the Christians upheld the Jewish teachings. "The Pharisees were scholars who wrested control of Judaism from the established authorities."[11] However, under the pressures of Roman colonization some created an internalized, inward-focused form of Judaism.

The religious leaders should be viewed by their role in the Jewish culture. Since Rome occupied Palestine it was important that leadership be delegated to other officials in the community.[12] The Pharisees and Sadducees existed because the nation wanted to avoid returning to the idolatry and sin that they had succumbed to when they were taken captive to Babylon.[13] In 165 BCE they rallied the nation to stand firm and resist the Greeks and Syrians who tried to desecrate the temple and slaughter many of the followers in Jerusalem. These leaders also opposed the Romans who tried to put an eagle statue or an image for Caesar in God's temple. The leaders took their role seriously and laid their lives down for Yahweh. These leaders saw their responsibility as leading and guiding the Jews to be faithful to God.

However, as leaders they were to maintain purity, peace, and safety for the people. If the Romans suspected a disturbance or unlawful assembly, they would investigate. The Jewish leaders, like many other leaders in occupied communities, wanted to avoid unnecessary involvement from the Roman government and many times kept a tight rein on the people and

---

11. Saldarini, *Pharisees, Scribes, and Sadducees*, 9.
12. Clark, *Jesus Unleashed*, 14–15.
13. Ibid., 8–9.

those suspected of leading rebellions. If those leaders became corrupt the tension would increase even more, but these leaders knew that to maintain order and peace, they needed to question anything out of the ordinary.

A Disturbance in the Community?

The religious leaders arrived while the crowd was listening to Peter speak concerning the resurrection (Acts 4:1). In their minds the Jesus matter was settled when they had him executed in such a cruel and brutal method. However, the story did not end at the cross. As with Jesus, Peter and John were put in jail and then questioned the next day by the same leaders who had judged Jesus. Their question was not about the teaching but the crippled man's healing. These men knew something had happened but they were not aware that these two apostles also had the power of the Spirit. Jesus did not perform miracles in their midst, but the apostles had.

> Then Peter, filled with the Holy Spirit, said to them: "Rulers and elders of the people! If we are being questioned today concerning good work done to a man who was lame and how he was healed, then you and all the people must understand that it is by the name of Jesus Christ of Nazareth, whom you crucified and whom God raised from the dead, that this man stands before you healed. Jesus is 'the stone you builders rejected, who has become the cornerstone.' Salvation is found in no one else, for there is no other name under heaven given to humans by whom we must be saved." When they saw the courage of Peter and John and realized that they were untrained, ordinary men, they were astonished and took note that they had been with Jesus. But since they could see the man who had been healed standing there, there was nothing they could say. They were ordered to withdraw from the Sanhedrin and then gathered/discussed. "What are we going to do with these men? Everyone living in Jerusalem knows they have performed a notable sign, and we cannot deny it . . . we must warn them to speak no longer to anyone in this name so that this will not spread among the people." (Acts 4:8–17)

It must have been an interesting scene that day. In the past the Jewish council, known as the Sanhedrin, would have heard many testimonies from rebel groups, political leaders, thieves, assassins, and common people. They would have heard the leaders of revolutions call them cowards, curse the Romans, and prophesy from God concerning the city's destruction. It is one thing to speak out in a crowd; it's another to speak in private to those who hold your fate. In this situation the leaders could use physical discipline in secret. When Jesus faced this crowd he was silent, except the two times he claimed to be Yahweh (Luke 22:66–71). The council examinations had a way of finding what one truly believed and could literally "beat it out of a person."

Boldness in the Spirit

Peter and John, however, argued their case with boldness and conviction. In Greco-Roman biographies and narratives courtroom scenes were common heroic themes.[14] The accused proved their innocence through long speeches that were used, by the writer, to vindicate them in the eyes of the reader and audience. Speeches were also used in Acts as Luke's way of representing the faith of the Christian community through the teachings and lessons of their leaders. The councils sometimes acquitted them, proving to be just, or condemned them, proving to be corrupt. Luke used this genre in his writings, especially with Peter and Paul's narratives.

However, Luke adapted this theme by suggesting that the evidence was the fruit of the church. Peter and John did not use clever arguments to persuade the council. First, *they relied on the hard evidence of the miracle before them.* Second, *they reminded these leaders that they unjustly murdered Jesus, who was God's son or Yahweh in the flesh.* Finally, *they boldly claimed that Jesus was Lord by using language common for Caesar and Yahweh.* Their statement "there is no other name" referred to Yahweh in the Hebrew Bible as well as the Emperor who claimed to bring salvation to all.

The council proved to be unjust. It attempted to prevent the spread of the miraculous healing, acknowledging that it could not deny this miracle. If these men were allowed to speak their use of "the name" for Jesus was a sign of blasphemy to the Jews and it became a source of treason for the Romans. The Jewish leaders operated out of fear both towards the apostles as well as their message.

The Holy Spirit operated in the courtroom as well. For Luke one major manifestation of the Spirit was boldness. The Spirit was to empower the early church to witness/testify and preach Jesus in any situation. In Acts 2 the Spirit empowered the Christians to witness cross-culturally. It also empowered them in this section to witness boldly with courage.

14. Schwartz, "The Trial Scene in the Greek Novels and in Acts," 105–38.

> The believers were united in heart and soul. No one claimed that any of their possessions was their own, they shared what they had. With great power the apostles testified to the resurrection of the Lord Jesus. Great grace was at work in them and there were no vulnerable persons among them. For from time to time those who owned land or houses sold them, brought the money from the sales and put it at the apostles' feet, and it was distributed to anyone who had need. Joseph, a Levite from Cyprus, whom the apostles called Barnabas (which means "son of encouragement"), sold his field, brought the money, and put it at the apostles' feet. (Acts 4:32–37)

Emerging movements thrive because they adapt to their environments. This was evident in the early Christian community. Woodward indicated that new movements become open, adaptable, grow in learning, distribute knowledge, practice servant leadership, and evolve between control and chaos.[15] The early Christians practiced this as well and became an emergent community in the ancient Jewish world. The apostle's witness empowered the church to reflect the Spirit again through reconciliation and redistribution. The wealthy of the group shared their blessings and provided for those without, which would have been a large portion of the group. This divine reversal was illustrated by a Levite named Joseph, who gave to the poor the proceeds from a piece of land he had sold. In the Hebrew Bible land was given by the people to the Levites, however here it was reversed. Barnabas's generosity earned him the Aramaic nickname "Son of a Prophet," which Luke translated "Son of Encouragement." This suggested that prophecy during this time was desired as a message of encouragement rather than judgment.

The Spirit continued to work within the community. Witnessing Barnabas's praise, a couple named Ananias and Sapphira tried to seek their own fame by imitating him and selling a field. Their sin was not in keeping some of the money but lying to the community, and the Spirit, and claiming to have given more than they had. While a story in the Christian Scriptures of two people being "struck dead" after a confrontation with a leader makes us uncomfortable, Luke's point is clear. The Holy Spirit seeks honesty, righteousness, and truth. As Paul wrote, "Do not allow what you consider good to be spoken of as evil. For the Empire of God is not a matter of eating and drinking, but of righteousness, peace, and joy in the Holy Spirit, because anyone who serves Christ in this way is pleasing to God

---

15. Woodward, *Creating a Missional Culture*, 62.

and approved by men" (Rom 14:16–18). The Spirit's desire is to create a community that reflects holiness and integrity. If Christian leaders wish the community of Jesus to be a witness to his integrity, we many times will have to be confrontational with those who threaten our reputation.

At the Agape Church of Christ we have a reputation in our community, and throughout the country, as being advocates for victims, whether they are homeless, poor, or victims of partner abuse or sexual assault. One issue we have faced is with men among us who are racist, misogynistic, or hold a cultural view of masculinity that shames "femininity."[16] There have been times when we as leaders (male and female) as well as our men at church have had to confront oppressive males. Those who stay become good men, fathers, and husbands. Those who leave have left a path of destruction in their life and the lives of others. Sometimes we are labeled as "angry feminists," judgmental, unloving, or uncaring. However, we are more concerned what our community, the county service providers, victims' advocates, and our own victims/survivors think about Jesus and us as a church carrying his name. Jesus' church must uphold the ethics and fruits of the Spirit in the community. Jesus' leaders must be willing to make the sacrifice to promote safety in our churches and be an advocate for safety in our communities.

Planting a church has been difficult, exhilarating, a struggle, joy, and the best job we have ever done. We have continued to reach out to the Portland community and yet take criticism for it. In 2012 we launched two new churches, losing five families to the new congregations. During that year we had four Christian couples involved in sin that we confronted and tried to protect the church. Our other ministers, Lori, and I were exhausted through this time, but we continued to reach new young people. In 2014 we again had an exodus of families while reaching many among the homeless community. Yet through it all we have learned that being a church in the way of Jesus involves struggle and requires a tremendous price. Leaders have to be willing to not only lay their lives down, but continue to do it—even if they are tired. We also have to be willing to confront sin and people who partner with sin even though it is emotionally and physically draining. This is what it means to be open, honest, and real. Those like Ananias and Sapphira who try to hide or justify sin for human praise will resent honesty and openness. However, Jesus calls leaders to promote truth and integrity in the congregation, as it is a reflection of Jesus to a hurting world seeking justice.

---

16. Clark, *Am I Sleeping with the Enemy?*, 28–29.

MINISTRY IN THE SPIRIT

> The apostles performed signs and wonders among the people. All the believers met together in Solomon's Colonnade. Few were bold enough to join them, even though they were highly regarded by the people. Nevertheless, more and more men and women believed in the Lord and were added to their number. As a result, people brought the sick into the streets and laid them on beds and mats so that at least Peter's shadow might fall on some of them as he passed by. Crowds gathered also from the towns near Jerusalem, bringing their sick and those suffering from unclean spirits, and all of them were healed. (Acts 5:12–16)

The early Christians gained influence in the community, as had Jesus, because people saw the power of the Spirit in their lives. Luke did not write that people flocked to their worship services in the temple. He mentioned that "few were bold enough to join them," or "many resisted joining them." However, he mentioned "the people" and "crowds" three times in this section. The power of the Holy Spirit was witnessed to by the church's ministry—not just its worship. Their leaders were not viewed as "great speakers" but people who were able to witness Jesus in their community outreach.

This is a challenge for the modern church. In the beginnings of Acts the power of the Spirit was not something only presented in a Sunday assembly. It was observed by the community. Large amounts of time, energy, and money have been invested in buildings for worship, programs for Sunday mornings, and the weekly worship. Hours are spent preparing for the Sunday sermon and weekly praise teams. Yet we continue to wonder why church attendance struggles and declines in the United States.[17] "Consequently, the main focus of middle-class churches turned inward toward worship, counseling, mentoring, and small groups. In and of themselves these are good things, but they entail the danger that church becomes one sided. The outward dynamic gets short shrift as churches in villages and cities cease to play a social or cultural role.... During the time of a mounting recession, dwindling middle class, and growing poverty, completely new, practical questions need to be asked of the church."[18]

In Acts 4:12–16, church worship was not attractional. Many people were not bold enough to attend or join. Yet they were willing to take part

---

17. Woodward, *Creating a Missional Culture*, 29; Robinson and Wall, *Called to Be Church*, 43.

18. Faix, "Toward a Holistic Process of Transformational Mission," 212–13.

in the daily outreach, healing, and respect of Jesus' people. Due to this, the church grew. Today Christians must focus upon weekly ministry out of the building, rather than just the Sunday morning assembly. Even more disciples of Jesus must see their spiritual lives outside of a building and in their homes, neighborhoods, vocation, and relationships. "Missional leaders don't see changing the church as central to their cause; they want to change the whole world."[19]

Leaders must also be men and women who "get their hands dirty."[20] Often I meet seminary/graduate school students who want to discuss preaching issues, styles of sermons, and definitions such as "missional ministry" or "attractional ministry." Male and female, the discussion of many concerns the Sunday worship, preaching, or teaching. Lori and I both have told males and females that the future of the church is not based upon how many more public speakers we train or bloggers who write and post on the Internet, but upon having men and women who are not afraid to lead others by living, loving, and caring for people in the community. The future is based upon whether our Christian leaders will be seen by our community as recluses or people who stand up and offer hope, courage, and guidance in our cities. It will not be viewed by leaders who only speak boldly, but those who are witnesses to the power of the resurrection both in their lives and the lives of those where they serve. I think that greatest compliment we have received as a church is when the county sheriff's deputy over Portland's human trafficking task force said, "Agape is a get-your-hands-dirty kind of church."

AN ADVOCATE

> Peter and the other apostles replied: "We must follow/obey God rather than humans! The God of our ancestors raised Jesus from the dead—the one you killed by hanging him on a cross [tree]. God exalted him to his own right hand as Prince and Savior to offer Israel repentance and forgive their sins. We are witnesses of these things, and so is the Holy Spirit, whom God has given to those who obey him." When they heard this, they were furious and wanted to put them to death. But a Pharisee named Gamaliel, a teacher of the law, who was honored by all the people, stood up

---

19. Frost, *The Road to Missional*, 21.
20. Shaw, "Vulnerable Authority," 121.

in the Sanhedrin and ordered that the men be put outside for a little while. Then he addressed the Sanhedrin: "Men of Israel, consider carefully what you intend to do to these men..." They called the apostles in and had them flogged. Then they ordered them not to speak in the name of Jesus, and let them go. The apostles left the Sanhedrin, rejoicing because they had been counted worthy of suffering disgrace for the Name. Day after day, in the temple courts and from house to house, they never stopped teaching and proclaiming the good news that Jesus is the Messiah. (Acts 5:29–42)

Gamaliel was a very wise teacher and leader among the Jews. The Apostle Paul credited much of his education to this man (Acts 22:3). He was also a well-respected rabbi and often quoted in the Jewish rabbinical texts (*m. Peah* 2:6; *m. Orl* 2:12; *m. Shek* 3:3; *m. Yeb* 16:7). It was written that "When Rabban Gamaliel the Elder died, the glory of the Law ceased and purity and abstinence died" (*m. Sot* 9:15). Gamaliel was viewed as a cautious interpreter of the Torah for people and the community, however he tended to lean toward mercy and favor for the vulnerable ones—especially women in cases of divorce (*m. Git* 4:2–3). He was also quoted as saying, "Provide thyself with a teacher and remove thyself from doubt, and tithe not overmuch by guesswork" (*m. Ab* 1:16).

Gamaliel was conservative and cautious, but cared about others. Luke shared that he was honored by all of the people (Acts 5:34). It is obvious that Paul received good mentoring from this man as he later became a powerful and loving leader in the church. However when the Jewish council found themselves face to face with the power of Jesus and the boldness of his followers, Gamaliel found an opportunity to intervene.

First, *the rabbi removed the men, whom he would have considered the problem, from the assembly.* This becomes a common method throughout Acts when an assembly becomes tense and begins to polarize (Acts 15:6; 22:24; 24:25; 26:30–31). Second, *Gamaliel took the focus off of the differing doctrinal issues and emphasized the fruits of their ministry and life.* As with other leaders the longevity of their work and followers was to be observed over time. For Gamaliel, if this was of God it would last. Finally, *he offered a reminder that Yahweh could be working in these men's lives.* As Jesus accused the Pharisees of blaspheming the Spirit, so Gamaliel warned that if Yahweh was working through the Christians, then the Jewish leaders should not fight against God (Luke 11:14–28).

While some might see Gamaliel as compromising on the issue, I suggest that he was honorable man and was careful to avoid resisting God. He quickly persuaded a group of corrupt and angry leaders (who had made sure Jesus was executed) to allow the apostles to continue to "blaspheme" (as they would have viewed it). The first resistance to the early Christians came from Jewish leaders operating out of fear, control, and a sense of regret over their decision to kill Jesus. They were losing their own to this movement and had to deal with the fact that this new church was doing more good for people in Jerusalem than they were. Gamaliel was a man who knew that change was coming, possibly by the hand of Yahweh, and that time would testify to the truth of this new movement. Luke will focus on "resistance" to this new Christian movement throughout Acts. However, Gamaliel was one who cautioned against resistance. He will represent the many Jewish leaders and people who do not resist the power of the Spirit but allow God's work to be shown in the church.

As an older minister of more than thirty years I appreciate Gamaliel and his offspring, men and women who over the centuries have found a way to persuade people to turn their anger outward and focus on the good Jesus has called them to do. As a young minister I was on the side of the Pharisees, trying to preserve and protect a church and youth group. Unfortunately it became controlling and motivated by fear and anxiety. Thankfully we all survived and realized that controlling others never led to peace and spiritual growth.

As a convert to Christianity I at times have found myself on the side of the apostles, calling for change, honesty, faith, justice, and peace. As a minister I have had a difficult time understanding why *change, transition, innovation*, and *adaptation* were negative words in the church. Many times those who have opposed this move were Christian leaders (whom I at times supported) who felt that God had called them/us to preserve, protect, and promote "the old paths," or "the traditional ways of the fathers." Conflict exists in many churches because both groups want what is best and in the end do the worst to each other. Gamaliel's advice is to let God work. Old wineskins preserve old wine while new wineskins produce new wine. Both are good. Both are needed. Both can draw together at the table of fellowship. The question is, "Will we be willing to let people choose which one they want?"

The council, however, still wished to prove a point. While it respected Gamaliel's advice, it did not respect the apostles. It had them tortured/

punished by whipping them with strips of leather that caused intense trauma and pain. Then they threatened them, something they knew would not work. Gamaliel was right, the apostles ignored the warnings and rejoiced that they suffered for "the Name" (Yahweh). This section ended as the book of Acts ended; the Gospel was preached in the city and no official could stop it. The apostles were now able to preach without pressure or opposition from the Jewish officials. It seemed, at this point, that they could do the work unhindered—yet we read in the following chapters that opposition will arise from new sources. The apostles, however, had found powerful ways to overcome this resistance.

First, *their boldness through prayer, faith, courage, and the Holy Spirit enabled them to preach the name, resurrection, and hope of Jesus.* They were able to call people to a decision and choice. The Spirit gave them the boldness to speak in various languages and publically for Jesus. Second, *those who opposed them finally backed down.* They had to resort to physical punishment and empty threats to stop them, which will not work. Finally, *there were those who, because of the apostles' courage and boldness, supported or joined the movement.* Thousands of people were baptized, one leader gave them an audience, and other leaders will later stand with the Christians in their witness of Jesus. Throughout Acts the apostles realized that Jesus had others in the community who would join or support the growth of his empire.

Today, Acts has a similar message for the modern church. First, Christianity, discipleship, and witness are based upon faith. This faith is not one that simply acknowledges that Jesus is Lord, accepts Jesus into one's heart/life, or makes a public confession of who we know Jesus is. This faith is one that is manifested through courage, conviction, and boldness. God's people are not intimidated by controlling, oppressive, and fear-based people. Jesus' followers do what he has asked of us but refuse to back down because others feel it is wrong. This is not a reference to "preaching about Jesus" when people don't want to listen, or asking that we respect everyone's right to believe. The faith and courage of Acts is one that proclaims that beggars should be cared for, the lame should walk or be protected, that people of other cultures have the right to know God is love, and that people should not be oppressed.

This faith and courage is also unwilling to back down from evil, whether it exists in our communities or (especially) in our churches. The Spirit is there to empower Jesus' followers to stand firm against evil and those who do evil and overcome it/them. The faith of the church is also observed by those in our community. When the Emperor Nero had Christians crucified and then lit on fire, put children in animal skins and threw them to the beasts, or tortured and murdered their parents, early Roman writers claimed that there was a sense of sympathy and respect for the Christians. Persecution was not just an illustration of the courage of Christians, it created a sense of empathy and support from their community. Many in the community would join their movement while others simply offered help.

Likewise American Christians today have a powerful opportunity to manifest courage and consistency in the midst of resistance. We can once again be a movement that thrives in adversity, as happens with those in other countries.

5

RESISTING THE SPIRIT: COMMUNITY RESISTANCE

For this is what Yahweh says: "To the eunuchs who keep my Sabbaths, who choose what pleases me, and take hold of my covenant; I will give them within my house/temple and its walls a memorial and a name better than sons and daughters; I will give them an eternal name that will not be cut off." (Isa 56:4–5)

In the last chapter we discussed the resistance that the apostles and early church faced from the Jerusalem leaders. As mentioned before, we should not view all of these leaders as corrupt, but understand that, as in any other form of government, there were some who were dishonest within this movement. They had the responsibility to lead the Jewish nation and make sure that they cooperated with the Roman government. Angry riots, uprisings, or political speeches would raise their anxiety. As the apostles began to heal people and preach, these leaders realized that something greater was present. Even after Gamaliel's advice they punished and threatened the apostles. This proved useless as the church began to grow while the apostles preached unhindered in Jerusalem. However, the early Christian community continued to face resistance, only this time it came from smaller groups also seeking to support the traditional faith community.

MEMBER CARE

> In those days when the disciples were increasing, the Greek Jews among them complained against the Hebrew Jews because their widows were being overlooked in their ministry. The twelve gathered all of the disciples together and said, "It would not be best for us to neglect the ministry of the word of God in order to wait on tables. Brothers and sisters, seek out seven witnesses from the men, full of the Spirit and wisdom. We will turn this responsibility over to them and will give our attention to prayer and the ministry of the word." This seemed good to the group. They chose Stephen, a man full of faith and of the Holy Spirit; Philip, Procorus, Nicanor, Timon, Parmenas, and Nicolas from Antioch, a convert to Judaism. They stood before the apostles, who prayed and laid their hands on them. The word of God spread and the number of disciples in Jerusalem increased rapidly, and a large number of priests became obedient to the faith. (Acts 6:1–7)

Luke's stories were favorable toward widows. He mentioned them in both books more than any other New Testament writer.[1] For Luke these women not only represented the more vulnerable groups in the ancient world, but also became some of the most active members in the early church. In addition to this it is probable that Jesus' mother, Mary, was a widow.

One of the first major issues that the church faced included concern for these women. The congregation had grown to the point where some widows were being neglected in the distribution of food. It is also possible that their conversion to the Christian movement removed them from their normal community care. They would have been paying a high price for their salvation. Not having males to lead or represent their family in the public square made it easy for them to be overlooked and ignored. This story has been understood as the first barrier that the church encountered and the fact that the apostles delegated their work was an indication of how to handle church issues. The appointing of the men (deacons) to help the widows seemed to suggest, to some, that the delegation of ministry duties was a major focus of effective leadership. This is true, and the church, at this time, was between 5,000 to 10,000 people. There was a need for the apostles to keep their focus on the preaching and ministry of the word, while others took care or "serving those in need" and other member-care ministries. In

---

1. Reid, "The Power of the Widows and How to Suppress It," 73.

this text the apostles not only delegated their ministry, but they encouraged the church to choose its own ministry leaders.

The congregation displayed their diversity by appointing Greek Jews (Hellenistic Jews) as evidenced by their Greek names. These men took care of the many widows and enabled the apostles to spend their time and energy with other ministries. This story indicated that effective church leadership required appointing others to care for the congregation. As Jesus appointed the twelve apostles, seventy disciples to go out two by two, and others to fulfill various ministries, so the apostles delegated responsibilities in the early church. Five thousand people were in the wilderness needing food. Jesus had said to the disciples, "You give them something to eat," enlisting all Christians to care ministries (Luke 9:13).

However, the point of the story seems to also involve the resistance. Luke wrote that the Hebraic Jews were neglecting the Greek Jews in the distribution of food. The resistance came from this group, which tended to be the ones who resented the Greek influence upon Jewish culture and were possibly the ones in Acts 2:13 who responded that the apostles were drunk. Rather than operating out of mercy they neglected the Greek Jewish widows and became a source of resistance within the early church. While the neglect of the widows was an issue or problem for the early Christians, it also became a sign of insensitivity and lack of care that some displayed for other vulnerable populations in Jerusalem.

The church decided to care for those in their community. This became another act of compassion that the Christians practiced as they shared possessions, distributed wealth to the poor, and cared for widows. Instead of avoiding care ministries for the greater good of reaching new people, they added this to their outreach. They realized that caring not just for their own, but those in need, was a sign of this new empire and justice/shalom of Jesus.

One of the classes that I teach at George Fox Evangelical Seminary is Pastoral Counseling. I always have a full class and many times have others who take the class online. In a movement that is bombarded with church growth, outreach, and evangelism materials there is a real need for care, counseling, and compassion for people in our churches. We are facing mental illness, depression, abuse, addictions, grief, family trauma, post-traumatic stress, and many other personal and family issues that affect our churches, members, and those in our community. Those who preach from the pulpit would do well to spend time waiting on tables before speaking to their people. In Acts 9 we will read that Peter also directly offered continued care to women in the movement. Even though he appointed others to the duty, he himself was not beyond directly helping people. This is what it meant to be a minister who was a witness for Jesus and of his power in the lives of others.

I was twenty-four years old as a youth minister in a church in Missouri. I was also considered an Associate Minister, which meant that the leaders wanted me to also visit the hospital, nursing homes, and widows to help the older minister who also had a busy schedule. One of the "widow ladies" I visited, Ruth, was a very sweet, caring, and supportive woman at our church. She would always offer me cake or something she had made when I would visit her. We would talk and I would pray with her. As with many of the older women I always felt like I was being cared for by them.

On one visit Ruth shared that she was going through "the change" known as menopause. She told me how she had felt and that many times she was exhausted, and would feel "hot flashes" that took her energy. I listened patiently and, as any twenty-four-year-old male would do, offered a bit of advice for her. "You know, when I feel that way I usually get up, take some aspirin, and run or work out in the yard to get a good sweat going." She looked at me a little startled and shook her head. "Maybe getting out in the garden and doing some work will help you in that, it seems to help me," I said. Ruth calmly said, "Well, we will see." We visited longer, prayed, and I left feeling very "pastoral." That is until I stopped at the office and shared with the minister's wife (Leigh) about my sound and wise advice.

Leigh gave me a lot (and I mean a lot) of advice at that moment. I don't remember everything that Leigh said, because she was talking so fast, but I do remember the phrase, loudly said, "Brother, if you are going to be any kind of help to women you need to learn compassion and to be a better listener." Feeling a little underappreciated, I met Lori, then my fiancée, for lunch and shared my wise advice with her. Oddly enough she said the same thing Leigh did, only with a little more intensity. Weeks later I visited Ruth and it seems that the elders' wives and Leigh had talked with her since I had visited. Ruth smiled and teased me about my advice while offering me more cake. I shared with her that I was sorry for giving her bad advice, to which she replied, "It's OK, I really didn't think you knew what you were talking about. I figured Lori would straighten you out. Looks like many others did that as well." She laughed and would remind me of that story every time I visited. Ministry is a learning experience, especially for younger, hard-headed males.

THE FIRST CHRISTIAN MARTYR

Soon after the disciples addressed the neglected widows, and while one of these deacons was doing ministry with them, he experienced resistance from others in smaller congregations. While the Jewish people regularly attended the temple in Jerusalem, synagogues were smaller communities throughout the city that were designed to facilitate spiritual, family, and personal growth. Some have suggested that these synagogues began in Babylon when the Jewish nation was without a temple.[2] Others indicate that they were a creation of the nation as they were scattered throughout Galilee. These communities were the heartbeat of the Jewish people within Jerusalem and especially in the areas where they were scattered throughout the Roman Empire. The synagogues were similar to modern churches in that they were small, reflected the temple atmosphere, and were places where the community met for weekly instruction.[3] In many places the synagogues were regionally located and met in someone's home or a rented hall. In Jerusalem some were located by ethnic groupings throughout the city where there were synagogues for freed slaves, Egyptians, and Asians (Acts 6:7–9). These Jews who had come from other parts of the world began to argue with the young servant Stephen. Instead of resistance coming now from the corrupted leaders, it came from local devoted worshippers.

> Stephen was a man full of grace and power, performed great wonders and signs among the people. Opposition arose, from members of the synagogues of the Libertarians [called freed ones], Cyrene, Alexandria, as well as those from the provinces of Cilicia and Asia. They argued with Stephen and were unable to withstand the wisdom the Spirit gave him as he spoke. Some men exaggerated, saying, "We have heard Stephen speak blasphemous things against Moses and God." They stirred up the people, elders, and teachers of the law. They seized Stephen and brought him before the Sanhedrin, with false witnesses testifying, "This fellow never stops speaking against this holy place and against the law. We have heard him say that this Jesus of Nazareth will destroy this place and change the traditions Moses handed down to us." All who were sitting in the Sanhedrin gazed at Stephen, and saw that his face was like the face of an angel. (Acts 6:8–15)

2. Harland, *Associations, Synagogues, and Congregations*, 182–85; Hoppe, *The Synagogues and Churches of Ancient Palestine*, 11–17.

3. Aviam, "People, Land, Economy, and Belief," 37; Hoppe, *The Synagogues and Churches of Ancient Palestine*, 21.

Stephen, like the apostles, was inspired by the Spirit with wisdom and boldness/confidence. The resistance of others could not overcome his spirit or knowledge and therefore they accused him of blasphemy, claiming that Jesus would destroy the temple, and that Christianity planned to change the Torah. While Jesus did claim that the temple would fall, changing the Torah was not part of his message. Stephen would have shared that there would be change, the temple would fall, and that Torah was going to be practiced differently. Luke did have a high regard for Torah and Christians were men and women who followed God's laws and practices. However, these religious zealots viewed Stephen as promoting an attack on the heart of their faith. Their belief in the temple and Torah was strong and they, like those against Jesus, felt that the Christians were trying to remove their laws from the Jewish community. Knowing that they were in place to protect what Jews for centuries had died for, it is understandable that people would have been anxious about the events that they were experiencing.

Stephen, like Peter and later Paul, preached a message from their Scriptures. This history he knew well as a Jewish man. However the common theme that Stephen used involved resistance, mistreatment, rejection, jealousy, oppression, and an unwillingness to trust Yahweh. Stephen wasn't telling anyone anything different. The Hebrew Bible is full of stories concerning human resistance and rejection of Yahweh. Throughout the prophets and Psalms God's people and others were reminded that they had failed to respect and trust their God, and their neighbor. Yahweh's mercy and forgiveness was their only hope.

The problem was not the story, it was the application of the story. Stephen compared the current resistance to those in the past. They resisted not only Stephen but the Spirit. He was not guilty of blasphemy, but telling the truth. They were no different than their fathers, something Jesus had also said, and they were destined to the same fate. This outraged the community leaders. They responded, as had the resistance throughout the Hebrew Bible and now with Jesus. They were angry, used violence, and compromised on their own truth. The crowd gnashed their teeth, screamed, and covered their ears, and out of anger and vengeance threw stones at Stephen in order to kill him. Stoning was brutal and the individual was physically beaten and pelted with rocks until they died. It was graphic and a horrible way to die. Those who would have witnessed this event would have been traumatized. The bruising, bleeding, and screaming of the victim would have been outdone only by crucifixion.

> When the members of the Sanhedrin heard this, their heart was furious and they gnashed their teeth at him. But Stephen, full of the Holy Spirit, gazed into heaven and saw the glory of God, and Jesus standing at the right hand of God. He said, "Look, I see heaven opening and the Son of Man standing at the right hand of God." At this they covered their ears and, yelling at the top of their voices, they all rushed at him, dragged him out of the city and began to stone him. Meanwhile, the witnesses dropped their garments at the feet of a young man named Saul. While they were stoning him, Stephen prayed, "Lord Jesus, receive my spirit." Then he fell on his knees and cried out, "Lord, do not hold this sin against them." When he had said this, he died. Saul approved of this event. (Acts 7:54–8:1)

Lest we become judgmental against the Jewish faith we must remember that Christian history is full of our own inner faith persecutions. Men and women have been burned alive for wanting the Bible to be translated into a common language. Women have been labeled "witches" because corrupt religious leaders were sexually attracted to them. Christian leaders and men who were abusive and controlling have threatened not only their spouses and other women, but those of us who stand against abuse and call men to accountability. People of color have been systematically oppressed by Christian leaders because they were viewed as being "nonhuman." Pedophiles have thrived in many church communities and yet manipulated leaders and ministries into forgiving them and offering another chance to reoffend. When we confront them for this behavior, they spiritually try to stone those of us who are promoting justice and healing in our communities. This is not an issue of religious beliefs—it is an issue of injustice, control, fear, and anxiety among corrupt and dysfunctional people from all religious groups.

Stephen, like the prophets of old, felt the wrath of the resistance. He died as Jesus had, asking for forgiveness and for God to not hold his executioners accountable for his death. He had finished his race and not only served like his master, but died like him. Luke did not share the response of the crowd. He did indicate that a young rabbi named Saul gave approval to Stephen's death. A Pharisee needed to be present to make sure that nothing disorderly happened and that the Roman officials were not disturbed by any uprisings. Though the Jewish council had warned the apostles not to preach and chose not to "fight against God," nothing was said about involving local citizens. Someone had to approve it so that the Romans would stay away. For Saul this was an opportunity to crush this rebellion and gain approval from the council.

The Heat Was On

The stoning of Stephen was like a drop of blood in a shark-infested pool. While faithful people buried Stephen's body, a persecution broke out against the church. Luke indicated that Saul was the leader of this attack. It might be that this was because Saul saw an opportunity to climb the corporate ladder and join the Jewish leadership. Or it is possible that Saul was zealous for God's law and believed that Christians should be exterminated. However, there is an additional possibility.

Research conducted on trauma and war survivors has indicated that witnessing a violent death, murder, or execution can traumatize an individual to the point that they respond out of anger, increased violence, and rage.[4] In the ancient world witnessing a public stoning, flogging, or crucifixion of others would have traumatized witnesses. Those who witness these events are psychologically affected. Luke indicated that Saul "breathed out murderous threats" (Acts 9:1) against the church. The Greek words suggest the behavior of a ravenous animal. Paul had become like an animal and hunted down, arrested, persecuted, and breathed violence against a peaceful people. He, like many war veterans I have known, went through a cycle and pattern of violent behavior and did many things he would later regret.

> On that day a great persecution broke out against the church in Jerusalem, and all except the apostles were scattered throughout Judea and Samaria. Faithful men buried Stephen and mourned deeply for him. But Saul began to destroy the church. Going into houses, dragging off both men and women, and putting them in prison. Those who had been scattered preached the word wherever they went. Philip went down to a city in Samaria and proclaimed the Christ there. When the crowds heard Philip and saw the signs he performed, they all paid close attention to what he said. With screams, unclean spirits came out of many, and many who were paralyzed or lame were healed. There was much joy in that city. (Acts 8:1–8)

Meanwhile, Saul was still breathing out murders and threats against the Lord's disciples. He went to the high priest and asked

---

4. Collie and Collie, *The Apostle Paul and Post-Traumatic Stress*, 14–15.

him for letters to the synagogues in Damascus, so that if he found any there who belonged to the Way, whether men or women, he might take them as prisoners to Jerusalem. As he neared Damascus a light from heaven flashed around him. He fell to the ground and heard a voice say to him, "Saul, Saul, why do you persecute me?" "Who are you, Lord?" Saul asked. "I am Jesus, whom you are persecuting," he replied. "Now get up and go into the city, and you will be told what you must do." (Acts 9:1–6)

Collie and Collie indicated that Paul's behavior was common for soldiers who witness a violent act in war.[5] Some respond by becoming hyper-violent for a period of time, typically thirty days. Many times the event that traumatized these individuals releases a sense of rage and violence that can be expressed through killing, destructive behavior, and using other forms of violence. This lasts for a few weeks until they come face to face with their actions and loss of control. Saul was no different. He responded to this event with rage, hunting down and arresting the Christians. This continued for a few weeks until he met Jesus. Then, the rage ceased.

Jesus' response to Saul was that he was not fighting humans, but like his teacher Gamaliel stated, he was opposing God. Jesus asked, "Why do you persecute *me*?" (9:4). Saul then spent three days reflecting on his actions, his experience, and possibly the trauma he placed upon not only the Christians but God/Jesus. Gamaliel was right: Paul was fighting God. Instead of being cautious like his teacher, he had been angry, impulsive, and reckless. While in this state Paul was vulnerable; he was blind, led by others, and in a town at the mercy of other Christians in Damascus. Trauma would have compounded Paul's emotions until Jesus gave him a "flash bulb" experience and altered state of consciousness.[6] For trauma survivors a sense of helplessness heightens a post-traumatic stress response as the normal adaptive systems have been overwhelmed and unable to function, and the individual shuts down.[7] Paul remained in this "altered state of consciousness" for three days. Jesus found a Christian named Ananias and sent him to Saul, who had been shown that he would suffer much for God's empire. Ananias, while cautious, was responsive, and Saul, the leader of the resistance, was healed by receiving his sight, and being baptized into Jesus.

---

5. Ibid., 30–33.
6. Ibid., 35.
7. McCarroll, *The End of Hope*, 88.

Holy Scattering

As with other forms of resistance the church continued to boldly witness to the resurrection with the help of the Holy Spirit. By facing and enduring persecution the Christian movement grew and was blessed in this section of Acts. *First, Luke suggested that the church was scattered (Acts 8:1; 11:19).* This word is similar to the word used in the Hebrew story of the Tower of Babel (Gen 11:1–9). God had commanded humans to multiply, spread, and cover the face of the earth (Gen 1:28; 8:17; 9:1, 7). Unfortunately in Genesis 11, they decided to build a city and stay home, "so that we may make a name for ourselves and not be scattered over the face of the whole earth" (Gen 11:4). God confused their language so that they would be "scattered" (11:8). The Tower of Babel was not a project of arrogance and self acclaim; it was a refusal to fulfill God's command to spread out. It was driven by fear rather than arrogance.

Jesus also commanded the disciples to pray that God "kick out workers" into the harvest to work and reap the crop (Luke 10:2). For Jesus, the empire spreads when God's people are pushed out of their comfort zones. Like those in Genesis 11 we tend to be driven by fear rather than faith. Jesus has sent us to "go" yet we many times "wait" for the Spirit. For Luke, Acts reminded the reader that the Spirit pushed (maybe shoved) people to go and fulfill Jesus' commands. After the death of Stephen, Luke wrote that the Christians were scattered through persecution and resistance. This scattering, while not directly God's doing, was something God allowed. As the first Christian martyr's body was buried Saul began his attack. Due to this the church fulfilled the plan of Jesus. They waited for the Spirit, were prepared and empowered, and then "went," even though it was forced. The scattering of the early Christians was a witness to the leading of the Spirit.

Holy Expansion

Second, due to this scattering people outside of Jerusalem joined the empire. The Samaritans were hated by the Jews and hated them as well. The Apostle John wrote that Jews did not associate or share eating utensils with Samaritans (John 4:8). Luke's parable of the Samaritan reflected an underlying dislike that the Jews had for the people of Samaria, especially one who would offer compassion and become the hero of a story (Luke 10:25–37). The Samaritans were descendents of the Northern tribes of Israel who were transported to Assyria and had their city repopulated with foreigners. They were not believed to be pure Israelites and had a history of disobedience toward God and persecution of the Jews in their rebuilding as a nation (Neh 4:1–3). They even built a temple at Mount Gerizim and had their own version of Torah, known as the "Samaritan Pentateuch." Samaritans were viewed as disobedient, ethnically mixed, and disloyal to God and the nation of Israel. "When they see the Jews in prosperity, they pretend that they are changed, and allied to them, and call them kinsmen, as though they were derived from Joseph, and had by that means an original alliance with them: but when they see them falling into a low condition, they say they are no way related to them, and that the Jews have no right to expect any kindness or marks of kindred from them, but they declare that they are sojourners that come from other countries."[8]

After Stephen was murdered Philip (another of the seven) was chosen to extend his ministry to Samaria. He came to this evil and magic-laced community providing a powerful witness to Jesus' resurrection. A magician named Simon controlled people with fear and his form of magic, yet Philip and the power of the Spirit offered a better alternative. Simon and many of the people were baptized into the Empire of Jesus through the spiritual witness of Jesus' resurrection. The conversions were so amazing that the apostles in Jerusalem sent Peter and John to see this work and view the city. Somehow only Peter and John were able to pass the gift and power of the Spirit to others; yet Philip, through this same Spirit, was able to testify to Jesus and lead many to Christ. The Spirit's power through Philip, Peter, and John was strong enough to convince Simon the magician to ask Peter for purchasing rites to this Spirit.

> Peter answered: "May your money perish with you, because you supposed you could buy the gift of God with money! You have no part or share in this ministry, because your heart is not right before God. Repent of this wickedness and pray to the Lord in the hope that he may forgive you for having such a thought in your heart. You are full of bitterness and enslaved to sin." Then Simon answered, "Pray to the Lord for me so that nothing you have said may happen to me." After they had spoken the word of the Lord and witnessed concerning Jesus, they returned to Jerusalem, preaching the good news in many Samaritan villages. (Acts 8:20–25)

---

8. Josephus, *Antiquities of the Jews*, 9:29 (9:14.3 in Whiston).

Jesus had commanded that the disciples witness the resurrection to Jerusalem, all Judea, Samaria, and the ends of the earth (Acts 1:8). They had been faithful at Jerusalem and now expanded their ministry to Samaria, a country that needed to be included in Jesus' empire. In addition to this, Philip and the other apostles proved to have a ministry like Jesus. At Samaria they confronted evil in the form of magic, fear, and control, and encouraged one of their leaders, a magician, to embrace this empire. Plato and other Greek authors felt that the magi were charlatans and fake. There was great skepticism concerning them because their goal was to manipulate people and gain money, rather than serve the gods.

> With such claims and contrivances they pretend to know something more and they deceive men by giving them sacred purifications, and most of their talk does not demonstrate their piety, as they believe, but rather their impiety, claiming as it does that the gods do not exist, while their supposed piety and their devotion to the divine is impious and unholy. . . . They make use of purifications and incantations and so do a thing that is quite unholy and ungodly, as it seems to me. For they purify those who are in the grip of disease with blood and other such things as if they were subject to pollution or avenging ghosts, or were bewitched by men, or had done some unholy deed. They should do the opposite to these men: they should sacrifice, pray, and bring them into temples and supplicate the gods.[9]

In spite of this Philip offered a magician a chance to repent and change his life. Peter and John further expanded the gospel throughout Samaria as they returned home to Jerusalem (Acts 1:25).

Holy Encounters

Third, the scattering led the disciples to people encounters in their country. After Philip's ministry in Samaria the Holy Spirit led him to a deserted road along Gaza. While there Philip overheard a court official from Ethiopia reading from the Hebrew Scriptures. Luke wrote that the man was a eunuch from Ethiopia and his queen's treasurer. He had visited Jerusalem to worship and would have tried to attend both the temple and synagogue. Africa was an important region for the Roman Empire and many Jews lived in the northern area of Egypt. In Acts, Luke shared that there were Lybians,

9. Hippocrates, *On the Sacred Diseases*, 1:27–28, 39–41.

Cyrenians, and Alexandrians in Jerusalem for festivals or who made permanent residence there. During the Babylonian captivity and dispersal Jews populated the northern Egyptian providence and would have spread their faith into Africa. It would not be improbable that an Ethiopian would make a pilgrimage to Jerusalem to worship at important festivals. Even more, his character as a eunuch helps to confirm Luke's emphasis that the church was a restored empire for Jesus. "To the eunuchs who keep my Sabbaths, who choose what pleases me and hold fast to my covenant—to them I will give within my temple and its walls a memorial and a name better than sons and daughters; I will give them an everlasting name that will not be cut off" (Isa 56:4–5).

Luke used the Ethiopian to first show that the church was the restored empire. Eunuchs were not allowed into the temple due to their physical disability and they were viewed as marred. However in the restoration from Babylonian captivity God promised that the community would welcome those whose faith was greater than their disability. Likewise Luke expressed the fulfillment of these prophecies through the encounter and conversion of the eunuch. Luke also used this story as an indication that the Gospel had gone to the ends of the earth. Ethiopia was viewed as one of the last areas of occupation by the Roman Empire.[10] Ethiopia lay on the outer edges of this empire and Luke was illustrating that the Christians had been faithful. The gospel had spread through Judea and Samaria, and would be spread through this Gentile convert to Judaism and now Christianity.

Philip had overheard the man reading from the Hebrew section of Isaiah (chapters 40–66) known as the Suffering Servant passages. The "servant" was first the prophet (in the Hebrew translations), next the nation of Israel (in the Greek translation), then finally the Messiah (in the Aramaic translation). Anyone hearing these Scriptures read may have heard three translations in the synagogue, with explanations, sermon notes, and quotes from the rabbis' interpretation of these texts. It would be confusing and this may explain why the eunuch asked, "Who is the prophet talking about, himself or someone else?" (Acts 8:34). No wonder he needed an interpreter.

> This is the Scripture that he was reading: "As a sheep led to the slaughter, and a lamb silent before its shearer, he did not open his mouth. In his humiliation he had no justice. Who can speak of his descendants? For his life was taken from the earth." The eunuch asked Philip, "Would you tell me who the prophet is speaking

10. Haya-Prats, *Empowered Believers*, 200–220.

about, himself or someone else?" Then Philip opened his mouth and began with that passage telling him the good news about Jesus. (Acts 8:32–35)

Philip interpreted the text for him and preached Jesus. This simple servant for widows taught the Ethiopian that Jesus was the Messiah, the one who became the servant to obey Yahweh and suffer for people. Even more, the tenor of the text could have applied to the eunuch, who himself was silent in the synagogue and temple, deprived of justice, without descendants, and humiliated because of his disability. Somehow Philip's message touched the official and he asked to be baptized. Baptism was not only a cleansing act for the Jews, but a way to prepare to meet God. The eunuch must have been moved enough to ask for conversion at that moment even though he would not have been allowed to do that at the temple. Both went into the water, suggesting immersion baptism. Immediately after this Philip was taken away by the Spirit and the eunuch went home happy. This wonderful story ended much differently than the others. At Jerusalem there was conflict. At Samaria there was conflict and corruption. At Gaza there was no resistance. A castrated foreign male returning from Jerusalem, reminded that he was not holy enough to enter the temple or experience conversion, completely embraced, obeyed, and rejoiced in a message from the Hebrew prophets. For Luke this was ironic.

THE EMPIRE SPREADS THROUGH THE VULNERABLE ONES

Each week I have continued to donate plasma at a local supply center as a form of outreach, giving back to others in need, and a chance to minister to those I know at the site. One of the technicians, Anli, is from Ethiopia. When I began to learn Ethiopian and work with some of the ancient texts she was a big help in my language, the culture, and telling me what she learned as a child living in Ethiopia and attending the church schools. However, one of her favorite stories was the "Ethiopian eunuch in Acts." She would tell me that he was the first convert who came to her country and started Christianity. While this is a common tradition, and some have claimed is simply a "story," it is amazing to me how a nation of Christ followers trace their spiritual conceptions to a single man, who could not have children, and who by the Spirit found Philip. It does reflect the simple truth of the gospel—insignificant people who were led by the Spirit (a servant of widows and a neglected eunuch) and upon meeting not only shared Christ, but embraced his empire. Through this the "mustard weed" gospel spread to a new country that continues to maintain beautiful texts of the Bible, wonderful people, and remind us that Jesus works through the most unlikely individuals.

Even more, Anli continues to be a bright presence in a location that sticks needles in people's arms, offers little compensation for both the workers and the donors, and tends to be riddled with anxiety, odors, and sometimes angry, rejected donors. Yet when I see Anli walk through the center loudly saying hello to people, everyone smiles. She continues to hum Ethiopian songs and laugh with people. Whether or not the eunuch's story is true, Anli is, in my opinion, the result of the good news going to the margins. She continues to bring it to people as well.

Spreading Through the Vulnerable During Resistance

As I finished and reedited this manuscript, I was struck by the news concerning the Christians in Mosul, Northern Iraq, and the terrorist group known as ISIS. While I agree that the Quran and Islamic belief systems are peaceful there are many groups that hold to this religious view who enact violence against others of different faiths (as Christians have also done for centuries). Our brothers and sisters in Middle Eastern countries have become vulnerable to many of these groups.

For the first time in over 1,600 years the churches in Mosul were not able to assemble for Christmas worship, ring their bells on Christmas Day, or live with the understanding that the Messiah brought "peace on earth." While we were opening presents with our children, many of the Christians were living in other cities due to the hospitality of Christians many miles away from Mosul. While we were singing "Joy to the World" and wishing for peace on earth, explosives were being placed on December 24, 2014 in one of the Mosul Catholic Church buildings to prevent people from coming to services on Christmas Day. While we were eating and enjoying a traditional feast on Christmas Day many Christians from Mosul were huddling together eating what was offered to them by their hosts who barely made ends meet. While we were cleaning up decorations and burning wrapping paper on December 26, explosives were detonated in the small Catholic church and a symbol for many Christians in that area was destroyed. I can't imagine the sorrow, trauma, and grief that these Christians must have experienced.

Even more I can't imagine how they can continue in the presence of persecution, threats, and violence. However, knowing what our movement is about, they will overcome the resistance. Faithful people will carry on and whether or not our world governments recognize that Christians are being persecuted even today, Christianity will survive. It will survive because even though there is resistance, there is hospitality, acceptance, courage, and faith. Jesus' people will rebuild and once again hear the bells on Christmas Day. When they hear the bells they will rejoice because the will remember what it was like to have them taken away.

I continue to read Internet posts, blogs, and discussions by Christians concerning whether or not we should attend church or find God in nature. I hear discussions from Bible scholars, authors, and influential Christian speakers about how they are "done" with the traditional church scene. I guess, as a person in the midst of ministry and leading people, it seems a little like quitting to me, although I know that making that claim would incite hard feelings from those I love who struggle with that discussion. I wonder how this helps us face the resistance and rise up to strengthen those suffering for their faith. Even more, I wonder what my brothers and sisters in Mosul would say. Would they see it as quitting or just practicing one's freedom in Christ?

The scattering of the early Christians due to the persecution brought further witness and evangelism for the early disciples. Again they were reminded to follow, not wait for, the Spirit as Christians spread the gospel over the face of the earth. That was faithfulness!

6

RESISTANCE FROM WITHIN

If they listen (they are a rebellious house) they will know that a prophet has been among them. (Ezek 2:5)

IN THE LAST SECTION Luke shared that the church was scattered due to the persecution from Saul of Tarsus. However, the use of the term *scatter* suggested that this is what Jesus had called them to do. They were to wait for the Spirit and then witness Jesus and his resurrection. Stephen's murder and the ensuing attack on Christians caused the movement to bring the message of Jesus to Samaria and an Ethiopian eunuch who lived on the margins of the Roman Empire (both geographically and culturally).

HEALINGS AMONG THE PEACEFUL

After Peter and John returned to Jerusalem, Peter began to travel throughout Palestine. As Jesus commanded the disciples to preach at Jerusalem, the surrounding area of Judea, Samaria, and the ends of the world, so Peter, after preaching at Samaria, focused on the Judean countryside.

> As Peter traveled about the country, he went to visit the saints who lived in Lydda. There he found a man named Aeneas, who was confined to a mat and paralyzed for eight years. Peter said to him, "Aeneas, Jesus Christ heals you. Get up and make your bed." Immediately he got up. All those who lived in Lydda and Sharon saw him and turned to the Lord. In Joppa there was a disciple named Tabitha (which means Dorcas); she was always doing good and

> helping the poor. About that time she became sick and died, and her body was washed and placed in an upper room. Lydda was near Joppa; so when the disciples heard that Peter was in Lydda, they sent two men to him and urged him, "Don't delay coming to us." (Acts 9:32–38)

Peter, like Jesus, continued to perform healing miracles in addition to preaching about the Empire of God. However, Peter gave glory to Jesus by simply stating to Aeneas that, "Jesus Christ heals you" (Acts 9:34). The healing of this man who was paralyzed and laying on a mat was similar to the story of Jesus' healing of the paralytic by commanding him to get up and take his mat. However, Jesus commanded the man to pick up his mat, while Peter commanded Aeneas to "make his bed," suggesting that he would leave behind his affliction. It was also similar to Acts 3 and Peter's healing of the lame man at the temple. While the leaders questioned Jesus in Luke, and Peter in Acts 3, at Lydda there was no resistance. These stories did have the healings and response of the crowds in common. For Luke, the healing of those who were crippled manifested Jesus' ministry which was announced in the Nazareth synagogue (Luke 4:16–19).

Peter next healed a young woman named Tabitha, who cared for the poor. She had died and was placed in an upper room with other widows who were mourning for her death. She was obviously of value to the disciples at the city of Joppa since they had sent two messengers to ask Peter to come. The people presented Peter with all the clothing she had made, while many people wept for her. As with Jesus and Jairus's daughter they were surrounded by mourners. The healing occurred in a small room, and involved the healer sending the mourners out of the room, taking the woman by the hand, and presenting her alive to the people (Luke 8:40–56). These two healing stories were intended by Luke to show the validity of the church in that it imitated the ministry and healings of Jesus.

Acts was not just a collection of stories of the work that the early Christians accomplished through the Holy Spirit. It was not simply a book that attributed all power to the Spirit working with completely passive Christians. Acts was proof that the early church not only witnessed Jesus' resurrection, but that it practiced the ministry and work of Jesus. In this section Peter was imitating Jesus and, as we will see with Paul later, saw this as the role of the church. The church was thriving as it overcame the resistance from the religious leaders, rogue groups, and angry individuals. However, the resistance continued, and now came from another entity.

THE RESISTANCE FROM WITHIN

> The following day... Peter went up on the roof to pray, since it was noon. He became hungry and wanted something to eat, and while the meal was being prepared, he fell into a trance. He saw heaven opened and something like a large vessel being let down to earth by its four corners. It contained all kinds of four-footed animals, reptiles, and birds. Then a voice told him, "Get up, Peter. Kill and eat." "Surely not, Lord!" Peter replied. "I have never eaten anything common or unclean." The voice spoke to him a second time, "Do not call anything common that God has made clean." This happened three times, and immediately the sheet was taken back to heaven. While Peter was wondering about the meaning of the vision, the men sent by Cornelius found out where Simon's house was and stopped at the gate. They called out, asking if Simon who was known as Peter was staying there. While Peter was still thinking about the vision, the Spirit said to him, "Simon, three men are looking for you. So get up and go downstairs. Do not hesitate to go with them, for I have sent them." Peter went down and said to the men, "I'm the one you're looking for. Why have you come?" The men replied, "We have come from Cornelius the centurion. He is a righteous and God-fearing man, who is respected by all the Jewish people. A holy angel told him to ask you to come to his house so that he could hear what you have to say." Then Peter invited the men into the house to be his guests. (Acts 10:9–23)
>
> The apostles and the believers throughout Judea heard that the Gentiles also had received the word of God. When Peter went up to Jerusalem, the circumcised believers criticized him and said, "You went to the house of uncircumcised men and ate with them." (Acts 11:1–3)

One of my favorite stories in the Bible is the conversion of Cornelius and his family. While Peter was living at Joppa, a town only thirty miles from Caesarea, he decided to stay in a home owned by a tanner. A tanner was a person who worked with dead animal skins and many times had to use urine (uric acid) to tan the hides for them to be useful. Animal skins were valuable and necessary for people to stay warm, and also needed for tents and other coverings. Dead animals were unclean in the eyes of traditional Jews. For Peter, staying at an unclean person's home, even though it was a gift of hospitality, meant that he would be unholy from his traditional faith standards. There were cleaning and purification rites for all people, but Peter knew he was in an unclean home.

An Apostle Searching

Thirty miles away in the city of Caesarea, lived Cornelius, a Gentile soldier who as a centurion (a leader in charge of more than 100 soldiers), showed compassion by becoming a follower of Yahweh. Luke wrote that he was a "God-fearer," meaning that he would attend synagogue, follow the Jewish customs and food practices, offer finances to help the synagogue maintain its purity codes, give to the poor, and bring his family/household with him.[1] However, circumcision was the final act an individual would do before baptism to become a full-fledged member of the Jewish nation. For obvious reasons this was an issue as it was not only painful for adult males, but dangerous. It was also an issue in that it caused Gentiles to become marked in their communities. While many of the Gentiles were attracted to Yahweh, the covenant of love, and the idea of serving one God, it was also convenient for the Jews to have a wealthy soldier who gave generously and helped them maintain their community, building, and safety in occupied Palestine.

Caesarea was a city that Herod the Great had spent large sums of money on remodeling as a Roman city.[2] The city was named after Caesar and Herod had redesigned the harbor to handle more ships. It was a wealthy seaside town. Wealthy soldiers retired to this city with comfortable incomes. The Persian god Mithrais was a favorite among males and soldiers. Mithrais was the most popular god among Roman soldiers, until Jesus became the more predominant God in the empire. It is not surprising that a citizen of this city, who was willing to care for the poor, was chosen by God to hear the Gospel of Jesus. Cornelius was a Gentile who had a heart for God as well as the people of Israel.

It was to this person that God sent Peter. Cornelius saw a vision of an angel during his three o'clock prayer. Since the Roman day began at six o'clock in the morning, the ninth hour was three o'clock in the afternoon. The angel had heard his prayers, as God had heard those of the priest Zechariah (Luke 1:12), and asked him to send messengers to Peter. As with Tabitha, two messengers were sent to Peter (Acts 9:38).

1. Witherington, *The Acts of the Apostles*, 341–43.
2. Johnson, *The Acts of the Apostles*, 181.

Peter, on the other hand, was praying differently the next day. God was teaching him a lesson in cleanliness. Throughout the Gospels Jesus had argued with religious leaders that being clean was a moral issue, rather than hygienic. Peter, however, was living in an unclean home, smelling food prepared by unclean hands, and arguing with God/Jesus whether or not he should eat unclean animals/food. Jesus was clear: what he cleans is clean. Peter almost sounded arrogant as he proclaimed his "holiness." He hadn't been much of a good Jewish follower of their purity codes before, but somehow he didn't see his issue.

As the story progressed one thing was clear. The resistance of the Christian movement was no longer centered in the religious authorities. It was no longer mobile with a zealous leader like Saul of Tarsus. It was not evil, magic, sickness, or homelessness. The resistance came from within. First, Peter (who was already unclean) resisted Jesus' command to eat three times. In each incidence God claimed that he had cleansed what was before him. The number three seemed to be common for Peter as he denied Jesus three times and struggled to tell him he loved him and would be his friend (John 21:15–19). Second, it only took the two messengers of Cornelius a few hours to reach Joppa, but Peter waited until the next day and journeyed an extra day to get there (Acts 10:8, 23–24). Third, upon meeting Cornelius Peter immediately reminded him that he was not to associate with Cornelius (10:28). This seems odd considering that Cornelius was not only a God-fearer but one who had prayed to God fervently. Finally, Peter's sermon was extremely passionless. Compared to his messages at Pentecost, to the Sanhedrin, and while at the Jewish temple, Peter seemed to act as if he was sharing facts rather than leading someone to follow and make a decision for the resurrected Lord. Peter later shared with the church leaders that he was opposing God (Acts 11:17). As Gamaliel had warned Paul and the Sanhedrin not to fight God, Peter seemed to be doing that very action.

An Apostle Struggling

I have sympathy for Peter. He spent much of his life learning to avoid Gentiles. He listened to countless messages, read many Scriptures, and knew stories concerning ritual purity, the ungodly Romans, and how brutal soldiers could be. I can imagine Peter and his crew standing outside Cornelius's house filled with cigarette smoke, football games on the big screen television, beer and ribs on every table, and people naming off their various deities. It would have been every Jewish person's nightmare. Or, even worse, one can imagine Cornelius as the Jewish community's favorite God-fearer going to the trouble to make sure everything was kosher; Nathan's hot dogs, yarmulkes, prayer shawls, and plenty of fish on clean pottery plates. There Peter would have stood, turning his nose up to the sky stating, "Of course, a *Gentile* would think this might pass as kosher."

Lori and I have had to bite our tongues often concerning how other Christians speak about the poor, homeless, those not part of our "denomination," not Christian or church attending, same-sex attracted, other ethnicities, and others who they refer to as "those people." It is difficult to not only hear this, but to believe that they can read the same Bible, have the same Savior and his Spirit, and continue to treat outsiders as "others." Sometimes we speak up. Other times we shake our heads. However, this attitude was one that Peter struggled with. Yet God's Spirit drove him to his knees so that he could become an advocate for the Gentiles. This can also be our prayer for others.

The Holy Spirit Intervenes

I think it would have been hard for Peter. Later the Apostle Paul wrote that Peter had compromised on this issue and abandoned the Gentile followers (Gal 2:11–16). He had denied Jesus three times, had responded to Jesus' threefold question "Do you love me" with, "you know I like you" and had denied food three times that Jesus had cleansed. He had a hard time getting the point. However, the beauty of this story is that the *Holy Spirit intervened*. When Peter resisted the Spirit pushed. If Peter took twice as long to get to Caesarea, the Spirit opened the way. If Peter was not going to pour his heart into a sermon, the Spirit would be poured out upon the listening hearts of these Gentiles. As Peter preached the Spirit overpowered the family of Cornelius and they spoke in languages. It must have been odd to see a Latin-speaking Roman leader speaking other languages. Yet for Peter and the team, it was a sign that God wanted them saved. Peter responded with, "Can anyone keep these people from being baptized with water? They have received the Holy Spirit just as we have." There it was. The Spirit was not only a witness to the resurrection of Jesus, it was a witness to the ministry of Jesus. God promised that Gentiles would flock to Jerusalem and present gifts at the temple (Isa 65:9–21). Cornelius and his household were close enough. Hardened Roman soldiers typically didn't support Judaism, even less a branch of it.

Yet this man was one who was open-hearted and Jesus wanted him in his empire. As Peter returned to Jerusalem he was met with criticism and resistance. He had withstood the Jewish rulers, a magician, and zealous Pharisees. Who would have thought that his own would have resisted this work? Somehow the early Christians believed that Jesus had sent them to witness the resurrection to only Jews throughout the world. However, the Spirit was working to show that Gentiles were part of that plan as well. What convinced them? The pouring out of the Spirit on Cornelius's household was that sign that the Empire of Jesus was all-inclusive.

Evidence was also streaming in through the other disciples. Antioch, one of the top four cities in the Roman world, was becoming a major hub for the resurrection of Jesus.

> Now those who had been scattered by the persecution when Stephen was killed went to Phoenicia, Cyprus and Antioch, spreading the word not only to the Jews. Some of them, from Cyprus and Cyrene, went to Antioch and spoke to Greeks, telling them the good news about the Lord Jesus. The Lord's hand was with them, and a great number of people believed and turned to the Lord. News of this reached the church in Jerusalem, and they sent Barnabas to Antioch. When he arrived and saw what the grace of God had done, he was glad and encouraged them all to remain loyal to the Lord with all their hearts. He was a good man, full of the Holy Spirit and faith, and a great number of people came to the Lord. Then Barnabas went to Tarsus to look for Saul, and when he found him, he led him to Antioch. So for a whole year Barnabas and Saul met with the church and taught great numbers of people. The disciples were called Christians first at Antioch. (Acts 11:19–26)

The followers of Jesus were now labeled with a Greek name. Jesus was Christ, not just Messiah, and the followers were taking on this name. *Christians* was the new term for these followers, a term that has continued for almost two millennia. Those scattered were taking the witness of Jesus to Syria, Asia, and Egypt/Africa. In addition to this Barnabas began to mentor the former zealot, Saul of Tarsus.

ONE LAST PUSH

The resistance came one last time from the king of the Jewish empire. The early Christians had weathered the resistance from the corrupt leaders, individual pockets of zealous followers, and themselves. The Spirit had worked in all of these instances and had given the believers boldness, courage, and the language to share the message of Jesus across cultures, ethnic discrimination, and physical maladies. The Spirit intervened by empowering them to be bold, speak a new language, heal and bring to life, and even to prove to an unbelieving apostle that all people need salvation. However, the final act involved a Jewish king and a major divine intervention.

> Then Herod went from Judea to Caesarea and stayed there. He had been quarreling with the people of Tyre and Sidon; they now joined together and sought an audience with him. After being supported by Blastus, a trusted personal servant of the king, they asked for peace, since they depended on the king's country for their food supply. On the appointed day Herod, wearing his royal robes, sat on his throne and gave a production for the people. They shouted, "This is the voice of a god, not of a man." Immediately, because Herod did not give praise to God, an angel of the Lord struck him down, and he was eaten by worms and died. But the word of God continued to spread and flourish. When Barnabas and Saul had finished their mission, they returned from Jerusalem, taking with them John, also called Mark. (Acts 12:20–25)

Herod Agrippa became a corrupt king. Even though he tried to put Peter in prison, an angel released him and brought him back to his community. Then, as Herod tried to claim his own deity and possibly conduct an empire-wide search for Peter, the angel struck him down and killed him. He died like another king (Antiochus IV) who had tormented God's people, with intestinal pain and worms (2 Macc 1:11–12, 17; 9:4–6, 11, 18; 7:31–36).[3] The resistance was over, the message was spreading, and everything seemed right with the world.

Luke ended this section as he had done in other sections: "The word of God continued to spread and flourish" (12:24). It seemed that the Spirit had done its job and so had the early Christians. They had witnessed Jesus to their own, their country, the Samaritans, and a few Gentiles who embraced the movement with excitement. They had overcome tremendous obstacles through the Spirit and the church was growing. All forms of resistance had

---

3. Yamasaki-Ransom, "Paul, Agrippa I, and Antiochus IV," 110–12.

been dealt with and the new empire was not only growing, it was reflecting the life and ministry of Jesus.

However, there was more to come. As beautiful and powerful as this was, it was just the tip of the iceberg. As glorious as this work had been there were more stories to come and lives to touch. Even more, it would be done by one of the most unlikely people, the Apostle Paul. He was the most controversial, but the most genuine. He was the toughest as well as the gentlest. He was courageous and humble. He was beaten, bruised, and carried the sins of his past and present with him. Even more he, like Jesus, had a calling to suffer, die, and raise with his Lord. He was led by the Spirit!

In 2003 I took my third trip to Albania to teach English and the Bible for World English Institute. I was also asked to teach Luke and Acts to the graduate and upper-level students at Nations' University. As usual I made an attempt to visit with students from my previous trips as well as families of Albanian friends from Portland. I brought gifts from the Portland families and individuals and made the time to meet in Albania while sharing how much we appreciated their children and how helpful they had been to our ESL ministry.

I was teaching in the capital city of Tiranë and stayed for two weeks. One of my Portland friends had family in the smaller city of Korça. On my past trips I found it easy to ride in one of the taxi minivans that took people to the various cities, the coast, or other sites. I spoke enough of the language to get around and visit with strangers. This trip I had decided to go to Korça, but unfortunately it was a two-hour trip. My plan was to ride to Korça, visit with the family, and catch the last taxi back to Tiranë, so that I could teach my class the next day. One of the younger evangelists, Bledi, offered to accompany me. He would translate for me, but I realized later that he knew I would not return that night.

While in Korça we met the family, exchanged gifts, visited, and had coffee together. The father was visibly bothered that I did not allow him to buy me something to drink, eat, or smoke. I found out that I would not leave that night. They had three more homes for me to visit, which included family, friends, and acquaintances. Bledi finally convinced me that my refusing hospitality, drink, or food was an insult. "Albania has a history of being the most hospitable country in the world," he would remind me.

I finally relaxed and enjoyed the evening. We visited, told stories, ate, drank, and shared about our church and our Bible teaching. Bledi shared his faith in Jesus with the mostly Muslim families. It was an exciting time.

However, I wondered where we would stay. Bledi told me that God would provide. One of the couples we visited were doctors and offered to drive us to Tiranë, so that we would not have to pay for a taxi home. "That's two hours," I said. Yet they insisted while Bledi encouraged me to accept their offer.

That night we returned to the small apartment of my friend's family. They lived in one room of a crowded apartment dwelling. The mother and two children went to stay at her parents while Armand made us a bed. They also fed us a small meal which consisted of a hot dog and French fries. Bledi and I were the only ones to be served meat, which was very humbling.

The next day the doctors Tehudi and Behum came to pick us up. I tried to offer something for our hosts but they refused and said, "Maybe next time you return, you will let us buy you something to drink. We are Albanians, we are the best in hospitality." Bledi kept nudging me to stop offering and get in the car.

The two-hour ride to Tiranë was fun. We visited, told jokes, laughed, and Bledi translated. At one point they had to stop to repair a radiator hose on their car. I mentioned to Bledi that I should offer them money for the trip. He told me three times, "Ron, whatever you do don't offer to pay them." After a half an hour as we drew closer to Tiranë I did it. I offered to pay them and asked what I could do. Tehudi looked back at me and made a spitting sound.

Bledi looked at me and said, "I don't think I need to translate that for you, do I?"

He and I later had a conversation about why men, especially American males, do not like to accept gifts, kindness, and hospitality from people. It was a good discussion. It also reminded me that as an American Christian I had much to learn from my Albanian brothers and sisters. Sometimes God is not able to work, nor are we able to see Jesus' glory, because we resist the work, compassion, and love of both the Spirit and others. I look forward to returning to Korça again, but this time I will learn to say "yes" and "thank you."

Peter was like many of us. He was raised with misconceptions of people and his own faith. Even after years with Jesus and leading this new movement he had to address his inner discriminations. While repentance for some means a radical change of behavior and destructive addictions, for others it means looking inward and dealing with their prejudices, pride, and unwillingness to be led by the Spirit. This involves change, viewing people differently, and even questioning what our parents, other church leaders, or teachers have taught us. It involves identifying the dysfunction and sin that has been transferred generationally to us and breaking the cycle of fear and anxiety and embracing love and the life of Jesus. This repentance may be different than that of others, however it produces the same people—men and women eager to reach others and give them the hope that they have been taught to withhold from outsiders.

AN EMPIRE
SENT BY THE SPIRIT

7

THE SECOND WAVE BEGINS

Then I will clean the lips of the people, that all of them may call on the name of Yahweh. (Zeph 3:9)

THE LAST SECTION OF Acts which we reviewed ended with hope. Hope that the resistance had been confronted. Luke indicated that Herod Agrippa, the corrupt Jewish leader, died by the hand of God. The religious leader Gamaliel had persuaded the Jewish leaders to observe the momentum of Christian movement, but not interfere. Outsiders began to embrace the gospel, while the internal prejudices and racism of these early Christians were addressed by the Holy Spirit. The church began to grow and witness Jesus' resurrection as it spread out of Jerusalem and to Antioch, the Roman world's third largest city.[1] Luke mentioned Peter and Jerusalem one last time before moving to the spreading of the gospel into the Gentile world (Acts 12).[2]

After Alexander the Great died he left his empire to four generals: Seleucus, Nicanor, Ptolemy, and Lysymachus.[3] The city of Antioch was conquered and named after Seleucus's father Antiochus, and was a powerful center for Judaism and Greek culture. Through time the Seleucid (Syria/Greece) and Ptolemy (Egypt) families became the major armies in Palestine and named many of the Syrian cities that Paul and Barnabas visited.

---

1. Tracey, "Syria," 239.
2. Johnson, *The Acts of the Apostles*, 217.
3. Fant and Reddish, *A Guide to Biblical Sites*, 143.

These cities had a heavy Greek influence. Many Jews were also brought to these cities to serve as mercenaries in the Seleucid armies. These cities had populations of faithful Jews who established communities and synagogues while absent from Jerusalem, in the diaspora.

Antioch was a mint for the Roman Empire. The emperor Claudius also established the Olympic Games of Antioch, which were held every five years and became a popular festival.[4] This location was also chosen by the government to have a governor, succeeding the Seleucid rulers.[5] It was culturally advanced and a safe place for the Jews. It is interesting that this city became a major hub for Luke's narrative. According to Jesus the gospel was to begin at Jerusalem and spread to the rest of the world. Jerusalem was to be the starting point of the mission yet later faded into the background, then near the end of Acts became the location for the judgment and betrayal for Paul, as it was with Jesus (Luke 22—23; Acts 22—23).

Since Jerusalem was not the hub of the growth in Luke's narrative, it is interesting to discover why Antioch became the major launching pad for the disciples' Gentile mission. First, followers of Jesus were "called Christians first at Antioch," *suggesting that the name of the movement was identified with Greek-speaking Jews* (Acts 11:26). Second, *the movement would share resources with these men and women along with their network of relationships throughout the Roman Empire.* Finally, *Antioch was located along major trade, travel, and postal routes in the Roman world and was viewed as a metropolis in Syria.* This opened the door for the spread of Jesus' message to the Greek-speaking world.

With the removal of *the resistance* it seemed that Luke's story would be smooth and that the gospel would grow unhindered, except for those who rejected Jesus or refused to believe the truth of the resurrection. It is important to remember that these followers of Jesus were practicing Jews who still upheld the Torah and Jewish way of life. The *resistance* was not simply Jews who were loyal to the Torah over Jesus. The resistance came from individuals who, overcome with anxiety and fear, used their own belief system to resist the followers of Jesus' message. In the early days of Christianity, Judaism and the followers of Jesus were not only compatible, they saw the law of God from similar eyes.[6] This was evident in the early Jewish diaspora

4. Ibid.
5. Tracey, "Syria," 239.
6. Zetterholm,"The Question of Assumptions," 91–92; Runesson, "The Question of Terminology," 76–77.

where the Christian movement began to rapidly grow. Therefore the church at Antioch was poised to launch another phase of Jesus' command to "go" (Acts 1:6–8).

> In the church at Antioch there were prophets and teachers: Barnabas, Simeon called Niger, Lucius of Cyrene, Manaen (who had been raised with Herod the tetrarch) and Saul. While they were worshiping the Lord and fasting, the Holy Spirit said, "Set Barnabas and Saul apart for the work which I have called them." Then they fasted, prayed, placed their hands on them, and sent them off. As they were sent out by the Holy Spirit, they went down to Seleucia and sailed from there to Cyprus. (Acts 13:1–4)

Luke set the stage for this second wave of outreach in the church. First, *there was a gathering of church leaders praying in one place*. This was a common theme in Acts (Acts 13:1–2; see also 1:12—15; 4:25–31; 12:12–14). Second, *the Holy Spirit was active in appointing individuals to carry out the message*. In the first chapter of Acts Joseph Barsabbas was not chosen to be one of the twelve. In Acts 13:1–3, Joseph (nicknamed Barnabas) had a similar name to Barsabbas. Both Josephs fade out of Luke's narrative while the other part of the duo, Matthias and Paul, become apostles in the church. Luke tended to focus on Paul and his writings, suggesting that this ministry to the Gentiles and Greek-speaking Jews was his main emphasis.

The Antioch prayer team was diverse and included a converted Pharisee, a Levite, a black man (Simeon Niger—possibly from Africa/Egypt), an Egyptian, and a Judean who was raised with Herod the king's family. Antioch became the church that modeled diversity and outreach through the witness of the Holy Spirit. This economic and cultural diversity became a mark of the Spirit-led church, rather than affluence. "Above all, cultures define their identity on the basis of similarity rather than difference; they seek association with those with the same color of skin and of the same social background, with the like-minded and the similarly-situated rather that with those of different views and life situations."[7] The Spirit offered a challenge to the ancient and modern church to promote diversity. *Finally, the Holy Spirit was active in the choosing/setting apart of faithful people, which began the launch of a new wave of growth, outreach, and proclaiming the message of Jesus.* Luke seemed to suggest that this was the beginning of the next wave of the Holy Spirit's witness.

---

7. Johnson, *Prophetic Jesus*, 130–31.

> When they arrived at Salamis, they proclaimed the word of God in the Jewish synagogues. John was with them as their helper. They traveled through the whole island until they came to Paphos. There they met a Jewish magician and false prophet named Bar Jesus, who was an attendant of the proconsul, Sergius Paulus. The proconsul, an intelligent man, sent for Barnabas and Saul because he wanted to hear the word of God. But Elymas the magician (for that is what his name means) opposed them and tried to turn the proconsul from the faith. Then Saul (Paul), filled with the Holy Spirit, gazed at Elymas and said, "You are a child of the devil and an enemy of justice.... The Lord's hand is against you and you are going to be blind for a time, not able to see the sun." Immediately mist and darkness came over him, and he groped about, seeking someone to lead him by the hand. When the proconsul saw what had happened, he believed, for he was amazed at the teaching about the Lord. (Acts 13:5–12)

After leaving Antioch Saul and Barnabas travelled to the island of Cyprus. They would have landed at Salamis, a major port and former capital for Cyprus. Similar to Jesus, Paul began preaching at the synagogue (Luke 4:16–19). They did not stay long in Salamis and quickly left for the current capital of the Island, Paphos. There were two travel routes from Salamis to Paphos. The northern route took 112 days while the southern route took 145 days. We can place them at Paphos around 47–48 CE.[8]

Cyprus had served as a bargaining tool between Egypt and Rome, but by Paul's day Rome listed Cyprus as an imperial providence. In 58 BCE, the Romans shifted the capital from Salamis to Paphos, which was a wealthy religious center housing the famous temple of Aphrodite.[9] Outside the city people sacrificed male and female animals for this deity.[10] It was also the location of a Roman garrison and boasted that the writer Cicero had been proconsul at one time.[11] While there they found favor with a Roman official

---

8. This estimate is based on Agabus's prediction of a famine in Jerusalem (Acts 11:27–29), after the flooding of the Nile River in 45–46 CE. The flooding affected the "breadbasket" of the Roman Empire, which within a year would have caused a shortage in the areas on the edges of the empire. Paul and Barnabas would have taken their contribution to Jerusalem, which was affected in 47 CE. They would have left shortly after this for Cyprus in order to be in Corinth during Gallio's leadership, which occurred from 50–52 CE.

9. Fant and Reddish, *A Guide to Biblical Sites*, 353.

10. Gill and Winter, "Acts and Roman Religion," 87.

11. Fant and Reddish, *A Guide to Biblical Sites*, 353.

named Sergius Paulus, who was proconsul/governor around 47–50 CE.[12] However, Luke indicated that the resistance came from a Jewish magi (Bar Jesus). The Romans did use Jews for religious and magical insight and Bar Jesus was obviously one serving in the court system at Paphos.[13] Paul, as Peter had done with an earlier magician, confronted this magician and cursed him with blindness (as Saul had been blinded). A pattern will continue throughout Luke's narratives. First, *there was the proclamation of Jesus' story involving the actions of the Spirit.*[14] Second, *there was resistance, followed by the boldness and courage of Jesus' follower(s).* Finally, *the gospel spread and the movement continued to grow.* Paul, Barnabas, and John Mark would have spent at least six months in Cyprus and found a sense of freedom preaching and teaching, as the head official was open to Paul's message. A church must have been established, since Barnabas and John Mark would later return to this area. However, Luke did not indicate how much longer this team stayed in Paphos.

The team next traveled to Psidian Antioch in the region of Galatia. Sergius Paulus had family at Psidian Antioch. "One of the wealthiest businesses families in Psidian Antioch was the family of Sergius Paulus, the proconsul of Cyprus whom Paul converted in Paphos."[15] This may explain why this city was chosen by the team. Psidian Antioch was a large city located along a trade route into Galatia. The city was named after the Seleucids who sought land to develop outposts against the Ptolemys of Egypt. Augustus later developed this region to reflect more the culture of Rome.[16] The temple of Augustus was the most dominant building in the city, during Paul and Barnabas's mission trip. The city also had a stadium, Roman baths, a large aqueduct transporting water from the nearby mountains, and a theater that seated 15,000 people.[17] Fant and Reddish indicated that about one-tenth of the population of the city would fit in the theater, bumping the estimates of the population to be 150,000 people. Psidian Antioch, while not the largest city in the world, was a major hub and trade route for the rest of Cilicia/Syria.

---

12. Nobbs, "Cyprus," 280–81.
13. Josephus, *Antiquities of the Jews*, 20:236–37.
14. Shepherd, *The Narrative Function of the Holy Spirit in Luke-Acts*, 16.
15. Hansen, "Galatia," 386.
16. Ibid., 394.
17. Fant and Reddish, *A Guide to Biblical Sites*, 158–60.

It is possible that Saul adopted Sergius's surname (Paulus) to become "Paul." The Bible gives us no reason for why he changed his name (13:9), but it is no coincidence that he was called "Paul" upon his acceptance by Sergius Paulus, and that he traveled, with his support, to a city where the official's family lived. It is also possible that Paul began to use his Roman contacts and government connections early on in his ministry. He did claim to be a Roman citizen from birth and showed little hesitance of using this right to further the gospel (Acts 22:28).

Paul also used his status as a rabbi to further the gospel. While attending a synagogue in Psidian Antioch he was chosen to speak. "On the Sabbath they entered the synagogue and sat down. After the reading from the Law and the Prophets, the leaders of the synagogue sent word to them, saying, 'Brothers, if you have a word of exhortation for the people, please speak.' Standing up, Paul motioned with his hand and said: 'Fellow Israelites and you Gentiles who worship God, listen to me!'" (Acts 13:14–16). It was possible that he was still considered a rabbi and Pharisee among the Jews. In Acts 28:21 the Jews at Rome indicate that Paul's reputation as a Christian had not been received by these Judean leaders. Since Antioch was on the margins of the Jewish community there would not have been many men to take turns reading or even to teach Torah. However, Paul was all too happy to read for and teach them. Even in the midst of the Antioch congregation, some of the individuals chose to oppose the team's message, and the work of Jesus. The resistance to Paul and Barnabas continued to follow them, as they moved from city to city.

Paul took the opportunity to speak in the synagogue concerning the Torah, Jesus, and the resurrection. His message, while somewhat similar to Peter and Stephen, was less filled with the nation's resistance, rejection, and neglect of God. For Paul the gospel involved opening a door to those on the margins of the Jewish community and offering an opportunity for grace. These individuals were not responsible for rejecting God/Jesus but had a chance to receive the promises, even though they were scattered throughout the Roman Empire. Even more they would have been viewed as marginalized because they were quite a distance from Jerusalem.

> Fellow children of Abraham and you God-fearing Gentiles, this message of salvation has been sent to us. The people of Jerusalem and their rulers did not recognize Jesus, yet in murdering him they fulfilled the words of the prophets that are read every Sabbath. Though they found no reason for a death sentence, they asked

Pilate to have him executed. When they had carried out all that was written about him, they took him down from the cross and laid him in a tomb. But God raised him from the dead, and for many days he was seen by those who had traveled with him from Galilee to Jerusalem. They are now his witnesses to our people. We tell you the good news: What God's promise to our ancestors has been fulfilled for us and their children, by raising up Jesus. . . . Brothers and sisters, I want you to know that through Jesus the forgiveness of sins is proclaimed to you. Through him everyone who believes is set free from every sin, a righteousness you were not able to obtain under the Law of Moses. (Acts 13:26–32; 38–39)

Paul's emphasis on "promise" was delivered to those Jews and Gentiles who sought the promise of full inclusion in the Jewish community, while living hundreds of miles from Jerusalem. They visited Jerusalem as guests and worshipped from a great distance. Even though Torah taught that they were still part of the Jewish community, the distance existed both geographically and spiritually. They were believers in a city of 150,000 people, trying to remain faithful to Yahweh while offering outsiders a chance to become part of their family. The Greek term *diaspora* referred to the scattered Jewish nation who were "exiled" throughout the empire. The "God-fearing Gentiles" among them were converts to Judaism, and would have been taking a tremendous step of faith. No matter what one teaches, to believe that Yahweh lived in another city suggested that there was distance in the relationship and community. It also required tremendous faith. People still had to travel to another city to offer sacrifice or celebrate Passover. Even though the synagogues tried to "look like the temple" they were not the dwelling place of Yahweh.[18]

Paul, however, suggested that Jesus came to people to offer grace, forgiveness, and healing. This continued for two weeks. However, the resistance came again as other disgruntled believers disrupted the team's teaching. Paul and Barnabas, who had dealt with resistance throughout their Christian ministry, indicated that rejection provided opportunity for others to receive the promise. Those who believed and would later rejoice illustrated a faithful response to salvation and God's empire.[19] Quoting from the Suffering Servant text in Isaiah, they indicated that the church was now the "Servant" of Yahweh.

---

18. Aviam, "People, Land, Economy, and Belief," 17–22.
19. Kuhn, *The Kingdom According to Luke and Acts*, 159.

> Then Paul and Barnabas answered them boldly: "We were compelled to speak the word of God to you first. Since you reject it and do not consider yourselves worthy of eternal life, we now turn to the Gentiles. This is what the Lord has commanded us: 'I have made you a light for the Gentiles, that you may bring salvation to the ends of the earth.'" When the Gentiles heard this, they were glad and honored the word of the Lord; and all who believed were appointed to eternal life. (Acts 13:46–48)

Paul and Barnabas left behind a community that understood the Torah, but now saw the fulfillment in Jesus' offer of reconciliation and hope. Paul and the team left a renewed community in Psidian Antioch, which not only received salvation but understood that it was open to all and remained to continue the work of Jesus' empire. There were many interpretations of who the "the servant" was in Isaiah 40—55, who was chosen by Yahweh to turn the nation back to their Lord. The servant was understood to be Israel/Jacob, the prophet, and Jesus—the Messiah. However, Paul and Barnabas viewed the church as the next *servant* by quoting the above verse found in Isaiah. "It is too small a thing for you to be my servant, to restore the tribes of Jacob and bring back those of Israel whom I have kept. I will also make you a light for the Gentiles that you may bring my salvation to the ends of the earth" (Isa 49:6). Paul's ministry was a reflection of his view that he and the renewed Christian community were Yahweh's servant, found in the prophets.[20]

The team next journeyed to smaller towns in the Galatian region. Augustus had built the Via Sebaste road in 6 BCE to connect many of the major cities in this area. The well-paved road was approximately three and one-half meters wide and served to accommodate wheeled vehicles as well as pedestrians and animal riders.[21] The highway connected Antioch to these towns, which were important colonies for the Romans.

Lystra, Iconia, and Derbe were areas that had the reputation of neglecting the gods. An ancient writer, Ovid, wrote a story concerning Zeus and Hermes as they visited a city in the form of humans, traveling and seeking hospitality.[22] They were unwelcomed in these towns, which were later punished by Zeus due to their lack of compassion and willingness to

---

20. Rosner, "The Glory of God in Paul's Missionary Theology and Practice," 158; Kim, "Paul as Eschatological Herald," 16–17.

21. Hansen, "Galatia," 384.

22. Ovid, *Metamorphoses*, 8:626–724.

offer comfort to strangers. This region was not interested in repeating that mistake.

As Paul and Barnabas entered Iconia they preached in a synagogue. As with Psidian Antioch they found a good reception by the listeners, until those of the resistance began to stir up the community.

> At Iconium they went into the Jewish synagogue. They spoke and a great number of Jews and Greeks believed. But the Jews who refused to believe stirred up the Gentiles and poisoned their souls against the brothers. Then they spent much time speaking boldly for the Lord, concerning grace, giving them the ability to perform signs and wonders. The people of the city were divided; some sided with the Jews, others with the apostles. There was a plot among both Gentiles and Jews, together with their leaders, to abuse them and stone them. But they found out about it and fled to the Lycaonian cities of Lystra and Derbe and to the surrounding country, where they continued to preach the gospel. (Acts 14:1–7)

In this story there are echoes similar to Luke's previous narrative and the persecution of Stephen. After the good news of Jesus was preached a few from the Jewish faith refused to accept the truth, making things difficult for the early Christians. It is interesting that these groups were not effectively growing in their communities and rather than viewing this new movement as an opportunity to work together, they blamed them for division. One reason might be that *the Christian team was attracting some of their people.* They may have felt threatened as they lost some of their stronger members. Another reason might be that *they felt hurt because they struggled to grow in this Gentile community.* This new movement, however, quickly developed a foothold and connected with outsiders. Instead of viewing this as an opportunity for new growth they interpreted the Christians as a threat and turned against them. Luke wrote that the community was divided, suggesting that not only the message but the conflict had become well known. How sad that two groups proclaiming the love and sacrifice of God could not work together to influence their town.

In addition to a small group of Jewish individuals resisting the Christian team, other Gentiles from the community joined the crowd. Paul was once again at risk for stoning, causing the team to leave town. This pattern of preaching among the Jews, resistance from the preceding town, and rejection of the gospel continued throughout Luke's narrative. The witness of Jesus required boldness because of the opposition of people who should have embraced the movement. However, new communities of Christians develop in the midst of this opposition, resistance, and persecution.

> When the crowd saw what Paul had done, they shouted in the Lycaonian language, "The gods are like humans and have come down to us!" Barnabas they called Dia [Zeus], and Paul they called Hermes because he was the main speaker. The priest of Zeus, whose temple was just outside the city, brought bulls and wreaths to the city gates because he and the crowd wanted to offer sacrifices to them. But when the apostles Barnabas and Paul heard of this, they tore their clothes and rushed out into the crowd, shouting: "Brothers and sisters, why are you doing these things? We are just people, like you. We are bringing you good news, telling you to turn from these worthless things to the living God, who made the heavens and the earth and the sea and everything in them. . . . He has shown kindness by giving you rain from heaven and crops in their seasons; he provides you with plenty of food and fills your hearts with joy." Even with these words, they had difficulty keeping the crowd from sacrificing to them. Then some Jews came from Antioch and Iconium and persuaded the crowd. They stoned Paul and dragged him outside the city, thinking he was dead. But after the disciples had gathered around him, he got up and went back into the city. The next day he and Barnabas left for Derbe. (Acts 14:11–20)

As Paul and Barnabas traveled to Iconia they encountered the myth of hospitality, the gods, and the community. This area also showed resistance to becoming fully Roman by keeping their natural language (Lyconian).[23] They were a people who held fast to their traditional way of life, which was more Hittite than Greco-Roman.[24] Paul healed a lame man, again a common action of Jesus and Peter, and manifested the power of the Holy Spirit in a Gentile community. The response of the city was that Paul and Barnabas were the incarnated Zeus and Hermes. Since Barnabas must have been older and quiet he was assumed to be Zeus, while Paul was identified with Hermes (known as the son of Zeus and a great speaker). This provides insight into the natures of both disciples and possibly their age difference. For Barnabas to take a back seat to the younger Paul as a preacher suggests that he truly was a man of encouragement and full of the Spirit. Paul, on the

---

23. Fant and Reddish, *A Guide to Biblical Sites*, 241–42.
24. Hayes, "Paul and the Multi-Ethnic First-Century World," 81.

other hand, would have manifested the Spirit through his giftedness and boldness in vocally witnessing to the resurrection of Jesus.

The crowd began to treat the two disciples as gods, which bothered both men. The crowd refused to act "inhospitably" and continued to sacrifice to and worship the supposed gods. However, the Jewish resistance evidently found Paul and Barnabas's location and stirred the crowd against them. It is odd that a crowd can be as fickle as this group and move from worship to hatred, but crowds have their own psychology. Paul and Barnabas were targeted and the crowd stoned the main speaker. As the corrupt religious leaders convinced the crowds to turn against Jesus and Stephen, so they manipulated a Gentile crowd to stone Paul, for admitting he was not a god. As these leaders convinced a Gentile king to crucify Jesus, so they moved a community to reject the object of their worship. Paul's sermon to the audience would have made any diaspora Jew proud, but these individuals had become hardened and blinded by rage. Paul became the scapegoat of this rage and suffered its consequences.

Paul suffered yet saw this as part of his ministry for Jesus. "Paul's references to his afflictions are designed to identify him with Christ's sufferings and crucifixion. Paul understands and portrays his sufferings as part of his discipleship and apostolic vocation—they were a part of his missionary activities and intrinsic to his calling. For Paul, living a self-giving life in participatory suffering with Christ is the model for ministry."[25]

Unfortunately for the resistance Paul lived. It is amazing that anyone could survive a stoning but even more amazing that Paul was mobile the next day. While I mentioned earlier that Paul was a trauma survivor by witnessing the murder of Stephen, even more he would have struggled as a violence survivor with post-traumatic stress. Shelly Rambo indicated that trauma survivors live in two worlds. "In the aftermath of trauma, death and life no longer stand in opposition. Instead, death haunts life. The challenge for those who experience trauma is to move in a world in which the boundaries and parameters of life and death no longer seem to hold, to provide meaning."[26] Paul would have mentally prepared for death during this experience and while Luke very quickly summarized his survival and return to town, psychologically one would understand that Paul's world would have been turned upside down. What would he have thought? Would he

---

25. Adewuya, "The Sacrificial-Missiological Function of Paul's Sufferings in the Context of 2 Corinthians," 89.

26. Rambo, *Spirit and Trauma*, 3.

have reverted back to Jesus' "showing him that he must suffer much for my name's sake" (Acts 9:15–16)? Would he have felt a connection to Stephen?

Unlike Stephen, Paul's "last" words were not recorded, nor was the anger and hostility of the crowd, as Luke had done with Stephen. However, the implications of the text are clear—Paul suffered a near-death experience and this would be the first of many traumatic experiences that he would face. Paul's ministry involved not only physical trauma but emotional and psychological suffering as well (2 Cor 11:25–32). His sufferings were the results of physical, verbal, and emotional abuse by those he wished to help. This experience will be a major theme in his personal life as well as his ministry.

The mission team left for the small city of Derbe and continued to preach in the surrounding villages.

> They preached the gospel in that city and won a large number of disciples. Then they returned to Lystra, Iconium, and Antioch, strengthening the soul of the disciples and encouraging them to remain in the faith and that we must go through many hardships to enter the Empire of God. Paul and Barnabas appointed elders for them in each church with prayer and fasting, and committed them to the Lord, in whom they had put their trust. After going through Pisidia, they came into Pamphylia, and when they had preached the word in Perga, they went down to Attalia. (Acts 14:21–25)

Paul and Barnabas were able to speak firsthand of their suffering and the cost of following Jesus. They would have known that a group from *the resistance* would be close behind them and that the call to enter the Empire of Jesus would come with a price. As it had been from the beginning of Luke's narrative concerning Jesus and the twelve apostles, so it continued through Acts. The accounts from Matthew and Mark quote Jesus multiple times, claiming that the Messiah would suffer and be rejected at Jerusalem (Matt 17:22–23; 20:17–19; Mark 8:31–33; 9:31; 10:33–34). Luke emphasized the rejection and suffering at least five times and mentioned that Jerusalem would be the seat of this rejection and resistance (Luke 9:23–27, 44; 13:32; 24:20; 2:35). As we read Acts this becomes a major theme for the author as Paul became the major model in this cost of discipleship. For Luke, Paul, and Barnabas, the Empire of Jesus came with a price and many times that price involved suffering, rejection, and death. On this first mission trip Paul and Barnabas remind the leaders and members of these new churches that suffering is a key component of discipleship.

The team began to appoint elders in each of these churches. The Jewish faith provided opportunity for those men who were older and mature to lead in their communities. The Hebrew word for elder (*zqn*) suggested a grey-bearded one or older man. These males led their people as ambassadors, fathers/grandfathers, wise advisors, and those who sat at the city gate offering judgment in local legal issues.[27] The Greek word for elders (today commonly called *presbyters*) was also used for those leaders in communities outside of the Jewish nation. These men were also referred to as bishops and pastors (1 Tim 3:1–7; 1 Pet 5:1–4; Acts 20:17–35). Typically "elder" was the title, while "bishop" (overseer—we get the word *Episcopal* from this) and "pastor" (shepherd) were descriptive of their roles in the community.[28] In order for the churches to survive Paul and Barnabas knew that they needed to appoint leaders to carry on in their absence.

The elders in these churches would have been fairly recent converts. Paul and Barnabas began their mission trip about 47/48 CE and returned to Antioch in 48/49 CE. This suggests that the churches in Galatia were one or two years old when Paul and Barnabas returned to Antioch, indicating that these elders would have had to be newer converts to Christianity. While they could have been Jewish or Gentile God-fearers, and familiar with the Torah, this did not have to be the case for all leaders. Many would have been Gentile in order to further the mission. However, I would suggest that Gentiles would have had a strong presence in these early churches because many were leaders in their local community and the resistance of some of the Jewish communities became strong. Since the synagogues were not prevalent in these cities it is likely that Paul and Barnabas would have focused their energies on Gentile converts.

As the team returned to Antioch they were able to bring good news of conversions, new churches, and the danger that they would have faced in the early stages of this global ministry. One would almost wish to have been present to see and hear loud cheers, their scars, and tears shed over God's work through this team. The first wave had gained another foothold in the Roman Empire and began to spread the news of the resurrected Jesus to Jews and Gentiles. The resistance was there but had not overtaken the

---

27. Revive, *The Elders in Ancient Israel*, 189 ; Willis, *The Elders of the City*, 307–8; and Clark, *Emerging Elders*, 38.

28. Clark, *Emerging Elders*, 39.

missionaries. Once again all seemed right in the world as Luke wrote that the mission team stayed in Antioch "a long time" (Acts 14:28).

These stories of success would continue, but with a price. Paul and Barnabas began to introduce into their teaching that Jesus was not the only one to pay a price for this new empire. These Christian leaders were also not the only ones paying this price. Faithful people were going to be called to suffer as well. In the early days of the gospel and mission of Jesus' empire people would need to lay their lives down for the message of Jesus and their missionary leaders. As early Christians would have heard the stories of Jesus they would, no doubt, have been taught that discipleship involved commitment, sacrifice, and sometimes suffering. The first wave was finished, but the war with evil was just beginning. *The resistance* also continued but soon found a way to ally and partner with those whose hearts were open to salvation, only to poison their minds and prevent the God who came to save them from changing their lives.

> Then he said to them all: "Whoever wants to be my disciple must deny themselves and take up their cross daily and follow me. For whoever wants to save their life will lose it, but whoever loses their life for me will save it. What good is it for someone to gain the whole world, and yet lose or forfeit their very self? Whoever is ashamed of me and my words, the Son of Man will be ashamed of them when he comes in his glory and in the glory of the Father and of the holy angels. I tell you, some standing here will not taste death before they see the kingdom of God." (Luke 9:23–27)

The growth of the Jesus movement thrived in the midst of suffering and conflict.

> Christianity arose during a time when there was already enormous religious curiosity on the part of Romans and other pagans about Eastern religions and divinities ranging from Isis to Jesus. It sought to take advantage of this curiosity, and it offered to pagans a religion that did not require certain rituals (such as circumcision or the keeping of food laws) that would have immediately alienated them in obvious observable ways from their fellow Gentiles. It did not require temples, costly animal sacrifices, priests—the very essence of much of ancient religion. It could meet in homes, and its rituals were flexible. It is not surprising that in the course of the next two centuries it came to be seen by pagans as a much more appealing religious option than Judaism, ordinary magic, or various other forms of traditional and popular religion that

existed in the Empire. The irony of course is that when Christianity was finally endorsed by the Roman emperor it was well on the way to taking on the very properties of other ancient religions with priests, temples, sacrifices, and the like. One must ask, then, whether in the end Christianity was more the bearer or the recipient of socialization in the Empire.[29]

It, like the movement of Yahweh and the prophets to restore the Judeans in exile, was born in resistance, conflict, and pain. The restoration of the nation of Judea arose out of the ashes of despair and suffering. This new nation was a remnant of faithful people who repented of their sins and the sins of their ancestors and celebrated the renewed covenant with Yahweh and the people. Jesus also came to a nation suffering for its sins and the sins of its ancestors. However, many of those on the margins of life were there because of the greed, corruption, and injustice of their leaders. Not only did Jesus renew a covenant/movement during this suffering, he himself suffered the price of coming close to humans. Yet, out of the ashes of death he rose to a new life, indicating that the people of God can, and must, rise out of their ashes of doom through repentance, baptism, and faithfulness. For Luke, the Spirit inspired others to continue that journey and survive *the resistance* and persecution of those who feared God's presence.

Modern Resistance

Near the end of the semester of my seminary class one of my students asked for prayer in the search for a ministry position, job, and calling. I typically began each class with prayer and solicited requests from the students. The individual spoke of how stressful it was not having a position and that he wanted to have a "good paying" ministry job. We all understood and know that this is a common concern for our students. Xiang was one of my students sitting by my desk. I noticed that she was also concerned and seemed troubled. Xiang had come from China to attend George Fox Evangelical Seminary while her husband and daughter stayed back in her country. Her goal was to become a pastor and return to help her church. Her English was very broken but she was learning the more she attended classes. "Xiang, can we pray for you today?" I asked. "Yes," she replied, "and for my pastor."

Xiang's pastor was routinely taken by government officials and their police officers, locked in a cell, and later released. This was something that

---

29. Witherington, *The Acts of the Apostles*, 389.

her church saw often and they would pray for his release, attend church the following Sunday, and listen to his stories of faith in the prison. As she finished the story I asked, "So, you are here to become a pastor and help him lead the church?' "Yes," she said. I then asked, "Does that mean you will be harassed as well?" "Yes, I hope to be. That way he won't have to do it alone," she said. I heard one of the students ask, "Xiang, your government must know you are here . . . ." Xiang responded, "Yes they do, and when I graduate I am expected to return. They will be ready for me." The room was silent. The student with the initial prayer request commented, "I guess this makes my anxiety over a job pretty insignificant. I think we should pray for Xiang." It is easy to forget that facing the resistance and persecution is not just for radically committed missionaries and serious disciples. Globally it is the least that Christians can do if they wish for peace and freedom in countries that outlaw the name of Jesus. For those of us in a country where practicing our faith is legal, it is easy to see it as a right, rather than a blessing. For those of us who can freely attend church without harassment, it should be a blessing—not something we seek for an excuse to miss.

"Suffering was not an academic subject with Paul. It was an experience he tasted ending with his death. Paul understood suffering as an integral part of his missionary calling and practice."[30] If this is true then it would be difficult to understand Paul's ministry, his writings, and his convictions if we choose a life of comfort and convenience. Even more, it would be difficult to understand a movement born in resistance and conflict as a people looking for a church to meet our needs. Today we must ask the question, can anything born out of convenience, materialism, and safety help us rise out of the ashes and sins of our lives and the lives of our ancestors?

---

30. Adewuya, "The Sacrificial-Missiological Function of Paul's Suffering in the Context of 2 Corinthians," 97–98.

8

A COUNCIL ON FOREIGN RELATIONS MEETS

In that day I will raise up David's fallen tent, and repair its broken places; by raising up its ruins and building it as before, so that they may possess the remnant of Edom and all the nations that carry my name. (Amos 9:11–12)

WE WERE TAKING OUR annual family trip to Missouri during the fourth of July. We enjoy the drive from Portland to Chillicothe, Missouri, which takes over two days. As usual we passed through Salt Lake City and spent the night. As we left early that morning we listened to a local Salt Lake radio station. This was during the time when television cooking celebrity Paula Dean had been accused of using racial comments that were offensive to some of her employees. Of course this was the topic of discussion on the local radio station. As Lori and I listened it became clear that all of the hosts and those calling in were Caucasian. It also became clear to us, as the show progressed, that they were eventually going to use the "N" word at some point in the broadcast.

The hosts of the show kept stressing that "any comment must be understood by the intent of the speaker." They very quickly pointed out that while people in the past were using the word along with other racist terms, they really didn't mean any harm by it—and people should understand this. They also pointed out, as many called in to express similar sentiment, that racist language is only racist if a person is being "mean about it."

Lori and I were livid and continued to speak loudly to the radio (as if anyone was going to hear us). I remember that one of us yelled, "This is the twenty-first century, I can't believe we are hearing this!" Our boys sat in the back and listened but, being nine and eleven years old, had little understanding of what was happening. Then it happened. The host used the racist word (which we *all* know is wrong), stopped, and said, "Well, I guess they will take me off the air, but there—I said it. Everyone knows I don't mean anything by it, and I'm just using it as a word." He was then supported by a barrage of callers who indicated that "some people will take this to extremes by being offended when he is truly a good person, only trying to stimulate conversation." We finally drove away from the signal and lost the station. We don't know how it ended but it was not a good view of that city, nor of that radio station.

It was obvious that no person of color was engaged in the conversation. It was also obvious that no one thought about how degrading this language has been for centuries, how people of color have for years been told to "understand," nor have they thought that *a speaker has the responsibility to clearly communicate* to their audience. Intent is not an excuse. The words we choose have the power to build up or tear down (no matter what our intent). Even more, Caucasian people have no right to tell people of color how they should understand racist language. Racism continues to exist in our country when people in a position of privilege and power ignore the feelings and feedback of those who are considered minorities and vulnerable others. While the good news of Jesus brought hope to the Jewish nation, those on the outside of Judaism also needed to hear the message; however, it had to be on their level of understanding as well.

TRADITION VS. FAITH

The church celebrated when Paul and Barnabas returned to Antioch to share the good news of their mission. As Jesus had promised earlier, the Holy Spirit was leading the church to witness and proclaim his resurrection to all including those outside of the Jewish faith (Luke 24:44–49; Acts 1:6–8). In addition to this the Gentiles were financially giving to those in need and bringing glory not only to God but to the nation of Israel. Isaiah's prophecy was being fulfilled as God had promised long ago to restore Jerusalem's glory and receive kings and Gentiles from other parts of the world (Isa 60:1–2). The church was expanding and reflecting this prophecy as Jews, leaders, upper-class men and women, and Gentiles were converted to Jesus.

> Some people came down from Judea to Antioch and were teaching the believers that unless you are circumcised, according to the custom taught by Moses, you cannot be saved. Paul and Barnabas came to a dispute and debate with them. So Paul and Barnabas were appointed, along with some other believers, to go up to Jerusalem to see the apostles and elders to seek this out. The church sent them on their way, and as they traveled through Phoenicia and Samaria, they told how the Gentiles had been converted. This news made all the believers very glad. When they came to Jerusalem, they were welcomed by the church and the apostles and elders, to whom they reported everything God had done through them. (Acts 15:1–4)

The dispute began as the church continued to grow. The resistance had been present throughout Luke's narratives. This resistance presented common themes. *First, there was concern with the traditional Torah (law of Moses), the temple, and issues of holiness.* Historically the nation of Israel struggled to uphold these issues. They had been taken to exile over idolatry, holiness, neglecting the law of Moses, not keeping the Sabbath, and defiling Yahweh's temple. The leaders were very sensitive to these beliefs and rightfully so. However, these also became convenient charges to place upon those who were viewed as troublemakers. Jesus, Stephen, and Paul, while upholding the Jewish customs, were charged with profaning the temple and/or law of Moses (Luke 23:1–2; Acts 6:14, 25:8).

Second, circumcision marked an important identity and tradition through conversion into the Jewish faith. The inclusion of Gentiles into the Jewish community required circumcision. Those who were not willing or able to take this step were considered *God-fearers*. Circumcision was a defining mark that separated Jews from Gentiles. To remove this symbol of faith, commitment, and covenant would have been viewed as a breach of Yahweh's covenant and a watering down of the Jewish traditions. Circumcision was also a symbol of God's promise to Abraham (Gen 17:1–8). It was a symbol of a nation returning to its God (Josh 5:2–8). It was also a sign of resistance to an evil empire during the Maccabee revolt and a sign of the covenant between God and humanity (Gen 17:3–8). One can understand why the Jewish Christians had become concerned with the inclusion of Gentiles through faith and baptism, without circumcision.

Luke wrote that some were stating "Gentiles must be circumcised." The resistance was not interested in discussion, dialogue, or examining the issue. These men had come from Judea (the central location of the Jewish community), and were teaching the Christians that salvation was dependent upon circumcision. One can understand why the Antioch church decided to respond. For the many Jews living in a foreign land there would have been concern that Gentiles were not only associating with Jews but too easily joining the faith without circumcision. They would have easily been persuaded by this form of resistance.

The church was faced with not only a conflict of tradition/Scripture, but a conflict of people groups. If Gentiles were being converted at a greater rate than under the previous system, was this good? Was this scriptural? Were the early Christian missionaries making conversion to God easier without demanding enough of a cost? Were they compromising Torah? Paul and Barnabas, however, must have worked through these issues on their first mission, and possibly while at Antioch. They had spent time with diaspora Jews and realized that reaching non-Jews was difficult and required understanding the law of God as it was to apply to Gentiles.[1] At Antioch they confronted the Judean resistance and became representatives for the Antioch church. On the way to Jerusalem, they took this opportunity to share the Gentile conversion stories as a way of addressing the circumcision issue.

Change

In the late 1980s church growth studies began to suggest that churches develop new methods of reaching new people, due to the higher rate of people leaving established congregations. So movements have promoted small house church groups, increased megachurches and satellite campuses, small community-based church plants, social justice or inner city churches that focus on the local community, or meetings that rent public schools, bars, coffee houses, or local community centers. Churches and faith communities are changing the way things have been traditionally done in the past. This is scary to some, troubling to others, and exciting to the rest. These newer methods of "doing church" have the goal in mind to reach new people where they reside. The key for many of these groups has been

---

1. Zetterholm, "The Question of Assumptions," 91–92; Nanos, "The Question of Conceptualization," 146.

an increased focus on theological study as well as studying the culture we have been called to reach.

Change is always difficult for humans, especially those who follow God, Jesus, or others. In reviewing history it is clear that even Christians have struggled to accept people who were different and challenged our ways of perceiving life. Living during a time when the United States has had its first African American president, I am still surprised at the underlying racism that exists among our churches, communities, and citizens. While many suggest that they are not racist we still struggle to repent of our attitudes, past beliefs, and injustices against others by ignoring our past history and assuming it has been reconciled. Even more, only a small percentage of Christian churches are "ethnically diverse" and we as a whole are unaware how we are perceived by those of another ethnicity.

I was asked to speak at a church in North Carolina concerning our work with abuse, abusers, and families affected by domestic violence. I was also asked to do a marriage workshop that Sunday afternoon for the congregation. Of the many couples present only one was African American. Since we boasted that Agape Church of Christ was an ethnically diverse church I felt that this would be an opportunity to not only reach couples but help them see that reconciliation involves more than just marriages—we are called to racial reconciliation as well. The workshop went well and I had given many illustrations of our work in Portland with abusive marriages, premarital counseling, and marriage mentor programs. I left that evening having enjoyed a great weekend with a good church and wonderful people.

The following week I received an email from a woman who attended the marriage workshop. She was upset that of all the images I used of couples, the only one of a black couple involved a man who was a drug dealer. She mentioned how insensitive it was and how I seemed to be oblivious to how hurtful that language was to her and her husband. She was right, I had used that illustration. As I thought about it I realized it was insensitive and racist. I felt sick and sad at the same time as I realized that the couple must have felt so alone in the group and maybe even targeted by me. I quickly responded by thanking her for her note, apologizing, and admitting that she was absolutely correct. I shared that I was insensitive and want to avoid this in the future. I promised that I would talk with our church people who would understand her position and work to change my language and illustrations. My brothers and sisters at church who were African American agreed with the email, her point, and how she must have felt. While they admitted that they knew me and my intent, they shared that this couple did not know me and my intent did not matter. They were alone in a group of Caucasians and I needed to represent all people with respect. The words were said and the words were heard. As hard as it was to hear, it needed to be addressed. I appreciate the feedback of those who have suffered from racism and discrimination.

I am thankful for those in my life who share with me how vulnerable they can be and how hurt they can feel when harmful words are said. They are not just words. They have meaning, regardless of the speakers' intent. However, if God's people wish to be ethnically diverse and reach out to those who are marginalized, we must first hear the feedback from those who hear our words and respond as people who desire to build *them* up, not *ourselves*.

Racism has been a stain on a history of an empire which began by reaching those on the margins of life. A movement designed to confront those who marginalized people has become a movement that resists the unifying work of the Spirit. Is it possible that we have become part of *the resistance* to Jesus' work in our world today? Is it possible that much of *the resistance* comes from bigotry, racism, and the unwillingness to admit and repent of the sins of our ancestors, rather than a religious belief?

Allowing God to Change Tradition

Since Jerusalem had been the location of the first outpouring of the Holy Spirit, it seemed consistent that this city should also become the place to resolve the circumcision debate. While welcomed by the church, Luke indicated where the source of controversy existed. "Then some of the believers who belonged to the party of the Pharisees stood up and said, 'The Gentiles must be circumcised and required to keep the law of Moses'" (Acts 15:5). As Luke wrote, the group wisely met without these individuals, but only with the apostles and elders. I have found that typically the first people to speak out at church meetings are the ones that tend to cause trouble. The elders and apostles met without the "Pharisaical Christians" to discuss the issue and find a resolution.

Peter shared the evidence and experience from the Holy Spirit, testifying to the Gentile acceptance into the Empire of Jesus. For this apostle, God's work was a sign of the new community. As Gamaliel had warned the council not to oppose the Lord, so Peter reminded the group not to test God providing evidence for Gentile inclusion (Acts 5; 15:10). Paul and Barnabas echoed his speech through their encounters and preaching. Their evidence on the mission field also held tremendous weight for the council.

Finally James, Jesus' brother, appealed to the prophetic text of Amos. "In that day I will restore David's fallen tent. I will repair its broken places, restore its ruins, and build it as it used to be, so that they may possess the remnant of Edom and all the nations that carry my name" (Amos 9:11–12). James added to the text God's "return" and that the "remnant" would seek God, as well as the Gentiles. For Luke, Amos's prophecy was adapted to reflect restoration from captivity as well as the restoration of Jesus' empire to the world. The text was a promise that the nation of Judah would be rebuilt after captivity so that those left over (the remnant) would wear the name of Yahweh. This remnant included the Gentiles. It was always God's desire to be inclusive rather than exclusive. As Johnson once wrote, "The Spirit-directed community understands that God is not restrained by the tradition of the Church and often works outside the boundaries of the community."[2] James, Peter, Paul, and Barnabas's testimonies were evidence that the prophets' real intentions were coming true.

The council came to a resolution due to the testimony and work of the Spirit along with the evidence of the biblical texts. In fact, the evidence and ministry of the Spirit and the missionaries was discussed first, before the Scriptures were consulted. They must have realized that this would be a difficult resolution for many Jews to accept. However, the Gentiles had an opportunity to prove to their new Jewish family that God's Spirit could transform them. Their fruit, behavior, and actions would provide an opportunity to prove to the Jews that they were "worth saving." The leaders suggested that they set a moral example and avoid the appearance of another stumbling block for the Jews. "It is my judgment, therefore, that we should not make it difficult for the Gentiles who are turning to God. Instead we should write to them, telling them to abstain from food polluted by idols, from sexual immorality, from the meat of strangled animals and from blood. From the earliest times the Law of Moses has been preached in every city and is read in the synagogues on every Sabbath" (Acts 15:19–21).

In some ways this small letter seemed to be a slap in the face to Gentiles, indicating that they did not have a moral code. However, it was an indication that the Gentiles seemed to feel that sexual immorality, and eating meat offered to idols as well as blood mixed with meat, were issues

2. Johnson, *Prophetic Jesus*, 71.

with which they struggled. While there is evidence that many philosophers opposed sex outside of marriage, the majority of people must have been practicing this. It is likely that the Gentiles would have seen nothing wrong with eating idol meat (as is evidenced in 1 Cor 8:1–13) and that sexual immorality (sex outside of marriage) may have been viewed as acceptable (Rom 1:18–32; 1 Cor 6:12–20). For the Jerusalem council, omitting circumcision as a requirement to be included in God's empire was going to cause strife in the Jewish Christian communities. However, if the Gentiles were willing to make additional sacrifices in other areas of life they would somehow prove to the Jews that they had been filled with the Holy Spirit.

Is Change Difficult Today?

There is an important lesson in all this. While those of us in conservative theological circles feel more comfortable consulting the Bible first, before we act, we should never disregard the work of the Spirit in our world. Often we spend hours deciphering an ancient text, which was not written to us in our culture, country, or period of time, and ignore the powerful work done by God on the lives and hearts of people. In a world where evil, selfishness, narcissism, abuse, exploitation of people, and despair reign, we would do well to realize that Jesus' task is to transform those behaviors by powerfully intervening and creating spaces for love, compassion, and mercy. The text gives us wisdom, but we read the text from our own perspectives. Listening to other voices, thoughts, and insights offers a broader view for God's Spirit (which requires that we believe the Spirit works in others rather than only in us). Over the centuries the sacred texts have been used to destroy lives, cultures, civilizations, and our own earth. This can only happen when people approach the text without seeing the cost and effect our interpretations have on ourselves as well as the people around us.

Often I am asked to speak to our county batterer intervention providers concerning abusive individuals and their use of the sacred texts to further oppress and abuse their partners as well as others. Since I am Christian, and many of them work with a diverse array of clients, I try to be more general in my presentations. We encourage the counselors to avoid arguing texts with individuals, but rather to understand that violent and controlling individuals use sacred texts to oppress others while peaceful and loving people use sacred texts to treat people with love, compassion, and respect. One of the counselors always reminds us, during the discussion, that we should ask our clients who use the sacred texts to justify their abuse: "How is your interpretation of that text helping you and your family?" For men who are mandated by the county court system to attend it is important for them to acknowledge that having family fear them is not the goal of God's peace in our lives. I find that this counselor has a tremendous amount of wisdom in his work and often comments that we must see the world around us in addition to the world of the texts. There should be peace, harmony, and safety when both worlds work together in our lives.

RESISTANCE AMONG FRIENDS

As the chapter came to a close it seemed that once again everything was right in the empire as the church experienced peace, harmony, and unity. Yet, Paul and Barnabas hotly disputed an issue that touched both of these men. For Barnabas, his cousin John Mark needed forgiveness, a second chance, and to go again into the mission field. This was Barnabas's gift as he had given Saul of Tarsus that same chance earlier in Acts, even though the other apostles resisted him (Acts 9). Early Christian tradition indicated that Barnabas's sister was Mary (Mark's mother), the woman who opened her home to Jesus at the last supper and to the apostles and early church in the beginning stages of the movement (Luke 22:12; Acts 12:12–14; 1:12).[3] The tradition also suggested that Peter was Mark's paternal uncle. John Mark held an important place in early Christianity as a relative of the early leaders, author of the second Gospel, and evangelist to Africa. Unfortunately in the beginning he had abandoned the mission team in their first trip near Perga (Acts 13:13). In spite of this Barnabas felt comfortable taking him along on the second trip.

> Some time later Paul said to Barnabas, "Let us go back and visit the believers in all the towns where we preached the word of the Lord and see how they are doing." Barnabas wanted to take John, also called Mark, with them, but Paul did not think it best to take him, because he had deserted them in Pamphylia and had not continued with them in the work. They had such a strong disagreement that they separated. Barnabas took Mark and sailed for Cyprus, but Paul chose Silas and left, commended by the believers to the grace of the Lord. He went through Syria and Cilicia, building up the churches. (Acts 15:36–41)

3. Oden, *The African Memory of Mark*, 84–85.

Paul did not share Barnabas' optimism. The text indicated that the two great leaders had a sharp dispute or what we would call a "falling out." In the past I was hard on Paul. I felt like he must have been too strict or expected too much. I had understood in this text that Paul must have forgotten that Barnabas had given him a second chance and that he must do the same for Mark. However, after planting a church and experiencing the heartache that comes with feeling abandoned by people both in leadership/ministry and as active members, I understand Paul's point. Paul may have felt that his ministry would be life-threatening and, as a trauma survivor, he needed people around him who would not abandon him. While he and Barnabas disagreed on Mark, they each had their appointed ministry from Jesus and were each highly gifted. More people would hear the news of Jesus because these two men would go different ways. Paul took Silas with him. He would be by Paul's side in prison, torture, and while preaching. Luke indicated that Silas was one of the men who was an encouraging prophet. Through time Mark would become Peter's companion and write the Gospel of Mark (1 Pet 5:13). Paul would later call Mark a fellow prisoner (Col 4:10). Mark became a great disciple but at this time, he needed to spend time being mentored by Barnabas. Paul needed a man like Silas who would join him in what would become a dangerous mission, while Barnabas needed a man like Mark.

Jesus' people are passionate. Sometimes they are so passionate that they fight, argue, and frustrate each other. Sometimes his people have to talk, reconcile, and work out their issues—for the good of the movement. Other times they have to set boundaries and give each other their own space. This space can give them time, but it also can help them to understand who they are and what they have been called to do. When they reconcile they will not be the same as before, but they will be working for the good of the movement. Others need to separate and go their own way. They may carry wounds or separate with scars but they can cover more ground when they are apart. However, if they are truly Jesus' people they will one day make peace, for the good of the movement. Even more, they will do more for the good of the movement while separated. The point is that we cannot force reconciliation. Sometimes God's people need boundaries not only with the sins of the world, but a potentially hostile relationship. All in all they are good for the movement.

The early movement had fought the resistance, especially among itself, and continued to focus on reaching those outside the borders of the empire of Jesus. While Paul and Barnabas went their separate ways they formed two more mission teams in the Antioch embassy. More people would be reached and Gentiles would continue to be included in the Empire of Jesus. However, Luke will focus his remaining material on Paul. One reason would be because Luke will join Paul on this next trip. Another reason would be that Paul became the main representative for the Gentiles and brought the message of Jesus to the Roman world. Paul would be the one to refuse to compromise on the inclusion of the Gentiles, and God needed his conviction for this mission. Paul also traveled to Rome and used the legal and political system to gain a foothold for the church.

Over the years studies on church growth, outreach methods, and evangelism have noted change, shifts, and adaptation. As Tickle mentioned, we seem to be in a transition period that will bring new life to our movement while helping the traditional church reform its ways of doing ministry and surviving.[4] As the twentieth century came to a close Christian churches in North America moved from a model of "excellence" and "baby boomer" generational "seeker" worship services while witnessing the exodus of the "millenial" generations. Authors mentioned that people loved Jesus rather than the church and saw Christians as judgmental and hypocritical.[5] This was viewed as one reason that people were leaving organized Christianity. Others indicated that the church had lost the focus on mission and continued to operate as an institution that felt called to control others. The emphasis on church planting and creating missional churches and communities was a powerful movement that helped to redefine churches, mission, and Christian leadership.[6] "Missional" language was eventually enhanced by changing to "missional/incarnational" as an attempt to move the church from a philosophy of mission to the practice of incarnational ministry as in the life of Jesus.[7] All of these writings have been strong attempts for Christian ministries, churches, and leaders to reach the many people not already attending congregations. Instead of being a church that "attracted" people the move was to be a church which "went after" or "engaged" people where they lived.

4. Tickle, *The Great Emergence*, 17.

5. Kimball, *They Like Jesus But Not the Church*, 41; Kinnaman and Lyons, *UnChristian*, 20–24.

6. Stetzer, *Planting New Churches in a Postmodern Age*; Guder, ed., *Missional Church*; Frost and Hirsch, *The Shaping of Things to Come*; Gibbs, *Churchmorph*.

7. Hirsch, *The Forgotten Ways*; Woodward, *Creating a Missional Culture*.

When I left an established church as the preaching minister to plant the Agape Church of Christ I began to read many of these works. I not only devoured the books, but found myself weeping at times as I had felt the way that many of the authors had claimed the church was moving. It was something that many of us in ministry had stated for years. I found myself agreeing with almost every page I had read from these authors and many others I had used as research.

I have watched the movement grow, struggle, face resistance, and experience both criticism and support. I have noticed that the very reason we all began this reform had become our biggest critique. We were moved to act because people had a negative view of God, Jesus, the Bible, and the Christian church. After years of focusing on social justice, engaging the community without pressure to convert, and developing relationships with "sinners and tax collectors," critique now seems to focus on the fact that the movement has not had enough conversions, is too focused on social issues, or has fallen short on the mission. My thoughts have been that if the mission was to change people's perspectives on Jesus and the church (Paul included) then shouldn't that be the measure we use for effectiveness? Are we facing similar resistance as the early Christians because we are trying something different? Are we accused of making it too easy for the Gentiles, becoming too close to the Gentiles, and/or becoming more Greek by name and the way we operate?

There is a second point that I have found. After years of trying to reach people, listening to the hurt and pain that has been inflicted by controlling or hypocritical Christians, and trying to reach people where they are located, something is happening to our message—or at least to what others want our message to be. Many of those who have been raised in a Christian home and struggle with rebellion also tend to want to point the finger at churches, yet they do not want to be accountable for their behavior. Many don't realize that the same Savior who stated "judge not" is the same one who stated "a good tree cannot produce bad fruit . . . by their fruit you will recognize them" (Matt 7:1, 18, 20). I have watched people leave the church and almost feel as if it is our responsibility to accommodate them so that they might return.

With the rise of the "non-affiliated" (also "unaffiliated"—those who do not choose to be in one denomination) or the "dones" (those who are done with church and attending weekly worship but still claim to be Christian), the Christian church is faced with a dilemma. Living in Portland, we have understood that we have one of the highest unaffiliated rates in the United States. On the one hand, we have the book of Acts that stresses discipleship through obedience, self-sacrifice, membership in a community, and generally laying one's life down for a Christian community and Jesus' vision. We have a book that stresses courage in resistance and hospitality by a community of others. Then we have the general view of Americans as both consumeristic and materialistic. Is the struggle for the modern church how we reach people, or is it having a compelling vision worth dying for? Is the struggle for Christians whether they feel comfortable in a congregation and with its children's programs, or is the struggle remaining faithful to a vision and group of people who are also struggling against the resistance, looking for the man or woman of peace who will embrace the movement, join us, and invite us into their home?

Will the future of our churches be based on how people see us, whether they join us, or what we do in a community where God is working in various ways?

9

WITNESSING IN GREECE

Yahweh is good, a safe place in times of trouble and one who knows those who take shelter from an overwhelming flood for those trust. (Nah 1:7–8)

PAUL'S SECOND MISSION TRIP began as the first one. The team of two left the Antioch church, however, this time Barnabas and Mark took the first leg of their trip through Cyprus. Paul and Silas focused on the Syrian and Cilician congregations by visiting those earlier established during the first wave of the mission work. Their main focus was to "strengthen the churches." They had earlier preached that Christians must enter the Empire of Jesus through suffering and this would have been a continued focus of their ministry. They would have also shared the letter from the Jerusalem church concerning the inclusion of the Gentiles.

> Paul came to Derbe and then to Lystra, where a disciple named Timothy lived, whose mother was Jewish and a believer but whose father was a Greek. The believers at Lystra and Iconium spoke well of him. Paul wanted to take him along on the journey, so he circumcised him because of the Jews who lived in that area, for they all knew that his father was a Greek. As they traveled from town to town, they delivered the decisions reached by the apostles and elders in Jerusalem for the people to obey. The churches were strengthened in the faith and grew daily in numbers (Acts 16:1–5).

It is interesting that Paul returned to Lystra, the city where he had almost been killed. However, he was willing to risk his life to encourage the churches in Derbe, Lystra, and Iconia. Instead of traveling to Psidian Antioch and moving south, they passed through Cilicia, which included Tarsus (Paul's hometown). Luke did not share if they stayed long in Cilicia. For Luke, Timothy joining the team was more important than what Paul had done passing through his home community.

Upon Paul's return to the area (in reverse order from the first trip), he met a young man whose Jewish mother had been married to a Greek. We can assume that his mother would have been active in the Jewish community without his father. Paul later wrote that this young man, Timothy, reflected the faith of his grandmother, Lois, and mother, Eunice (2 Tim 1:5). No mention is made of his father's faith or that his father was a God-fearer or proselyte. This might suggest that Timothy's father was not a follower of Yahweh, and later Jesus. Timothy would have been one of the many young men who was brought to worship, practiced his faith at home, and who carried a deep spirituality because of his mother. Because his father was a Greek Timothy was not circumcised, also suggesting that his father was not concerned with passing this tradition on to his son. However, Timothy was a young man of outward faith, as shown by the fact that the church respected him.

Timothy was not a person of "faithful" words but one of action and obedience. Because of this Paul chose him for the team. He also had him circumcised so that Timothy could be an example to the Jewish Christians. While they had a letter from the Jerusalem council indicating that circumcision was not a requirement for Gentiles, Paul knew that Timothy's example was still important for the Jewish believers. Even more Timothy's trust and obedience, and willingness to sacrifice for future followers, may be why Paul would later write: "I have no one else like him, he takes a genuine interest in your well-being. Everyone looks out for their own interest, not those of Jesus Christ. You know that Timothy has proved himself and has served with me, as a son with his father, in the work of the gospel" (Phil 2:20–22).

I often remember my earlier days in ministry and how I was blessed to have men and women of faith who could model not only a Christian marriage, but a healthy desire to reach people for Jesus. Like Timothy my mom took (dragged is more how I remember it) my brother and I to church because my dad was atheist. While he was in Vietnam it was difficult for my mom to raise my brother and me and take us to church, especially as we continued to be a problem for the Sunday school teachers. However, I remember the regular visits from the Presbyterian minister (Pastor Groves) to our apartment, his talking with me, and when he gave me my first Bible. I also remember the many times in my life when ministers talked to me about being a Christian man, having sexual self-control and honor, while modeling healthy marriages.

My dad once said, "You're just a damn jock—you would probably pass up sex with a girl just to lift weights. Date a freshman, she'll let you do what you want." That was my role model of manhood, character, and respect for women. There were guys on my football and wrestling teams in high school who were Christian and talked to me about purity, faith in Jesus, and being a Christian man. When I became a Christian I had good brothers and sisters in the congregation who taught me and helped me to see faith in action. While unfortunately there were many males who disappointed me as both a young Christian and later a church leader, I often remember the men who became spiritual fathers in my life. I would never do anything to hurt them or disappoint them, not because I feared them, but because I knew that they loved me, as well as my family, and wanted the best for us. Lori and I are where we are today because of many of these men and women who helped to heal the father wound I had.

This is ministry, and this is the calling that Christian men and women have. For Timothy, Paul filled that gap that his father must have created. For Paul, Timothy was one of those individuals who proved that loving and investing in people paid off. Even though they had a letter from the Jerusalem council concerning circumcision, Timothy accepted the difficult task that Paul requested. While there may have been many who resisted or abandoned Paul, there were those like Timothy who reminded Paul (and us) that it was worth the work, patience, and effort. Even more, Timothy had men like Paul who modeled a life of courage, faith, and devotion.

There are times when ministry requires us to make personal sacrifices. Paul wrote extensively in 1 Corinthians 8—10 that ministry called him to be concerned with others more than his own freedoms. For Timothy the issue was not whether he needed to be circumcised, but that his circumcision and sacrifice would go a long way in building rapport among those who were going to struggle with the inclusion of the Gentiles. From his sacrifice Timothy could help them to have compassion. Even more, since he was circumcised he would not be advocating non-circumcision from his own best interest.

ON TO ASIA

The Holy Spirit prevented Paul and the team from entering Asia. The team had to bypass the regular route and take a longer journey to Macedonia. Twice Paul tried to enter that region (16:6–7). He was persistent and pushed the envelope on the mission field while God's Spirit was patient with him and guided him where Jesus wanted them to be. The team followed one of the Roman postal routes and walked along the border of Asia to Mysia and then to Troas, a beautiful and popular city along the coast. Troas was founded by one of Alexander's generals (Antigonus) in 310 BCE. Nine years later the Macedonian king Lysimachus killed Antigonus and named the city after Alexander.[1] Since the city reminded them of Troy it was named Alexandria Troas.[2] Julius, Augustus, and the later emperor Constantine loved the city to the point of considering to make it the capital of Rome. The city had a temple to Asklepius (the god of healing) as well as a major medical school within its walls. It seems likely that Luke would have met Paul in this city.

Paul did not stay long as the Holy Spirit led them away from Asia to Macedonia through a vision of a man calling for help. Luke claimed that this vision helped the team conclude that the Spirit had called them to preach the gospel there. Notice that here Luke switched to a first-person plural designation, indicating that he must have joined Paul and the team at Troas. Whether Luke was a proselyte or God-fearer is uncertain. Physicians were typically slaves and those well educated in the healing arts. This education would have included the ability to research (Asklepions had libraries within them). In the Roman Empire many physicians received their best training with armies during combat.[3] Luke would have been familiar with trauma, wounds, and other injuries, something that the early Christian team would have experienced often.

PHILIPPI

The team first arrived at the Greek city of Philippi. This was an older city that had been named after Philip of Macedonia, the father of Alexander the Great. In 42 BCE Augustus and Mark Antony defeated Brutus and Cassius

---

1. Fant and Reddish, *A Guide to Biblical Sites*, 332.
2. Trebilco, "Asia," 358.
3. Faulkner, *Ancient Medicine*, location 47.

(who assassinated Julius Caesar). The city then became a Roman colony and was settled with veterans from the Roman army.[4] Many of the Macedonian soldiers were recruited from Philippi for Caesar's private body guard, known as the Praetorian Guard. The Via Egnatia became a major Roman route through the city opening the way to Corinth and Athens in Southern Greece, connecting Rome with the Eastern provinces.[5] It was also famous for its school of medicine which sent graduates throughout the Roman world.[6]

Philippi was one of the most prominent of the Roman colonies. The city had the reputation of reflecting much of the Roman way of life in its desire for honor and prestige over wealth, pride in Roman citizenship, and its Roman culture.[7]

> We traveled to Philippi, a Roman colony and the leading city of that district of Macedonia, and stayed there several days. On the Sabbath we went outside the city gate to the river, where we supposed was a place of prayer. We sat down and began to speak to the women who had gathered there. One of them listening was a woman from the city of Thyatira, Lydia, a dealer in purple cloth and a worshiper of God. The Lord opened her heart to respond to Paul's words. When she and the members of her household were baptized, she invited us to her home saying, "If you consider me a believer in the Lord, come and stay at my house." She persuaded us. (Acts 16:11–15)

Acceptance

While in Philippi the team met at the river on a Saturday (Sabbath) for prayer. If there were not enough Jewish males to establish a synagogue the small Jewish community would gather at a river. In addition to this, Philippi allowed Roman gods and the Caesar cult at the city forum, while pushing the Greek and other religions outside the city walls.[8] This may be one reason why the team expected the Jewish community to meet outside the city. While there the team met only females, suggesting that there were

4. Gill, "Macedonia," 11; Hellerman, *Reconstructing Honor in Roman Philippi*, 69–70.
5. Fant and Reddish, *A Guide to Biblical Sites*, 101; Witherington, *Acts*, 488.
6. Witherington, *Acts*, 490.
7. Hellerman, *Reconstructing Honor in Roman Philippi*, 46–49.
8. Ibid., 84–86.

no Jewish males gathering on the Sabbath. Philippi was a Roman colony and Luke claimed that it was the leading city of the district (this boasting may suggest that he was from or had lived in Philippi). This major city did not have a strong Jewish presence, which is surprising. However, most of the cities where Paul preached did not have large developed Jewish communities. Even more, Lydia was a woman who was a "worshiper of God," indicating she was a Gentile convert or God-fearer. Her Greek name also suggested that she was Gentile and her common trade as a dealer in purple textiles (something sold to royalty and upper-class individuals) meant that she would have been a businesswoman who worked with dyes and had dirty/unclean hands. Even though purple cloth was a common product for upper-class or royal individuals, she was not necessarily a wealthy business owner. Her trade was very common and most business owners in the ancient world worked hard and made just enough money to barely make ends meet. Since she was mentioned without a husband she was either, like Timothy's mother, the spiritual head of her family or one who was unmarried/widowed. However, she was a leader among the women.

Luke spent time in this section writing about those who, unlike the resistance, received the gospel. First, *he wrote that Lydia's heart was opened by God*. She was open and receptive to the Holy Spirit. Second, *she and her family were baptized*. Not only was she a woman of faith but she was seen by others as a woman of faith and integrity. In the ancient world family (household) involved children, extended relatives, slaves, and sometimes those in need. While the relationships within this family involved debt, blood, and marriage ties, those who were baptized with Lydia would have done so by their choice because of her influence. Finally, *she proved her faith by offering hospitality to the mission team*. Luke wrote that this was a test of Lydia's faithfulness and their willingness to embrace her in the faith. While Paul and the team had been delivering the Jerusalem letter to the churches Lydia wanted them to show trust and relationship through accepting the hospitality of a Gentile. Her comment, "if you consider me a believer in Yahweh," was one that must have persuaded them.

Resistance

The team continued to practice meeting by the river for prayer but next encountered a different woman. This woman was a slave and fortune teller. While the Holy Spirit opened Lydia's heart the evil spirit opened the slave woman's heart. She, unlike Lydia, was not a believer and had been exploited by her owners. Luke indicated that she followed Paul and the team for many days, testifying to their message. In the early stages of Acts Jesus stated that the Spirit would testify to him through the church, not a demonic fortune teller. Her continual testimony irritated Paul to the point that he performed an immediate exorcism (16:18). While this would have brought emotional relief to the team, it brought financial ruin to her owners.

These Gentiles at Philippi resisted not the message of Paul but his choice to help this woman. Their pocketbooks stirred them against the team even though the men presented no immediate threat to them. As usual a riot occurred and the mission team suffered at the hands of angry, unjust people. The resistance had a new face.

> About midnight Paul and Silas were praying and singing hymns to God, and the other prisoners were listening to them. Suddenly there was a violent earthquake that the foundations of the prison were shaken. Immediately the prison doors opened, and everyone's chains came loose. The jailer woke up, and when he saw the prison doors open, he drew his sword and was about to kill himself because he assumed that the prisoners had escaped. But Paul shouted, "Don't hurt yourself! We are all here!" The jailer called for lights, rushed in and fell trembling before Paul and Silas. He then brought them out and asked, "Sirs, what must I do to be saved?" They replied, "Believe in the Lord Jesus, and you will be saved—you and your household." Then they spoke the word of the Lord to him and to all the others in his house. He gathered them that that hour of the night, washed their wounds; then immediately he and all his household were baptized. The jailer brought them into his house and set a meal before them; he and his whole household were filled with joy because they had come to believe in God. (Acts 16:25–34)

Paul and Silas were both dragged through the streets, falsely accused of crimes, stripped, beaten, and thrown into stocks in the jail. There would have been no cleaning of their wounds, no place to use the toilet, and no way to keep warm. These two were placed in a dark inner jail with their hands and feet fastened to wooden boards. If the beatings were not bad enough, the uncomfortable settings in the jail would have been worse. The psychological trauma and humiliation would have been incredibly brutal. Paul later complained that he and Silas were Roman citizens, which should have provided them protection from this cruel torture and humiliation

(Acts 16:37). However, the Roman leaders did not take the time to examine the evidence. Paul and Silas both were unjustly treated and found themselves in a bad situation.

Acceptance—Again

The story did not end or focus on their mistreatment. As with others who were imprisoned for their faith (Joseph, Gen 39; and Daniel, Dan 6) the two disciples were vindicated by God. The text explained that they were singing psalms at midnight. With their wounds becoming infected, feet and hands in an uncomfortable position in the stocks, and the trauma from the beatings it would not be surprising that the two could not sleep. Ancient prisoners suffered from overcrowding, putrid air, extreme heat, limited toilet access, diminished food and clothing, deep darkness, heavy chains around their neck, feet, and hands (usually at night), and psychological trauma due to the suffering, conditions, and darkness.[9] David wrote in the Psalms that he would awaken in the night and sing or think about Yahweh, which may have been why the two missionaries were singing in the night (Ps 16:7; 77:2, 6; 119:55). It would have been an interesting sight to see the other prisoners crying out to their gods but these two singing praises. As with Peter and the others Paul and Silas felt blessed to suffer for the name of Jesus. However, in this case God responded. An earthquake happened (common in this area) and destroyed the well-built city jail. Instead of escaping (as Peter had Acts 12:6–11) the two stayed in the prison.

Soldiers and those law enforcement individuals in charge of prisoners, confiscated loot, or public projects were under strict orders to insure the security of these buildings or individuals. In this story the security guard thought that this open prison would have sent criminals back to the streets and he would have had to answer for the loss of them. In the ancient world cities were also punished for the loss of prisoners.[10] He also would have been a man who was expected to have a sense of honor in his occupation. He attempted to do what many men would have done in this situation. In order to avoid the shame, humiliation, and torture for abandoning his job he decided to take his own life. In ancient cultures this was not shocking but expected. However, the two missionaries prevented this from happening. They saw an opportunity to remain in the jail and save his life, as well as

9. Rapske, *The Book of Acts and Paul in Roman Custody*, 196–224.
10. Ibid., 16.

the lives of his family. Luke wrote that they offered the man another way. To believe (obey, follow, trust) Jesus would be the only way his life and honor (as well as that of his family) could be salvaged.

Paul and Silas shared the gospel with the man and his family (wife, children, slaves, associates, relatives) and then baptized them. The story was similar to Lydia's in that her faith and decision influenced her household. However, the jailer initiated the act of love first by washing their wounds and then offering them food. It must have been an interesting sight. This Roman family offered compassion to these two smelly and blood-crusted prisoners by bathing and washing them, then being bathed and washed in Jesus' name by the clean missionaries. This is a beautiful story of reciprocity as the family cared for the two men, offered love to ones they kept behind bars, and later fed them. The early acts of grace and love were evidenced at Philippi by the generosity and love of Lydia, the security guard, and their families. Even more, it was a sign that in spite of the resistance, there were those who offered acceptance, safety, and support.

Paul and Silas must have returned to the jail and proven to the jailer, his family, and the public officials that they were not intending to escape—nor would they let others escape. It is surprising to me that more prisoners were not baptized, but not everyone's heart was open at that time. The city officials understood that they had humiliated Roman citizens (they were probably told this by the jailer) and offered to send the two away secretly. The process of stripping, flogging, and putting men in bonds was a humiliating act, especially for those who were Roman citizens.[11] Politics, ancient and modern, are not much different from each other and this was an opportunity to avoid "bad press," especially from those wanting support from Rome. However, Paul and Silas requested an apology (so that they could move freely throughout the empire without any charges) and traveled on to the next town.

THESSALONICA AND BEREA

After the humiliation suffered at the hands of the citizens in Phillipi, the mission team's next stop was the city of Thessalonica. This city was also a Roman colony and the capital of Macedonia (Northern Greece). Cassander, one of Alexander's generals, named the city after his wife Thessalonike, who

---

11. Ibid., 284–90.

was also Alexander's half sister.[12] Thessalonica was host to many historical figures such as Alexander, Cleopatra, Cicero, and Pompey (who hid his army from Julius Caesar in this city). The city also had a strong presence from the Imperial cult.[13] Caesar Augustus's image replaced Zeus's image on the city's coins.[14]

Acceptance and Resistance

> Some of the Jews were persuaded and joined Paul and Silas, and many religious Greeks and quite a few prominent women. But other Jews were jealous; so they gathered some bad characters from the marketplace, formed a mob and started a riot in the city. They rushed to Jason's house in search of Paul and Silas in order to bring them out to the crowd. But when they did not find them, they dragged Jason and some other believers before the city officials, shouting: "These men who have caused trouble all over the world have now come here, and Jason has welcomed them into his house. They are all opposing Caesar's decrees, saying that there is another king, one called Jesus." When they heard this, the crowd and the city officials were troubled. (17:4–9)

As will become a common issue, the witness of Jesus would be met with acceptance followed by resistance. Paul's preaching and message were able to persuade those familiar with the Torah (Jews, proselytes, and possibly God-fearers) as the movement gained a foothold. Then others would come along and create friction. However, as the story progressed the tension and resistance became more and more violent. At Thessalonica one of the members of the team or community (Jason) was dragged before the public officials for examination. As with many riots there was no basis for any charges or accusations and the crowds were dismissed.

Unlike in the persecutions of Jesus, Stephen, and Peter and John, the Roman government in the outlying areas refused to be involved in riots and public matters of judgment. This did not suggest that Rome was truly interested in justice, it only meant that they knew that riots were opportunities for communities to show independence from their occupiers. Those to whom Rome delegated authority were to make decisions that maintained

---

12. Fant and Reddish, *A Guide to Biblical Sites*, 133.
13. Gill, "Macedonia," 415.
14. Witherington, *Acts*, 203.

peace, promoted loyalty to the empire and emperor, and allowed the city to prosper. In Greece, Rome kept a tight rein on their colonies in order to keep the Persians and Egyptians at bay. The church likewise tried to avoid violence and oppositions by sending the team to another city when conflict arose.

Acceptance

> As soon as it was night, the believers sent Paul and Silas away to Berea. On arriving there, they went to the Jewish synagogue. The Berean Jews were nobler than those in Thessalonica, because they received the message eagerly and examined the Scriptures every day to see what was true. As a result, many of them believed, as did many prominent Greek women and many Greek men. But when the Jews in Thessalonica learned that Paul was preaching the word of God at Berea, some of them went there too, agitating the crowds and stirring them up. (Acts 17:10–14)

Luke only devoted a few sentences to the establishment of the church at Berea. Berea was a city forty miles west of Thessalonica. Little is known of the city other than that it was the second major city in Macedonia. The Macedonian *koinon* (athletic games in this region) were held here regularly and supported by the Roman Empire.[15] However, there was a small Jewish settlement in Berea.

It is interesting that those from the Jewish community at Berea were considered nobler than the previous communities and that they studied the text eagerly. In light of the turmoil and trouble that Paul and the team faced, a time of peace would have been viewed as an important stopping point in the journey to Rome. They did not resist and offered spiritual hospitality.

Thriving in Resistance

Luke highlighted the growth and thriving of the early church in the midst of turmoil, persecution, resistance, and conflict. This is an important message for the church today. Too often we long for safety and security and place tremendous emphasis on peace and compliance, when in actuality the story of Acts occurred during a time of resistance and conflict. Even

---

15. Gill, "Macedonia," 415.

during this resistance and conflict, Luke focused on the receptivity and faith of the believers as a place of peace, rest, and healing for the people of God. It was always important to find people of God and people of peace.

In Zechariah the prophet called the nation of Israel to repentance at the beginning of the book (Zech 1:1–6). The book was concerned less with the rebuilding of the temple and more with the relationship between the community and Yahweh. Yahweh was mentioned seven times in this section while repentance (*shub*) was mentioned four. The nation was called to "return" or "repent" to Yahweh and be different than their ancestors. This section was followed by six cycles of visions and dreams and reminded the prophet that the people were forgiven (1:7—6:8). The section began and ended with the desire for "rest," which meant that the nation would be safe and at peace. In the midst of the Persian Empire's control of the nation, God offered rest, peace, and safety. This came at the costs of repentance and faithfulness from the people. This safety and rest/peace was a common theme in restoration language as Luke, throughout Acts, interrupted the resistance episodes with times of peace, faithfulness, and acceptance. Even more Luke intentionally placed this "hospitality" in the midst of resistance. Those who were hospitable and accepting were found by the message and searching of the apostles in Luke's story.

Continuing Through Resistance

Once *the resistance* found where the missionaries were meeting they followed them, stirred up trouble, and "agitated the crowds" (Acts 17:13–15). This time Paul departed and left Timothy and Silas in Berea to not only deal with the corrupt groups, but protect and build up the church. When reading 1–2 Timothy and Titus, it is common to find that Paul called these missionaries to be firm, strong, moral, and build up the Christian community. It must have been tough for Silas and Timothy as they faced the opposition and possibly harm. However, it would have been a growing opportunity for them as well, as evidence that Paul's leadership had developed to where he had "entrusted the message and ministry to faithful Christians."

When I was a youth minister in a small town, Chillicothe, Missouri, I had come at the invitation of an older minister known by the community as "Brother Jim." He had been their preacher for over twenty years and even though he did not have a Bible education, he was a powerful speaker, great at personal evangelism, and viewed by the other seminary-trained ministers as a "human Bible concordance." He was well loved by the town and had also developed a powerful ministry, school, and many new churches in Ghana, West Africa. He visited Ghana every two years and would be gone for six weeks. His year to return to Ghana was during my fourth month as a new youth minister. There were things he left for me to do and other things he forgot to tell me to do. I would get a call from him (through the secretary) and he would say, "Hello brother, I forgot to tell you to do . . . ." This involved marrying a couple, being in charge of a picnic for a care facility, and speaking at a local event. He would always end with, "I know you will do a great job—I have confidence in you." During that time I preached regularly, continued my work with our youth, learned to drive a school bus of retired adults for a retirement home picnic, conducted premarital counseling and married an older couple, continued to work with our elders and their wives to visit many of the families who were sick, and addressed church discipline issues. I was converted to Christ my senior year in college. I had a bachelor's degree in chemistry and biology, with a minor in agriculture. There was no religious studies in my curriculum. My only serious Bible study was to have read the whole Bible three times, all of Josephus's works, and the first ten volumes of the Ante-Nicene Fathers. I knew little but understood that the work needed to be done while he was gone. When he returned we had long conversations about the work in Africa, Chillicothe, and my future in ministry. For me that was a powerful test that proved to him (and Jesus) that I was called to ministry. The elders laid their hands on me that next month and appointed me an evangelist. For me it was not only a test, but an opportunity to learn more concerning ministry. It was also an opportunity to prove that this was what Jesus needed me to do.

While some might think that Timothy and Silas were "thrown into the fire" the Pastoral Letters (1-2 Timothy and Titus) illustrated that Paul not only prepared people to do ministry in his absence, but intentionally pushed them in that direction. Luke indicated that for the Empire of Jesus to grow, men and women needed to be empowered not only by the Spirit, but other Christian leaders, to face the resistance and prove to be faithful.

CHRISTIANITY IN THE MARKETPLACE: ATHENS

Paul's next stop was at the "seat of culture in the Roman Empire." While Athens was not the most populated city in the Roman colonies, it was still considered the most educated. The Romans became involved in ruling the city in 86–88 BCE when the people rebelled against them.[16] There was a heavy Roman temple presence there even though it was a city "full of idols/statues" to their Greek gods. It was also the center for education, arts, and southern Greek culture. While Rome ruled the world, Athens was allowed to exist as a colony. The Romans sent their children to Athens for philosophical education.[17] Greek culture still dominated the Roman world as most people continued to speak Greek rather than Latin.

> While Paul was waiting for them in Athens, he was frustrated in his spirit seeing that the city was full of idols. He reasoned in the synagogue with both Jews and religious Greeks, as well as in the marketplace daily with those who were there. A group of Epicurean and Stoic philosophers debated with him. Some of them asked, "What is this babbler trying to say?" Others remarked, "He seems to be advocating strange demons/deities," because Paul was preaching the good news about Jesus and the resurrection. They brought him to a meeting of the Areopagus and said, "We want to know about this new teaching that you are presenting. You are bringing some strange ideas to us and we would like to know what they mean." . . . When they heard about the resurrection of the dead, some of them ridiculed, but others said, "We want to hear you again on this subject." Paul left the Council, yet some of the people became followers of Paul and believed. Among them was Dionysius, a member of the Areopagus, a woman named Damaris, and a number of others. (Acts 17:16–20; 32–34)

While in Athens Luke indicated that Paul was "distressed" or "very irritated" by their many idols. This was a term also used for God's displeasure toward the Jews and their worship of idols while in covenant with their Lord (Deut 9:18; Ps 106:29; Is 65:3; Hos 8:5).[18] In viewing the city from the marketplace he would have observed statues of human gods, athletes, gods in the shape of sexual organs, animals, and altars dedicated to "invisible" gods. Luke mentioned that Athens "was full of" or "was covered with" idols. These statues would have been tucked away in any small area in Athens, giving the sense of a city cluttered with idols in every location. Even more there was a tradition that the Athenians were cautious not to miss or offend a god, and created an empty pillar as a reminder that "all outsiders and their deities were welcome." One of the struggles that ancient people in

16. Gill, "Achaia," 441–43; Fant and Reddish, *A Guide to Biblical Sites*, 14–15.
17. Fant and Reddish, *A Guide to Biblical Sites*, 12.
18. Witherington, *Acts*, 512.

the "all-welcoming" Roman Empire faced was *syncretism*. Syncretism occurred when deities were introduced from many cultures and overlapped with other local deities in responsibilities, names, and status.

One example was Isis. Isis was an Egyptian goddess who, because of the expanding Egyptian and Roman kingdoms, mixed with other religious cultures. Along with Cybele, a goddess from Syria, these deities were mixed with Demeter and Isis to create hybrid gods and goddesses. While they were hybridizing and adapting to the average immigrant, it would have been confusing and created much anxiety. In addition to this, others in the empire found themselves questioning the existence of deities, demons, and spirituality.[19]

While Athens was the intellectual center of the empire Paul found an opportunity to converse with the popular scholars about God, gods, and humans. The Epicureans were a school who believed that happiness was the greatest good, while Stoics suggested that spirituality was manifested by tremendous acts of self-control, reason, avoiding pleasures, and many times living without homes or responsibilities. Both groups had their religious followers and had a prominent position at Athens. It was here that Paul, being irritated by the many statues of gods and goddesses, took the opportunity to discuss the resurrection of Jesus. For Paul, the center of Christian preaching lay in the unique nature of Jesus as God in the flesh who died and came to life in order to judge all nations. For those in Athens this was language of both the Roman Caesar, Dionysius the god of wine, and Asklepius the god of healing. However, Paul's message was such that he was invited to speak to the city council (Areopogas) at the place known as Mars Hill. Mars was the god of war and this location was the place where people shared stories, wisdom, and beliefs. It was also the main "council chamber" of the city. Typically this was done at the city gate, but in Athens it was done among the city council. Rome had put their hand into the politics of the city and located "wisdom" in the chambers of the "god of war." This was a reminder that the Roman military machine was the favorite of Mars.

Paul was able to discuss his views with the council through their own terms. First, *he referenced their superstition*. He used a word that indicated they were "superstitious," suggesting not faith but anxiety. Second, *he quoted two common philosophers*. Plato, in his work *The Symposium*, had one of the guests (Agathon) state, "He lives and moves among the softest of all living things, he has established his dwelling in the characters and souls

19. Klauck, *The Religious Context of Early Christianity*, 80.

of men [humans]."[20] Paul also quoted Aratus, who was a Stoic from Paul's home country of Cilicia in his statement that "We are his offspring."[21] He was suggesting that they had philosophers who admitted that God was relational. Finally, he challenged them by suggesting that a god did not need to live in a temple but was in all humanity.

In the ancient world humans were typically a by-product of creation and designed to serve the gods.[22] However, Yahweh was relational and not only sought to be worshiped by people (as they knew in their culture) but would offer salvation to those who believed in the resurrection of the "man appointed." In the ancient world Dionysius was murdered during a drinking party and later came to life through the mercy of his father Zeus. However, for Paul, the death and resurrection of Jesus was intentional and one that proved God's power and judgment. Jesus, the man appointed, did not die accidentally but intentionally so that others could be saved.

At the end of the sermon some were willing to follow Paul's teaching. Oddly enough the council member Dionysius, named after the resurrected Greek god of wine, along with a woman named Damaris (also possibly on the council), and others believed the message concerning the resurrection. It seemed that Luke was indicating here that those converted and who requested Paul to speak again were men and women of high financial status, and who held honored positions in the community. While Christianity had become a movement in the synagogue, and also among slaves and the lower class, at Athens Luke illustrated the rise of this movement among the upper-class Gentiles. The church grew at Athens and even though Paul left before Timothy and Silas had come, an influential community was formed. One interesting note was that the resistance had yet to come to Athens.

CHRISTIANITY AND THE CITY OF SAILORS

Corinth was an ancient city that was considered to have an immoral and excessive culture. Due to rebellion against Rome in 144 BCE, Lysius Mummius's troops leveled the city and left it empty for 100 years. In 44 BCE Julius Caesar rebuilt the city as a Roman colony. Other than the squatters living in the ruins as well as the priests for the temple of Apollo (which survived the destruction of the city), Corinth was repopulated with slaves,

20. Plato, *The Symposium*, 69.
21. Fant and Reddish, *A Guide to Biblical Sites*, 17.
22. Clark, *Am I Sleeping with the Enemy?*, 6–7.

Roman veterans, and many foreigners.[23] Corinth was known for its artwork, craftsmanship, and the Isthmian Games. These were second only to the Olympics. Even more, this city had developed a reputation of struggle and competition. This was prevalent among the athletic games as well as the economic classes. Slaves were constantly struggling to buy their freedom, find power, and gain honor. Paul's letters to the Corinthians indicate that those in the church also struggled with each other for power, honor, and status.[24]

I believe that God must have had a sense of humor in sending Paul to Corinth. Paul even wrote to the Corinthian Christians that he was uncomfortable at his first visit: "I came to you in weakness with great fear and trembling" (1 Cor 2:3). It must have been interesting to see a former Pharisee who was clearly skilled at setting boundaries with "sinful people" journey to Corinth. However, Luke indicated that he stayed with Priscilla and Aquila, a couple who made tents. These tents would have been important for the Isthmian Games that occurred every four years. Paul would have worked in the small unventilated shops each day and shared the story of Jesus with the many people who came to conduct business. During this time he visited the synagogue, taught Jews and Gentiles, and baptized many. He stayed in a home with a God-fearer (Titius Justus), which would have fueled the fire of the Jewish people who resisted Paul's message. Somehow two synagogue leaders were converted (Crispus and Sosthenese), which was evidenced by Sosthenese helping Paul to write 1 Corinthians (1 Cor 1:1–2).

Peace During the Resistance

"One night the Lord spoke to Paul in a vision: 'Do not be afraid; keep on speaking, do not be silent. For I am with you, and no one is going to attack and harm you, because I have many people in this city.' So Paul stayed in Corinth for a year and a half, teaching them the word of God" (Acts 18:9–11). Those who did not believe formed a resistance (Luke does not indicate that there were those who had followed them from Macedonia) and stirred up a riot in Corinth. However, Jesus had found those who would offer acceptance to the messenger and practice peace, and he reminded Paul that they were present in the city

---

23. Clark, *The Better Way*, xvi–xviii.
24. Ibid., xxii.

> While Gallio was proconsul of Achaia, the Jews made a united attack on Paul and brought him to the place of judgment. "This man is persuading the people to worship God contrary to the law." As Paul was about to speak, Gallio said to the Jews, "If you were making a complaint about some infraction or serious crime, it would be reasonable for me to listen to you. But since it involves questions about words and names and your own law—settle it yourselves. I will not consult on these things." He drove them off from the place of judgment. Then the crowd there turned on Sosthenes the synagogue leader and beat him in front of the proconsul; and Gallio showed no concern. (Acts 18:12–17)

The riot did very little to stop the movement. Gallio, who was present in Corinth in 50 CE, was the leader placed in the city by the Roman government. He had a very short career and was the brother of the well-known philosopher Seneca.[25] His response suggested that Paul's message, while seen by some as anti-Roman, was not one that the government officials found threatening. On the outer borders of the empire government officials would have been sensitive to anti-Imperial rhetoric, but here Paul did not threaten them. Paul's message has continued to be appropriate for the government in power, but not for those believing that Jesus was not the Messiah.

The church at Corinth began during turmoil, struggle, and suffering. When reading 1 and 2 Corinthians it becomes clear that Paul addressed a community that imitated their culture. Corinthian culture not only honored competition and struggle, it devalued people. The church consisted of Jewish followers, Gentile converts, and most likely Gentiles who left the synagogue. Paul indicated in his letter that the church also consisted of slaves, prostitutes (male and female), those dealing with recovery issues, and a very small number of people with financial means. Yet the turmoil in the beginning came from the community and those jealous of the Christian missionaries' success. The issues were less about doctrine and more about people, and those willing to follow Paul's message. One can envision Paul working hard with Priscilla and Aquila in one of the small shops.

Paul would have worked with his hands making tents for one of the upcoming Isthmian Games while sharing Jesus and the Torah. It was a very simple ministry that did not involve flashing lights, smoke machines, large bands, and big auditoriums. It was a humble ministry that did not involve high-level executives, famous people, and young attractive families. Paul's

25. Ibid., xxiii.

ministry at Corinth was one that was reflected in his first letter to the Corinthians, "Think of what you were when you were called. Not many were wise by human standards, not many were influential, and not many were born to a noble family" (1 Cor 1:26). Paul's own teaching ministry was one that brought suspicion from elite teachers because he worked with his own hands. However, Paul's ministry reflected Luke's narrative of Jesus. He, like Jesus, brought a message of hope to people in the worst areas of the Roman Empire.

Even more, Paul's time in this location was a reminder that God lived even in the wicked city of Corinth. When Paul was rejected at the synagogue Jesus told him, "I have many people in this city" (Acts 18:10). Paul not only stayed in Corinth because Gallio offered protection for the movement, but because Jesus had people there. Some would suggest that this meant there were Jews who were willing to believe. Others might suggest that Jesus saw the future and knew that others would believe. These are true, however the verse also reminds us that God's Spirit is always working even in places where we haven't been. Jesus works in lives that have not confessed him as Lord, or that haven't heard the good news. They provide acceptance and support as the empire thrives in the midst of resistance.

The Spirit at Work

I find it common that when Christians "go" and begin to connect with people in our neighborhoods, work, community, or other places, we find that many are already thinking about God. These are the ones who tell us, "We were just talking about going back to church the other day," or "I started praying again this week and . . ." or "I've been wanting to ask you about your faith, I am at a crisis in my life." These are individuals who the Spirit has been preparing for us. While Jesus told the apostles to "wait" (in Acts 1), once the Spirit was poured upon the early Christians we were called to "go." The Spirit isn't interested in waiting for us, but for us to go. Whether we go or not, *the Spirit of Jesus will do his work*. We have the option to either obey and go, or wait for someone else to do it for us. However, the Spirit isn't waiting for us to show up. God seeks reconciliation with others. The question for us as Christians is "will we go and join the Spirit in this act of reconciliation?"

Paul told the Corinthian church that the fear of God motivated him to persuade people to follow Jesus. "We must all appear before the judgment seat of Christ that each one may receive what is due them for the things done while in the body—good or bad. Since we know what it is to fear the Lord, we try to persuade people . . ." (2 Cor 5:10–11). Archaeologists have uncovered the judgment seat (Bema) in Corinth where Gallio may have sat while hearing the case of Paul and the Christians. This would not only have been a fresh reminder to Paul but the early Christians as well. They would have daily passed by this judgment seat and been reminded that Rome ruled their city and that they needed to not only follow the law, but encourage each other to do the same.

The early Christians would have also been reminded that they had a purpose, task, and role. God was already present and the judgment seat was visible. Yet it was their role to help others reconcile and finish the task of healing and ministry. Paul called this a message of reconciliation (2 Cor 5:19). Today the Spirit continues to work in the lives of others calling for reconciliation and peace. The Spirit also calls us to work in their lives as well and speaking the message, "Be reconciled to God!" (2 Cor 5:20). We practice this reconciliation weekly by taking communion in our churches and developing, repairing, and maintaining relationships during the week.

Experiencing the Work of the Spirit

I think often about the advice I was given years ago in church growth classes and seminars. I think about the times when the teachers would indicate that if we wanted large and fast-growing churches we would not do pastoral counseling. This eats at precious time that can be used working with teams, committees, and outreach. Even though most large church ministers that I know do not connect with people to do their own outreach, they have found a way to mobilize others to connect and draw people to the community. I appreciate their giftedness and ability to help so many people connect with the body of Christ and find peace and spiritual growth in their churches.

However, I have found that when counseling ministry is actually done, it is real, it is personal, it is Spirit led, and it reflects the nature of Christ. It also provides the opportunity to know people and understand what they deal with both in their families and in their family history. There the gift of patience is necessary. I can't list how many times I have wanted to shout, "What is wrong with you?" or "What are you doing?" but I don't. There are times when I have had to confront a parent, child, spouse, or grandparent for their behavior. To push and keep confronting their resistance to do the right thing, and to do what is best is not only difficult, it can become risky. To find other ways to readdress the issue that they continue to avoid takes time, compassion, and courage.

> To hear the screams and cries of a victim who unpacks their story and has to admit that it is more painful than they have been admitting, traumatizes the listener. To hold someone's hand as they walk the road to conquer their fears, confront a bully, or make amends for their sins takes compassion, empathy, and faith. To persuade someone to make good choices and do what they know they need to do is difficult as there will always be a fine line between persuasion and coercion, patience and force, love and anger. It is also a great gift that we can give to our people. When they're being true to their calling, pastors urge Christians to do the hard work of reconciliation with one another before receiving communion. They lead people to share in the suffering of others, including people they would rather ignore, by experiencing tough circumstances—say, in a shelter, a prison or a nursing home—and seeking relief together with those in need. At their courageous best, clergy lead where people aren't asking to go, because that's how the range of issues that concern them expands, and how a holy community gets formed.[26]

I am concerned because this is the ministry our ministers and Christian leaders should be doing. While it is important to delegate and stay focused on church growth and working with committees or teams of church leaders, it is in these quiet sessions where I have learned about people, their faith, and the God who can transform them. I have also learned more about myself as well. It is in these quiet and sometimes tumultuous sessions that I have learned from them the courage to face resistance, the courage to push through and work through resistance, and the courage to help others find peace, acceptance, and hospitality with their own lives, the lives of others, and the life of Jesus. It's a shame that we no longer encourage ministers to counsel others or be active in their community by holding positions of leadership. We are creating speakers, bloggers, and pundits rather than witnesses who can testify to what they have seen, the healing power of Jesus in the lives of others. Maybe this is why so many struggle to connect with people, or why our sermons many times lack passion. Paul was one who was able to state that he put his heart and soul into others. He did this in the quiet and intimate moments of the small shops, apartments, and small

---

26. Frost, *The Road to Missional*, 71.

campfire gatherings with his mission team. Even more he must have passed this on to others who likewise practiced care for their members.

10

WITNESSING IN ASIA

Arise, Shine, for your light has come, and the glory of Yahweh rises upon you. See, darkness covers the land and thick darkness the people. Yahweh's glory rises and appears over you. Gentiles will come to your light, and kings to the brightness of what is rising upon you. (Isa 60:1–3)

PAUL IN ASIA

Paul remained in Corinth for many days. Then he left the brothers and sisters and sailed for Syria, accompanied by Priscilla and Aquila. Before he sailed, he had his hair cut at Cenchreae because of a vow he had taken. They arrived at Ephesus, where Paul left them and went into the synagogue, debating/discussing with the Jews. When they asked him to spend more time with them, he was not able. He left promising, "I will come back if it is God's will." Then he set sail from Ephesus. When he landed at Caesarea, he went up to Jerusalem and greeted the church and then went down to Antioch. After spending some time in Antioch, Paul set out from there and traveled from place to place throughout the region of Galatia and Phrygia, strengthening all the disciples. (Acts 18:18–23)

The next phase of Paul's mission involved Asia and return trips to strengthen the churches. Earlier Paul had twice been prevented by the Holy Spirit from entering Asia (16:1–6). Now, possibly five years later, God opened the door for the mission into this part of the world. Paul was accompanied by his Corinthian friends Priscilla and Aquila to Ephesus, considered the fourth largest city in the Roman world. After a short stay and preaching in the synagogue Paul left the community in the hands of this couple and traveled to visit the other churches.

Again Paul delegated ministry to his Christian team of Priscilla and Aquila, who were originally Paul's hosts and coworkers at Corinth. This couple became leaders in the Christian movement and hosts to the church community (1 Cor 16:2). Paul indicated that they had the church meeting in their home, suggesting that they were people with better finances than most. As tentmakers they would have had an apartment above or behind their shop. They also continued to teach for Paul in his absence and eventually encountered an intelligent man named Apollos. He was Jewish and had come from Alexandria, where a large Jewish population thrived. Alexandria, Egypt was the second largest Roman city and later became a strong foothold for Christianity and Christian education. Apollos was well educated in the way of Jesus or the Messiah except on one point. Luke indicated that he *only knew the baptism of John*. This suggested that he was baptized by John and baptizing people in the *name of the one who was coming*, rather than in the name of Jesus and the Holy Spirit. However, John's baptism was similar to Jesus' in that it was immersion for the forgiveness of sins (Luke 3:3; Acts 2:38). Apollos may have been taught and baptized by John rather than Jesus. Therefore, according to Apollos, baptism prepared the recipient for the one coming (Messiah) but provided no promise of the Holy Spirit (Acts 2:38-39). Priscilla and Aquila invited Apollos to their home and "taught the way more accurately," suggesting that they taught about Jesus and being filled with the Holy Spirit. Apollos accepted their teaching and then went to Greece to build up the church at Corinth and "confront the resistance."

Baptisms at Ephesus

One question might be important in this section. Luke typically indicated that the reception of the Christian message involved baptism. He made it clear that baptism was part of the conversion/salvation process. However, at Ephesus it seemed different. Apollos was not rebaptized yet another group of disciples, in Acts 19, who followed John's baptism were rebaptized.

> While Apollos was at Corinth, Paul traveled through the interior and went down to Ephesus, where he found some disciples. He asked them, "Did you receive the Holy Spirit when you believed?"

They answered, "We have not even heard that there is a Holy Spirit." Paul asked, "What baptism did you receive?" "John's baptism," they replied. Paul said, "John's baptism was a baptism of repentance. He told the people to believe in the one coming after him, that is, in Jesus." On hearing this, they were baptized in the name of the Lord Jesus. When Paul placed his hands on them, the Holy Spirit came on them, and they spoke in languages and prophesied. There were about twelve men in all. (Acts 19:1–7)

First, *Apollos, like the apostles, may have been baptized by John the Baptist and, along with the early disciples, did not need to be rebaptized.* Somehow John's baptism before Jesus' ascension was sufficient. *After this, baptism in the name of Jesus became the normal practice* (Luke 24:45–49; Acts 2:38). As Paul returned to Ephesus he encountered disciples who would have been taught by Apollos. It is no coincidence that Luke had earlier mentioned Apollos at Ephesus preaching the baptism of John (Acts 19:1–6).

These disciples, like Apollos, had an incomplete understanding of Jesus' message, but they would have been baptized after the ascension of Jesus. Paul simply completed their belief by naming Jesus as the Messiah and baptizing (or rebaptizing) them. They, like Cornelius and his family, were immersed and empowered by the Spirit to preach in languages. The number of twelve men was also Luke's way of testifying to an Israelite restoration.

Ephesus

Ephesus was a city that was one of the largest in the empire. Lysimachus, one of Alexander's generals, ruled the city from 301–281 BCE until he was assassinated by Seleucus I, who moved the city to higher ground due to flooding.[1] In Paul's day it lay by a harbor that attracted many ships, merchants, and travelers. The temple of Artemis was an imposing structure that greeted those entering through the harbor. The temple was a major landmark in the city until it burned in 356 BCE. Alexander offered to finance the rebuilding of the temple, which the citizens tactfully declined stating that it was not fitting for a god to build the temple of another god.[2] Ephesus had many shops, paved roads, theaters, and temples, making it a tourist attraction and a seat for the Roman Empire. Artemis had become

---

1. Fant and Reddish, *A Guide to Biblical Sites*, 178.
2. Ibid.

a hybrid goddess and was a deity for childbirth, hunting, sailors, and presided at weddings.[3] She was the "head" and "mother" of the city and cared for the people. While the Roman Caesar made various attempts to build temples that overshadowed hers she continued to prevail and Rome eventually bowed to the Artemisians.[4] The temple also contained great wealth and as a banking center provided funds for outlying Artemisians in other Asian cities.

The city had a major university (the School of Tyrannus) where some of the great philosophers and poets lectured. This university connected with the outlying Asian cities and became an important hub of information for them. Ephesus was also a place of magic, mystery religions, and various deities. Because the city had attracted so many visitors its spiritual beliefs merged with many other foreign cultures so that the religious climate was extremely diverse. Even more, the Roman government allowed Ephesus to become a city that was "guardian of Artemis" (Acts 19:35).[5]

While in this city Paul, as he had done previously, spent time in the synagogue until he and the message were resisted by those who refused to believe. However, Paul and his church moved their location to the School of Tyrannus, one of the major institutions in Asia. Luke indicated that Paul's teaching spread to "all of Asia," probably through the students and their sharing of this new story. Churches later appeared in Colossia, Laodicea, Smyrna, Thyatira, Sardis, Philadelphia, and Pergamum due to this message (Col 4:16; Rev 2—3). Paul claimed that he had not seen many of the people in these churches, indicating that this mission was carried through the work of others.

The message of the early Christians grew during Paul's two-year stay in Ephesus. Three times Luke mentioned that the movement's reputation and power spread throughout Asia (19:10, 20, 26). Jesus had mentioned that faith was like a mustard weed/bush that grew out of control (Luke 13:18–19), and so it was in Asia. Luke recounted the stories where Jesus' power worked through Paul due to his faith and obedience to God.

> God did miracles through Paul's hands, so that even handkerchiefs and aprons that had touched him were taken to the sick, and their illnesses were cured and the evil spirits left them. Some Jews who went around driving out evil spirits tried to invoke the name of the

---

3. Xenophon, *Ephesian Tale of Anthia and Habrocomes.*
4. Treblico, "Asia," 324–27.
5. Ibid., 349–50.

> Lord Jesus over those who were demon-possessed, saying, "In the name of the Jesus whom Paul preaches, I command you to come out." Seven sons of a Jewish chief priest, named Sceva, were practicing this. One day the evil spirit answered them, "Jesus I know, and Paul I believe in, but who are you?" Then the man with the evil spirit overpowered them all, attacking them so that they ran out of the house bloody and naked. When this became known to the Jews and Greeks living in Ephesus, they were all afraid, and the name of the Lord Jesus was honored. Many of those who believed came and confessed what they had done. A number who had practiced sorcery brought their scrolls together and burned them publicly. When they calculated the value of the scrolls, the total came to fifty thousand drachmas. The word of the Lord spread widely and grew in power. (Acts 19:11–20)

Ephesus had been the seat of power and magic, yet the church confronted this power and proved to be greater. Unfortunately this new power presented a threat to those who produced statues/idols to prey upon others' fears. Instead of the unbelieving Jews causing trouble, the city's business and religious leaders incited a riot. Gaius and Aristarchus, from Paul's team, were drug into the 20,000-seat theater and had to listen to the chant "Great is Artemis of the Ephesians." It would have been frightening to be there as these two men were helpless.

However, a public official dispersed the crowd by reminding them that Rome frowned upon public disturbances. The riot ended and the Christian movement had proven that it was not only here to stay, but did not back down from its faith and conviction. Ephesus became a base for Paul's team while he prepared to return to Jerusalem to visit the churches in Asia and Galatia.

REVISITING OLD FRIENDS

In Luke 19:28, the writer mentioned that "Jesus set his face to Jerusalem." For Luke, Jesus began the journey to Jerusalem at Luke 9:51, but spent the next section preparing the disciples for ministry through sending out the seventy, feeding thousands, and preparing them for his crucifixion. Paul also traveled to Jerusalem and visited the churches, preparing to return to the city for a final ministry (Acts 20:1—21:18). Later he sent for the disciples, encouraged them, bid farewell to them, and went to Macedonia, as well as Jerusalem. He, like Jesus, not only had a vision for the *journey to Jerusalem*, but he prepared the disciples to carry on in his absence.

First, *Paul returned through Greece to visit and strengthen the churches.* His team consisted of Sopater, Aristarchus, Secundus, Gaius, Timothy, Tychicus, and Trophimas (we don't know what happened to Silas). These were men who joined him while on the mission field and who were sent to communicate and minister with the churches. As Jesus sent out the disciples to prepare his way, so Paul sent disciples to encourage the churches (Luke 10:1–3; 19:30; 22:8). It is possible that during this time Paul wrote 1–2 Timothy, Romans, 1–2 Corinthians, Ephesians, Colossians, Philippians, and 1–2 Thessalonians (Acts 20:2–5). This would have been an active time for Paul's ministry as his team would have been busy teaching, reading the letters, confronting problems in and out of the congregations, and collecting money for the movement.

Second, *Paul spent time preaching and teaching in the churches.*

> On the first day of the week we came together to break bread. Paul intended to leave the next day and spoke to the people until midnight. There were many lamps in the upstairs room where we were meeting. A young man named Eutychus was sitting in the window. He fell into a deep sleep as Paul spoke. When he was sound asleep, he fell to the ground from the third story and was picked up dead. Paul went down, fell upon him, put his arms around him, and said, "Don't be alarmed, he's alive!" Then he went upstairs again and broke bread and ate. After talking until daylight, he left. The people took the young man home alive and were comforted. (Acts 20:7–12)

In this story worship was expressed as a time to "share a meal each week," and listen to a message from this missionary. Jewish communities believed that Sunday began at sunset Saturday evening (Saturday was the Sabbath), which would explain the late-night preaching, the exhaustion of Eutychus, and their gathering weekly for communion and a meal. As was common in the gospel the young slave boy was healed and restored to his place in the community.

Finally, *Paul used this time to prepare and appoint church leaders.* While at Miletus (a city about forty miles from Ephesus), Paul had a retreat with the elders of the Ephesian congregations. Miletus was a city with four harbors and a major port both during war and peace time.[6] It provided a

---

6. Fant and Reddish, *A Guide to Biblical Sites*, 244–45.

safe retreat area outside of the regions where the resistance may have continued to exist.

Challenging the Elders and Leaders

In the Bible elders were leaders of their community. Their roles were to shepherd (pastor) and oversee/watch (bishop) a church (Acts 20:28). The resistance was present both in the community and churches and Paul knew that each congregation needed leaders who could protect the sheep and confront the wolves. "I served the Lord with great humility and with tears and in the midst of severe testing by the plots of my Jewish opponents. You know that I have not hesitated to preach anything that would be helpful to you but have taught you publicly and from house to house. I have proclaimed to both Jews and Greeks that they must turn to God in repentance and have faith in our Lord Jesus" (Acts 20:19–21).

First, *Paul used his own life as a pattern for their leadership ministry.* Paul served Jesus and the church through the humiliation and did not quit. He also taught repentance and integrity to the people in the face of resistance. In addition to this Paul reminded them that his ministry would involve rejection and cost his life. This apostle knew from his conversion that he would suffer for Jesus' empire, and this was always present in his faith. He, like Jesus, would go to Jerusalem to suffer. Second, *Paul commissioned these elders to not only imitate his life, but be appointed by the Holy Spirit.* These leaders were to face the resistance with the same integrity, courage, and faith that Paul had. Finally, *the resistance might arise among them.* As shepherds they were to protect the sheep, confront the wolves, and care for the weak/vulnerable. This commission was not only from Paul but the Holy Spirit.

It must have been a moving experience to witness as the leaders, family, and mission team knelt by the shore to pray, shed tears, and say goodbye to both a leader and old friend. While there has been much written to suggest that Paul was harsh, judgmental, and controlling, the following scenes are Luke's reminder that Paul developed intimate relationships with those churches he planted and those which others had begun. While Paul had been clear that his destiny was to go to Jerusalem and face those who "resisted the message with violence," it was also clear that the followers of Christ tried to persuade him to not follow the journey of Jesus.

> When Paul said this, he knelt down with all of them and prayed. They all wept as they hugged his neck and kissed him. What grieved them most was that they would never see his face again. Then they accompanied him to the ship. (Acts 20:36–38)

> When we heard this, we and the people begged with Paul not to go up to Jerusalem. Then Paul answered, "Why are you weeping and breaking [troubling] my heart?" (Acts 21:12–14)

These last two stories, before Paul left for Jerusalem, display the tension that must have existed between congregation and leader. Paul was willing to suffer and die because he knew that this was the ministry given to him by the Holy Spirit. The church seemed to want Paul to avoid this fate and live to serve them another day. However, Luke indicated that Paul, as leader, showed his integrity by offering his life for the mission, vision, and life of the Christian community. He, like Jesus, willingly laid his life down so that the bigger picture could be fulfilled.

Leadership Today

It was one o'clock in the morning as I drove to the small house in my town. People were gathered on the street, there were flashing lights from the sheriff's deputy's patrol car, and Karen ran to my car. "Mike's inside and won't send Stevey out. He has a gun. I am sorry to have bothered you."

I had graduated from college, was working at McDonald's, and turned down graduate school in biochemistry to help a small church in my hometown. I was not paid but started working with this nineteen-person church and saw growth from new couples, singles, and teens. The preacher was an older man who traveled from a nearby city to speak to the church while I organized and taught Sunday night and Wednesday night classes. I was not a minister but some called me a preacher. I had no experience in ministry but offered to help a church that was ready to close its doors. I invited many people to the church, conducted Bible studies with others in their home, and baptized those who wanted to give their lives to Jesus. One couple who came to church had been restored after having fallen away from Jesus. Karen and I worked together at McDonald's while Mike worked at the local Tyson plant. They had three children. Mike was an alcoholic and was abusive. Eventually Karen left him. We tried to work with both in the small church. Mike would get drunk and call me in the middle of the night with repeated attempts at suicide. I and one of the older men from church would talk to him, pray with him, then he would sleep off his night's intake of beer. It was a continuous cycle.

Karen tried hard to keep her boys safe. We would help with the supervised visitation but Mike would always push the envelope. I was twenty-two years old and struggled to manage my finances, my spiritual walk with God, and time between work and helping a church. Even though the church was slowly growing it was hard for people to understand what was happening in this family's life.

Karen had called me in the middle of the night because she had come to pick the boys up from Mike's house, and he would not return the youngest son. He had a gun and had been drinking. As I groggily drove to the home in this small town I could see the patrol car's lights from a block away. As Karen met me at the car I walked to the house. I was still tired and thought, "I'm too tired for this." In some ways I thought that I shouldn't have been dealing with this. In other ways I believed that this is what it meant to be a church. I told Karen I would talk to the deputy and went to him. In a small town everyone knows the police and they know everyone else. Since I had been to high school in this town he knew who I was. He smiled at me and told me Mike was inside with a loaded weapon. There were no threats but he was responding to a call with only the basics of the situation.

In a small town people don't check a minister's credentials nor do they ask what school one attended. While I wasn't a minister Karen's statement to the deputy, "He's our preacher," seemed enough for him. He also smiled as if thinking, "You are a minister now—God does change people!" "He's harmless," I said. "He does this as a suicide attempt often and we have gone to help him many times." The deputy listened and replied, "Maybe, but we can't be too careful. He is not supposed to have firearms so I am going to have to arrest him. I am waiting for backup to go in there." I offered to go in and talk to Mike as I knew him and believed nothing serious would happen. The deputy was hesitant and said, "I don't plan on going in alone, and I don't want you to get hurt either." I assured him it would be fine and I would talk Mike out of any threats, and then we could all go home and go to bed. "OK, but I'm going in with you son, this is pretty serious."

We went in and I knocked on the door. I told Mike it was me and he said, "Come on in, Ron, what's all the noise about?" He had Stevey on his lap and there was no gun in sight. Stevey looked anxious and Mike had a beer on the table and music playing loudly. "Mike, Karen says you won't send Stevey back and you are threatening people," I said. "Naw, Stevey doesn't want to go and he says he wants to stay with me," Mike responded. Stevey shook his head yes. "Hey Stevey, your mom's waiting for you outside, you can come see your dad next time. Your brothers are there too—why don't you go out there and see them?" I said. Stevey looked up, smiled, and said, "OK Ron, bye Dad." They hugged and the boy left. Mike said, "See, no problem."

I told Mike he wasn't supposed to have a gun and he grabbed a twenty-two caliber rifle from the other side of the room. "Oh this old thing, here you can have it," as he removed the two tiny shells and handed me the gun. That was it. It was over that quickly. All of the noise, all of the lights, all of the commotion were gone as soon as the boys left with their mother and the deputy and I walked out.

The deputy thanked me for getting involved. I am sure he had seen these situations escalate into violent confrontations. I am sure he worried about people getting hurt during these events. I am sure he appreciated the help. There was nothing heroic about what I did. I didn't feel afraid, noble, or even a rush of adrenaline. I was just tired. I was emotionally and physically exhausted from my job, doing ministry as a volunteer, and the constant stress of trying to help this man and his family. I wanted Mike to stop treating his family and himself the way he did. I wanted Karen to get a break and the boys to have a dad that loved them and treated them with respect. I wanted the boys to see that a father loves their mother and honors her. Even more I wanted a couple from our church to be a reflection of God's light. Unfortunately that wasn't happening and Mike was causing stress and pain to his family, his church, and his community. While I was not a "paid minister" or given the title of leader, I knew that Christian leadership requires that we become close enough to people that we act even when it is risky. Unfortunately none of the other male members in that church, including the older men who stressed that I was too young for ministry, chose to become involved in helping the family. However, that experience has shaped my ministry. I decided that night that if I was going to be in ministry, I was going to be someone who was willing to take risks because I cared about people.

Paul's travels at Ephesus and Asia illustrate the power that the movement of Jesus can have in any world. A city such as Ephesus that had resisted Roman domination, financed their own rebuilding projects, become the seat of magic and demonic activity, and was an intellectual center for

Asia still embraced the simple message of Jesus and the resurrection. The city will also become a major hub for the Christian movement historically. Even more than that, the Apostle Paul became a hero in this highly charged community. His presence, power, and preaching not only offered people hope but it provided healing to those under the power of evil.

Today the church can manifest the same power. However, it will begin with leaders. Paul was more than a preacher during his time at Ephesus. He was more than a Christian leader or former rabbi. The man who taught in the School of Tyrannus was more than a scholar with a powerful message. Paul was a man of courage. He confronted evil, visited people's homes, mentored leaders, wept with others, and promoted a vision with courage, faith, and conviction. The reason the church manifested that power in Acts 19—20 was because they had a leader who manifested that power and courage.

Years later I entered full-time ministry. I was often trained by observing smaller town ministers and I was fortunate to see men and women work with people personally. I saw them visit homes, sit in the hospital, offer words of comfort to grieving people in a cemetery, attend events that the children of their church performed in, and put their hands on me and pray for me. I knew that they counseled people and couples, married couples, confronted men, women, and teens, and even offered a prayer when a public official sinned and wept for forgiveness. I witnessed their tears when people left the church, thanked them for sending people my way (who were looking for a younger minister), and worked with them as we handed out food, clothes, and toys during Christmas. I saw their smiles. I saw their glasses become foggy as someone cried and thanked them. I saw these men holding hands with their spouses as they attended events together and offered the prayer for the group. I saw them serve at community work days in coveralls, boots, jeans, and T-shirts (although some of the older ones still came in slacks and open-collar shirts). I saw them visit our church and hold their tongue when my preaching was a little too narrow or inaccurate, as they smiled and said, "Good job, young man." They were/are small church ministers in small towns, big towns, and suburbs. Even more they represented their community. They were part of our communities. They carried a high level of respect because people knew that they were men and women of influence, power, and holiness.

They delegated. Many had interns, youth ministers, or members (lay members) who worked with them side by side. They developed friendships with these men and women. They passed on wisdom and respect to these members. This is why so many members struggle with leaving or changing to another minister. They have been touched by the presence of a holy leader and they struggle to trust another. As a young minister I learned very quickly that if I wanted people to walk with me, I had to prove worthy of the task. No one carried a handkerchief away from me because I was a minister. They would only do it if they saw the influence, respect, faith, and courage that had been shown to them previously. Ministry is about influence, not language.

I also remember sitting in church growth classes hearing that effective large churches have pastors that focus on meetings, committees, delegation, leadership development, systems, style, feedback groups, and taped sermons (now podcasts). These were the tools of growing churches. These were the skills that were required for churches to grow. These were the men who were going to lead us as a movement back to growth in America. Sometimes I wonder why it is difficult to listen to those who are the main speakers at large events and conferences. It is difficult when I hear that they are showing us the way, yet spending much of their time in committee meetings and locations "away from the public."

I'm not being critical of church growth materials, megachurches, large church pastors, or podcasts. I am thankful for what I have learned from many of these leaders and churches. There is tremendous wisdom in what we hear. However, as a minister in my community I do believe that we are quickly losing something in our movements. I go to conferences and classes and hear wonderful talks, lectures, and sermons from people who speak in the confines of the church building. I hear great presentations from people whose contact with unchurched people are only through Facebook, Internet chats, or what their members tell them. I listen to podcasts from those who talk about "problems" that are not Ephesian problems but upper-class American problems. My students often tell me that they are frustrated with the large systems because they don't really connect with people who are outside of the church walls. When I teach sessions concerning community problems such as counseling women in prostitution, victims of abuse, those with addictions, suicide patients, those with depression, or adult survivors of abuse, some say, "I won't be dealing with this in my ministry." I have even heard my wife, a women's minister, tell younger female clergy and interns that we need more women to be involved in abuse prevention and working with women in counseling, rather than becoming bloggers and speakers only. She receives the same reaction I do when I suggest to male clergy and interns they do the same thing.

Is this true? Are they correct? Is this the direction of our church leaders? Do we have those who, like Paul, say, "I have personally invested in you what it means to do ministry?" I sometimes wonder where I would be had I not witnessed these men and women who showed me hands-on ministry. I sometimes wonder where I would be had I avoided counseling, connecting with people, or even being an active coach in my community.

Would we be leaders who are guided solely by the vision and mission of Jesus?

ENDURING RESISTANCE FOR THE SAKE OF THE EMPIRE

11

ON TO THE PROMISED LAND?

The one who is not with me is against me and the one who does not gather with me scatters. (Luke 11:23)

IN LUKE'S GOSPEL JESUS set his face to Jerusalem, knowing that there he would meet his end. As in the ancient classical writings, the hero was compelled to follow a journey to a city, fort, or battle to meet his destiny. Typically this meeting involved violence, testing/temptations, and courage. Jesus, too, followed the journey to Jerusalem where he was rejected, humiliated, tortured, and murdered. However, as was written at the end of Luke's gospel and the beginning of Acts, he conquered by ascending to heaven.

PAUL'S JOURNEY

Paul, like these literary characters, had his own journey. While we often read Acts and view the missionary trips/journeys as the focus, for Luke the road to Jerusalem, and later Rome, was the main emphasis of this work. While Jesus met his end at Jerusalem, Paul would find a way to continue the mission to the capitol of the world. However Paul, like Jesus, suffered, faced rejection, was tried as a criminal before a corrupt religious leadership, physically beaten, and had death threats against him. He was accused of violating the Torah, traditions of the Jewish nation, and the integrity of God. He was delivered to Gentiles, but these Romans protected him. Throughout his missionary travels he had faced severe persecution, but when he went to Jerusalem, his home, he was rejected. While Jesus had come to Jerusalem and overturned the merchants in the temple, Paul had come to preach to the people that God desired the Gentiles to have salvation. However, Paul did do his share of upsetting and turning over things while he was in Jerusalem.

Paul met with the church to share the good news of salvation that went out to the non-Jewish people throughout the Roman world.

> When we arrived at Jerusalem, the brothers and sisters received us. The next day Paul and the rest of us went to see James, and all the elders were present. Paul greeted them and reported what God had done among the Gentiles through his ministry. When they heard this, they praised God. Then they said to Paul: "Observe, how many thousands of Jews have believed, and all of them are zealous to observe the law. They have been informed that you teach all the Jews who live among the Gentiles to turn away from Moses, telling them not to circumcise their children or practice our customs. What shall we do? They will hear that you have come, so do what we tell you. There are four men with us who have made a vow. Take these men, participate in their purification rites, and pay their expenses, so that they can have their hair cut. Then everyone will know there is no truth in these reports about you, but that you keep the law. As for the Gentile believers, we have written to them our decision that they should abstain from food sacrificed to idols, blood, the meat of strangled animals, and from sexual immorality." (Acts 21:17–25)

Paul and Resistance

As I read this section I can almost see Paul sighing and rolling his eyes thinking, "Well, well, well. Here it comes. While we have many Gentiles you all want to talk about thousands of Jews. While we are on the theological borders of interpreting the Torah for them, you are worried that we have crossed the line." I envision Paul as a man who had decided to pick his battles. Any other time he would have taken a stand and not backed down. The man who wrote Colossians and Galatians and warned the Gentiles to not allow the circumcised Christians to judge them or hold them to the law of Moses, was the same man who followed the advice of these Jewish Christians. However, this was Jerusalem and Paul must have understood that this was not a battle to fight. As he had written to the Corinthian Christians that he was willing to become all things to all people (1 Cor 9:20-22), at Jerusalem he made the decision to submit and fulfill their wishes. While the Jerusalem church may have seemed to be acting out of fear rather than faith, it lived in the heart of the Jewish nation, and its best form of outreach was to be respectful and follow the Torah. Even more, Luke would suggest that Christianity involved upholding God's laws rather than disregarding them.

> "When I returned to Jerusalem and was praying at the temple, I fell into a trance and saw him [the Lord] speaking to me. 'Leave Jerusalem immediately, because they will not accept your testimony concerning me.' I replied, 'Lord, these people know that I imprisoned and abused in the synagogues those who believed in you. When the blood of your martyr Stephen was shed, I stood there giving my approval and guarding the clothes of those who were killing him.' "Then he said to me, 'Go; I will send you far away to the Gentiles.'" The crowd listened until he said this. Then they raised their voices and shouted, "Get rid of him! He doesn't deserve to live!" (Acts 21:17-22).

The conversion story of Saul of Tarsus was written three times in Acts. Luke somehow felt that this story was not only worth repeating, but one that needed to be placed in the mouth of Paul. Stories retold in Acts are the conversion of Cornelius and his family (Acts 10—11), the letter from the Jerusalem Council (Acts 15:22-29; 21:20-25) and Saul's conversion (Acts 9, 22, 26). These stories support a powerful theme for Luke. First, *Cornelius's conversion placed emphasis on the inclusion of the Gentiles in the new faith*. This was illustrated by the Jerusalem Council's willingness to state that the Gentiles were to be saved and did not need to practice circumcision. Second, *the Cornelius story and Jerusalem Council letter also illustrated the resistance to the freedom of the gospel by some in the Jewish community*.

Paul's conversion story also shared these two themes. First, *in all three stories Jesus called Paul to reach the Gentiles* (9:15-16; 22:21; 26:17-18). However, in each successive account Jesus' emphasis to Paul was that he was commissioned to bring this message to those outside of the faith.

> This man is my chosen instrument to carry my name before the Gentiles and their kings and before the people of Israel. I will show him how much he must suffer for my name. (Acts 9:15-16)

> Then the Lord said to me, "Go; I will send you far away to the Gentiles." (Acts 22:21)

> I will rescue you from your own people and from the Gentiles. I am sending you to them to open their eyes and turn them from darkness to light, and from the power of Satan to God, so that they may receive forgiveness of sins and be with those who are sanctified by faith in me. (Acts 26:17–18)

Second, *the stories also build upon the theme of resistance by God's chosen people.*

> "When I returned to Jerusalem and was praying at the temple, I fell into a trance and saw him [the Lord] speaking to me. 'Leave Jerusalem immediately, because they will not accept your testimony concerning me.' I replied, 'Lord, these people know that I went from imprisoned and abused in the synagogues those who believed in you. When the blood of your martyr Stephen was shed, I stood there giving my approval and guarding the clothes of those who were killing him.'" (Acts 22:17–20)

> "King Agrippa, I was persuaded by what I saw from heaven. First to those in Damascus, Jerusalem, all Judea, and then to the Gentiles, I preached that they should repent and turn to God and prove their repentance by what they do [how they live]. That is why some Jews seized me in the temple courts and tried to kill me. But God has helped me to this day; so I stand here and testify to small and great alike. I am saying nothing more than what the prophets and Moses said would happen—that the Messiah would suffer and, as the first to rise from the dead, would bring the message of light to his own people and to the Gentiles." (Acts 26:19–23)

For Luke the resistance from the chosen people (Paul included) furthered an opportunity for those outside the Jewish faith to receive the gospel. Even more, their acceptance and hospitality proved that they not only offered peace to the Christians, but to Jesus himself. Throughout Acts God's grace for all was met with resistance. However, the Empire of Jesus continued to grow in spite of this.

These two themes were prevalent while Paul was at Jerusalem and the surrounding area. Paul's experiences during meetings of councils, local trials, and before Roman officials indicated that he was suffering "unjust treatment." Trial scenes were a common format for ancient hero stories. In these scenes the hero was someone who faced false allegations. Sometimes the defendant was silent and faced an unjust death. Other times the defendant spoke up and proved his innocence. However, the trial scene was an opportunity for the reader to join the author in the drama of injustice and the struggle for truth.[1]

Enduring Resistance

During Paul's encounter of resistance he prevailed in various ways. Paul was able to escape injustice by appealing to his rights as a Roman citizen (Acts 22:22–29; 23:12–35; 25:12). Paul was not foolish; if he could avoid a beating he would, and his appeal to Caesar and Rome offered him protection from riots, assassination plots, and an unjust judicial system. Paul even used trickery to confront the high priest and pit the Pharisees and Sadducees against each other. The resistance spoke against Paul as Luke indicated that their abuse of power could not condemn him. "Paul looked straight at the Sanhedrin and said, 'My brothers, I have completed my duty to God in all good conscience to this day'" (Acts 23:1).

Gentile Inclusion

The theme of Gentile inclusion was prevalent in this section. Paul stirred up the group during a corrupt religious court of appeals. The next night Jesus told Paul: "Be courageous, as you have been my witness in Jerusalem, you will also testify in Rome." (Acts 23:11). From this point forward, the Gentiles became a willing audience for Paul's message concerning Jesus' resurrection. A Roman commander had him abducted from a riot and protected in the Roman quarters. In addition to this Paul received an armed military guard when an assassination plot by some of the corrupt leaders was uncovered. The guard escorted him to Caesarea during the night with the belief that "there was no charge against him that deserved death or imprisonment" (Acts 23:29). Felix, a Roman governor of Caesarea who had convinced a teenaged Jewish girl named Drusila to leave her husband King Aretas of Gamarsa and live with him, granted Paul a private audience. He as a Roman leader of this area later heard his case and kept Paul in protective

---

1. Walton, "Trying Paul or Trying Rome?," 123–25; Schwartz, "The Trial Scene in the Greek Novels and in Acts."

prison. While he was an unjust and corrupt leader, Paul continued to challenge him concerning his own morals.

Later the succeeding governor, Festus, the Jewish king Agrippa, and his sister Bernice heard his last defense against the Jews as well as an appeal to Caesar. Paul's conversion story and testimony of a divine commission caused the Roman official, Festus, to proclaim that he was crazy, while the Jewish king scoffed at Paul's invitation. "Do you think that in such a short time you can persuade me to be a Christian?" (Acts 26:28).

Paul had become an apostle to the Gentiles in both his missionary journeys as well as his journey to Jerusalem and Rome. While his trial at Jerusalem bore resemblance to Jesus' (appearing before the Jewish council of Ananias the high priest, a Herodian king, and a Roman official) he, unlike Jesus, found justice from the Roman government. For Luke Jesus was rejected by corrupt Jewish leaders and vindicated by God. Luke's emphasized resistance and inclusion of Gentiles as not only part of God's plan, but one by human choice. There were those who chose to reject the gospel and there were others who chose to listen and promote justice for the gospel. Whether they were willing or unwilling parties, the Empire of Jesus survived.

Can We Also Endure Resistance?

The story of Paul at Jerusalem has many applications for the church today. *First, resistance is not something we seek but we should not be surprised if the message of Jesus is rejected, even by those who should be its biggest advocates.* Beginning with Acts 20:22–23, resistance was mentioned twelve times by Luke (20:22–23; 21:11, 21, 27–36; 22:17–20; 23:2, 12–22, 27; 24:6–10, 22; 25:1–12; 26:1–32). For Luke, it was not the message or messenger alone that was being rejected but Jesus. One common statement in all three of Paul's conversion accounts was, "I am Jesus . . . whom you are persecuting . . . ." Luke reminded the early reader that rejecting the message of Jesus and his resurrection was a rejection of God. "It is concerning the resurrection of the dead that I am on trial today . . ." (Acts 24:21). Even though Gamaliel, in the beginnings of the movement, had warned his colleagues not to fight with God and the message, this seemed to be common throughout Luke's narrative. Not all of the Jewish leaders opposed the movement, but those who did tried to carry more authority than they had.

Second, the church's response to resistance should not be to retreat but to boldly proclaim the message of Jesus and practice his lifestyle. Paul found opportunities to share his testimony with high Gentile officials, those soldiers accompanying him (Phil 1:13; 4:22), and other Jewish political leaders. Paul always had opportunities as God based the spread of the message upon open hearts, rather than resistant ones. Additionally Luke's narrative provided the reader with many opportunities where Gentiles and Jews accepted and offered hospitality to the movement, message, and men on the early mission teams.

Third, *we will be surprised at who will reject the message.* To be a "friend of sinners and tax collectors," and "apostles to the Gentiles," will bring conflict from some who name Jesus as Lord. These Christians resist because human nature typically rejects outsiders and causes us to form our own close-knit communities. However, the call to risk our lives and relationships for Jesus will be ignored by those preferring comfort and security in their faith.

Finally, Paul found opportunity to be prophetic in his message. Imagine Felix standing with his teenaged wife/partner, whom he had manipulated and exploited out of lust. Imagine how this man as an official represented the worst in moral justice and Roman integrity. Yet Paul held nothing back as he preached concerning "righteousness" (a social justice term), "self-control" (something Felix lacked), and "God's judgment." Luke wrote that Felix became alarmed (worried) at what Paul was saying. Even more, Paul chose to be under house arrest rather than buy his own freedom. God's people must have a strong moral code if the church plans to go public. This would have been a challenge to Theophilus who, like Felix, carried the honorific title "most excellent." Theophilus needed to know that the movement, while being prophetic, could not spread if it was immoral. This was a reflection of both the ministry and resurrection of Jesus.

> The task of the members of faith communities is to be "witnesses" to Jesus. This means more than simply telling one's personal story of faith or transformation, as important as that may be. To be Christ's witnesses is to bring forward into our own time and place the truth of the gospel. Just as Matthew, Mark, Luke, and John each took the words, teachings, deeds, life, death, and resurrection of Jesus and brought it to bear in their particular time and their communities, so the church's essential calling and task is to bear witness to what God has done and is doing in Jesus, to this outpouring of grace and healing, to this victory over the myriad powers of death at work in the world and in us—to witness to the

power of Jesus to heal all that distorts, disfigures, and diminishes God's dream for life.[2]

I love ministry and ministering to people. When I was a single youth minister working with "Brother Jim," his wife, Leigh, took me aside one day. The first two months of my new position at the church I lived in their home until I found my own place to live. She talked to me about being a moral example as a young man and minister. While it was important for me as a single man, and even more as an older minister, I often remember her words. However, she also mentioned something to me that afternoon that Lori and I continue to appreciate. "The reason you need to be a moral and spiritual example is because of what you will hear. We know things about people because they tell us. We also know because others tell us. There are things we know that are dark, shameful, and can ruin someone's life if we shared them. Even more, it is hard for us because we know things about people who continue to portray a public presence that is fake and hypocritical. We could never have called these people to holiness if we were like them. We have also been able to forgive because we know that this is what some need in order to move forward."

These *are* wise words. Some would call her judgmental, although the truth is that she is correct. Lori and I know things about people that are dark, shameful, evil, and humiliating. We know this because they have told us, their families have shared this, others in the community have come to us, or their behavior has become flagrant enough to be seen by all. Some carry a fake presence of Christianity, moral integrity, and family values. Due to Facebook and other forms of social media, it has become easy to "look spiritual" within a community that only sees our words rather than our actions. I would be lying if I didn't write that there were times we wanted to let the world know and put them in their place. Even more there continue to be times where we want to go to their homes and unload our hurt, frustration, and anger upon them. Yet we know that it will solve little. However, we can share our hurt with each other, and sometimes other friends in ministry, and deal with the emotional strain together. It is a blessing that Lori and I are partners and can help each other through the hard times in ministry.

Others have struggled and confided in us, and sharing this news would wreck the hard work they are doing to make things right in their lives and the lives of others. Still others have unashamedly walked away from our churches and are arrogant in their attitudes. Sharing what we know would

2. Robinson and Wall, *Called to Be Church*, 43.

humble all of these people. Knowing what we know can bring tremendous stress, anger, sadness, and frustration. It is exhausting but we still must be examples of Jesus' resurrection both morally and spiritually.

Leigh was right.

Leaders and Resistance

I was having lunch with a local author whom I respected and enjoyed reading. We had met a few times before and had developed good conversations concerning "what seemed to be wrong" with American Christianity. This meeting was a good discussion and the time seemed to slip away quickly. It was my turn to pay for the meal so I asked for the check and began do the usual "closing discussion" before we went back to our work and planned for the next meeting.

My friend asked, "What are your plans for the weekend?" I responded, "It's Easter weekend, I will be tied up preparing for our outreach, worship, and follow-up. I am assuming you are going to church, but you are welcome to visit Agape since we will have many guests and friends attending." "Oh thank you," he said, "my wife and I plan to hike this Sunday and get out in nature. We don't go to church often." My jaw visibly dropped and I could see he noticed it. "You're kidding me," I laughed, "this is the biggest day for inviting friends to church, and you're not going?"

He smiled and mentioned that it was hard to find a church. We hugged and went our separate ways.

I'm not judging my friend. I know he is a wonderful man and loves God. He is well respected in the community and I still enjoy what he has written. I have read over the past few years many articles, blog posts, and stories concerning academics and religious authors and their hesitance to attend church. I have heard how it seems boring sitting and listening to a preacher, especially one that may not be interesting; or that we can serve God in nature. I have listened to many share the faults of our churches, evangelical and American Christianity, and how they feel disconnected. In many ways I understand. As a student in graduate school it was hard to be learning advanced theology, Greek, and Hebrew, and attend church each week to listen to a minister who at the time hadn't studied much of what I was learning. It was a hard two years for me and I struggled, sometimes forcing myself to listen. There were many men in my graduate school classes that I knew had not become involved in a church. Others did and they are great leaders in their churches today. However, it was tempting to take a position preaching at a small church an hour from Memphis and doing my own ministry. But, I don't regret the decision to stay active in a local congregation.

I know how wonderful it was to sit next to Lori each week, help her with our newborn son, and develop relationships and conversations with men and women who weren't learning what I was. They would be nice and ask me how school was going and I would tell them. Then after ten minutes I noticed the glazed look in their eyes, and realized I was talking too much. They were being nice and I needed to learn to live in community. I still have friendships with many and remember how much they loved me, and how many of the guys helped me to be a good father. I also remember the monthly Monday night visitation dinners we had where our team had dinner together and then left to visit those who were guests that previous Sunday morning. They were common people who loved God and served in their church. I was also a common person who needed to love God and serve in my church.

After my lunch meeting with my friend I called the minister back in Memphis where I had gone to school and attended church. He has since finished his doctorate and served in the church for over twenty years. I had a good visit with him and told him how much I appreciated his heart, leadership, and preaching. He was there when Lori was hospitalized, he was there to hold our new son, and he was there to congratulate me when I graduated. I told him how much that meant to me.

He thanked me and then said something that really touched me. "Ron, I appreciated that you were there. It must have been hard but you were an encouragement to me." I know that he was sincere and I know that he was aware that many of the students didn't attend church. I know he bit his tongue when I would share some of the new theology I was learning and how we needed to do a better job preaching from the text. He was patient, even though we were only five years apart in age. He accepted me as an intern there and worked with me.

I think that there is something about being active in a church. Sometimes community is where we learn what really matters and what doesn't. The community requires patience and a willingness to sit, listen, and obey; yet it also offers blessing. The community reminds us that no matter what we know, we need to be effective at helping people know Jesus. The community reminds us that all our learning, wisdom, and academics are only valuable when we can live in harmony with people. While it is true we can experience God in nature, it is interesting that the Apostle Paul felt more called to a crowded room than an open forest. Even more, Luke seems to share more concerning the meetings and gatherings than what Paul taught on the road, in the open country, or around the campfire.

I wonder how many other leaders we, who are skilled and trained, can bless by simply listening to and supporting them in ministry. The resistance is not only outside our churches, it is among those who should be supporting and uplifting the Empire of Jesus.

Leaders Enduring the Resistance

First, we, like Paul, must endure the resistance by being examples in our faith, integrity, morality, compassion, mercy, love, and holiness. While it is a struggle, and we many times have had to ask forgiveness in our lives, we have to stay faithful. There are times when we have to speak the truth in love, or simply share that Jesus is justice and that we must be examples and prepare for the judgment day. Some will call it judging but this is what God has called us to do. There is a temptation to become like those we help. It would have been tempting for Paul to pay the bribe or walk away from the trials; however, he knew that he was not called to that. God had given him a mission and expected it to be completed.

We cannot forget that while there are those corrupt individuals promoting injustice and weak morals in our world, there is a larger population of people who are honest, hardworking, love God, and seek to be led by those who do so in holiness, honesty, and love. It is this group of people who need us to love them and guide them. They are the majority and they are the ones we many times forget, because we worry about Felix rather than the myriads of people who follow, love, and practice our faith and values. They are the ones who offer acceptance and hospitality to the message, mission, and mercy of Jesus. They are the ones whom Jesus puts in our lives to make our stay in prison comfortable, protect us at court, and be the army who rides with us to make sure we are safe. These are the men, women, and children whose hearts are opened by the Holy Spirit and who will receive the words and resurrection of Jesus in their lives daily.

Second, we who live in the United States have every reason to be open about our faith. Those of you who live in other parts of the world where Christians are persecuted have my prayers every week. I find that even in persecution you continue to openly share your beliefs in Jesus. You do not fear humans because you know that God will provide. I also know that you would be thankful to have the freedom, as we in America and other places do, to practice your faith without being attacked, harassed, or abused. Those of us in places where it is not illegal to be Christian should realize that this is a movement born out of suffering, struggle, and pain. I do not believe that we need to seek persecution, or try to create it, but we need to realize that any movement arising out of resistance will struggle in safety and peace. This is not an excuse, but a reminder that we cannot seek our own comfort nor can we try to force Christianity to become a self-pleasing or comfortable belief. The crucifixion of Jesus reminds us that our faith is one that involves sacrifice, love, and sometimes becoming countercultural.

Finally, this countercultural message many times calls us to be prophetic. *To be prophetic means that we not only speak for God, but we try to create an alternate world where justice, love, compassion, and mercy thrive.* This is especially important for men and boys. To be a masculine Christian does not mean that we copy cultural masculinity, placing manliness in testosterone, sexuality, or physical size. To be a manly Christian is to have men who uphold the biblical truths, values, and ethics of love, compassion, mercy, grace, and courage to be loving in the face of evil and hatred. To be prophetic in American masculinity means that we are concerned with Jesus' qualities rather than those of our actors, athletes, and business leaders. To be prophetic in American masculinity means that we, like Paul, mentor others and show them how to love others, how to forgive, and how to have a ministry of reconciliation.

12

PAUL GOES TO ROME

Do not stop him, whoever is not against you is for you. (Luke 9:51)

KING AGRIPPA'S FINAL WORDS seem to resonate to the end of Luke's work: "This man could have been set free if he had not appealed to Caesar" (Acts 26:32). This is true. Paul could have walked away from Caesarea, avoided years of turmoil, and continued to strengthen the Gentile/Jewish churches in Asia, Greece, Italy, and Syria. He could have been set free and been a great blessing for all Christians and maybe written many more letters and baptized thousands of others. He could have established more churches, possibly even in China and Persia. Yet, Luke reminded us that Paul was concerned with Jesus' mission, not comfort or glory. He was concerned with obedience rather than safety.

> Now, bound by the Spirit, I am going to Jerusalem, not knowing what will happen to me there. I only know that in every city the Holy Spirit said that prison and hardships await me. I consider my life worth nothing; I want to finish the race and complete the task the Lord Jesus has given me; testifying to the good news of God's grace. (Acts 20:22–24)

> Then Paul answered, "Why are you weeping and breaking my heart? I am ready not only to be bound, but also to die in Jerusalem for the name of the Lord Jesus." (Acts 21:13)

The following night the Lord stood near Paul and said, "Be courageous! As you have testified about me in Jerusalem, so you must do so in Rome." (Acts 23:11)

I will rescue you from your own people and from the Gentiles. I am sending you to them to open their eyes and turn them from darkness to light, and from the power of Satan to God, so that they may receive forgiveness of sins and a place among those who are sanctified by faith in me. (Acts 26:17–18)

Luke has mentioned that Paul was "bound" seven times in the previous section (20:22; 21:11, 33; 22:5, 29; 24:27; 26:29). For Luke, Paul was bound to Jesus' mission and plan to reach all people. He did not have a choice to obey or not, to suffer or find safety, to go or stay. Thankfully Paul chose "bonds" over freedom and comfort.

BOUND AT SEA

The next section is an interesting one in Acts. First, sailing and sea voyages were common themes for ancient hero journeys.[1] At sea the hero usually encountered a threat of death, storms, and shipwrecks, was stranded on islands, or experienced tribal conflict. Paul, like these ancient characters, was a hero on a spiritual and divine journey.

In the Roman world Egypt was "the breadbasket" of the empire. Alexandria was a major shipping port for this cargo and Rome offered hefty rewards for merchants who could get extra grain to Rome before the "storm season" shut down the seaways.[2] Many a captain was willing to push the boundaries and get that extra grain to Rome for the compensation. Likewise, many bushels of grain were lost at sea due to these captains who took the risk.

Paul's team boarded one of these ships. Luke and Aristarchus accompanied Paul along with a centurion named Julius. Roman soldiers on "Caesar's business" could board any ship they wished. Desiring to hurry to Rome they found this risky grain ship from Egypt.

They paid the price for this risky journey. The ship struggled with the storm, ran aground on an island, and broke apart. However, throughout this story of fear, anger, death, and material disaster Paul presented a calm

---

1. Johnson, *The Acts of the Apostles*, 451.
2. Rapske, "Acts, Travel, and Shipwreck," 22–23; Crossan, *God and Empire*, 38.

presence. In Jonah the Jewish man on a Gentile boat hid from the storm, confessed his unfaithfulness, and was thrown overboard. In this story Paul stayed calm, offered advice, and served communion.

> Men, I envision that our voyage is going to be perilous and bring great loss to ship, cargo, and to our own lives. (Acts 27:10)

> After they had gone a long time without food, Paul stood among them and said: "Men, you should have taken my advice not to sail from Crete; then you would have spared yourselves this loss. I urge you to keep up your courage, because no one will perish, only the ship. Last night an angel of the God to whom I belong and whom I serve stood beside me and said, 'Do not be afraid, Paul. You must stand before Caesar; and God has given you the lives of all who sail with you.' Be courageous, for I have faith in God that it will happen this way." (Acts 27:21–26)

> Then Paul said to the centurion and the soldiers, "Unless these men stay with the ship, you cannot be saved." So the soldiers cut the ropes that held the lifeboat and let it drift away. Just before dawn Paul urged them all to eat. "For the last fourteen days," he said, "you have been in constant suspense and have gone without food; you haven't eaten anything. I encourage you to take some food. You need it to survive. No one will lose a hair." After he said this, he took some bread and gave thanks to God in front of them all. Then he broke it and began to eat. They were all encouraged and ate some food themselves. Altogether there were two hundred seventy-six of us on board. When they had eaten what they wanted, they lightened the ship by throwing the grain into the sea. (Acts 27:31–38)

In the heart of a storm Paul reflected his own peace, security, and faith in God. Paul's faith was not in his own safety but because he had a gospel meeting planned with Emperor Nero.

As they were stranded on Malta Paul was able to do as he had done on his earlier mission journeys. It seemed that while Paul was on trial, in prison, and on the run we had forgotten that he was still an evangelist and apostle. Luke reminded the reader that Paul's journey was not only to Caesar but those Gentiles needing Jesus. "I will rescue you from your own people and from the Gentiles. I am sending you to them to open their eyes and turn them from darkness to light, and from the power of Satan to God, so that they may receive forgiveness of sins and a place among those who are sanctified by faith in me." (Acts 26:17–18)

Paul showed miraculous power by helping people. His recovery from a snake bite piqued the interest of the natives who had been hospitable toward the survivors (Acts 28:2, 7–8). Luke often wrote concerning the hospitality of those outside the Jewish faith. Paul also healed Publius's father (Publius possibly being a Roman official). He then healed those on the island who were sick. One not only must laugh at the irony of an island seeing Jesus' miracles, but also of the surviving ship passengers who, until this moment, must have wondered if Paul was more of a "blowhard" than a true apostle.

Hospitality and Reception

There is one interesting note in this section of Acts. This story is unique in Luke's narrative. First, *Paul did not preach to the Maltese people.* Second, *there were no recorded baptisms.* Luke typically emphasized preaching and baptisms/conversions in Acts. However, no such events took place. This suggested that while preaching and teaching are important functions of the church, the result was not always baptism or conversion. *Sometimes God's people simply do good things for others because it is the right thing to do.* Luke also mentioned "hospitality" three times, indicating that these islanders, while probably not followers of Jesus, were more loving and compassionate than some of Paul's own contemporaries. The people offered acceptance and hospitality.

It is interesting that Luke's sea voyage occupied such a large space in his narrative but chronologically covered such a short time. Compared to the rest of Paul's journeys Luke devoted much attention to a short trip. It seemed that Luke was suggesting that the ship was slowly reaching its end. As the ship docked at Rome Paul was given an apartment (under house arrest) with a soldier, entertained guests, and shared the message of Jesus with the Jewish community and others that were interested in listening. This would support the belief that Rome was the end of Luke's story, Paul's journey, and the goals of the Empire of Jesus. The stories and travels of Paul covered vast amounts of time, but on the way to Rome the story slowed down, covered more detail, and ended abruptly. Some have suggested that Luke intended to write part three but didn't complete it. Others have suggested that he only intended to do two books. Either way his omitting the death of Paul, Peter, and the Christian persecutions is interesting.

BOUND AT ROME

First, *Luke indicated that the gospel mission had been fulfilled at Rome through Paul's preaching to the Jews who were there.* He gathered the leaders together and first asked if *the resistance* had preceded him and given them a negative report.

> They replied, "We have not received any letters from Judea concerning you, and none of our people who have come from there has reported or said anything bad about you. But we want to hear what your views are, for we know that people everywhere are talking against this sect." They arranged to meet Paul on a certain day, and came in even larger numbers to the place where he was staying. He witnessed to them from morning till evening, explaining about the kingdom of God, and from the Law of Moses and from the Prophets he tried to persuade them about Jesus. Some were convinced by what he said, but others would not believe. They disagreed among themselves and began to leave after Paul had made this final statement: "The Holy Spirit spoke the truth to your ancestors when he said through Isaiah the prophet: 'Go to this people and say, "You will be ever hearing but never understanding; you will be ever seeing but never perceiving. For this people's heart has become calloused; they hardly hear with their ears, and they have closed their eyes. Otherwise they might see with their eyes, hear with their ears, understand with their hearts and turn, and I would heal them."' Therefore I want you to know that God's salvation has been sent to the Gentiles, and they will listen!" (Acts 28:21–29)

After preaching, Paul again referred to Isaiah the prophet and the Christian movement as the servants of Yahweh. He, like Jesus, warned his hearers that the resistance was opposing God, the Messiah, and the renewed covenant for Yahweh's people. His message echoed Jesus' confrontation with the Pharisees and those who "opposed the Holy Spirit." Luke shared little concerning their conversion, acceptance, or rejection of the message. Typically Luke's accounts involved baptisms, new converts, and the resistance stirring up trouble. Due to this Paul and the mission team had to flee the city and proclaim to other locations.

However, this was not how the story ended at Rome. "For two whole years Paul stayed there in his own rented house and welcomed all who came to see him. He proclaimed the kingdom of God and taught concerning the Lord Jesus Christ—with all boldness and without hindrance!" (Acts 28:30–31). For Luke the story was complete. *First, there was no resistance.*

Paul was able to speak the message of Jesus without fear, resistance, or persecution. While we know that the story continued past Rome, Luke wanted the reader to know that the gospel reached its full end not at Jerusalem but Rome. Paul had been faithful to Jesus and was given the opportunity to live out his years preaching and teaching.

Second, the gospel ended not at the seat of Judaism but that of the Gentile world. The message was not meant for Jews only but for those on the margins and those formerly excluded from the covenant of Yahweh. One can almost imagine the soldier guarding Paul's apartment overhearing the conversations, asking questions, and maybe even staying after he was relieved of his guard. Paul was in an apartment, probably near the heart of the city sharing Jesus' message with the diverse populace.

Finally, the gospel ended with hospitality. Throughout Luke's writings, those who opened their homes, served food, or offered care for others became models of the Christian faith. While Luke's gospel began and ended at the temple, Acts began and ended in an apartment/upper room. The vehicle for Christianity was the small group, house church, or family atmosphere. Joseph Hellerman indicated that Christianity grew rapidly in the ancient world because it used the model of the family/household to spread the message and virtues of hospitality and love to others.[3] Paul was no different and it was amazing that a former rabbi, who worried about being Kosher or separate from others, opened his home to strangers at Rome. Paul was a man on a mission and was radically transformed by Jesus' love, call, and vision.

Paul left behind thousands of new people who were followers of the way. He planted many new congregations that grew and spread the news of Jesus to some of the darkest areas of the Roman Empire. The Empire of Jesus penetrated many ethnicities and Paul was able to teach through lessons, letters, and his life that the resurrection of Jesus was real in the lives of people. For Luke, Jesus' empire spread in many directions through many people, all working to be led by the Holy Spirit.

Leaders (men and women) were trained to carry on the work. After the death of the apostles and other witnesses of Jesus, the church continued to fulfill the mission of Jesus. People would suffer and die, like Jesus and the apostles. Even during persecution people would step into leadership and lead the disciples to become like Jesus. Luke would return and write

---

3. Hellerman, *The Ancient Church as Family*.

his narrative of Jesus and along with Acts, would live in the hearts of people for centuries.

However, Paul would not end his life in a glorious building, with a high leadership post in the government, or as a wealthy man. He would die living in a small rented apartment sharing his faith with the soldiers who guarded him. He would end his days serving people a meal and sharing Jesus with them. Some would respond, while others would scoff. That would be the pattern of the gospel. Paul would continue to do what he had always done, share the message and show love in the midst of resistance. History claims that Emperor Nero had his head removed. A humiliating act to a brilliant humble man. However, this would be the cost for proclaiming Jesus.

The Humility of the Gospel, Empire, and Ministry of Jesus

I was traveling on an airplane to Texas to speak at a conference. A young man sat in the seat next to me and we began to visit before the plane departed. Sometimes God places people next to me who have no desire to talk, and I am able to finish my reading or get other work finished. Other times God leads someone who wants to talk. This was one of those individuals. He was a young man attending a state university who had not grown up attending a church, but while in college enrolled in a few religion classes. He had learned much about Christianity, world religions, and even some of the Bible stories while in the classes. He had a positive view of Christianity and had many discussions with Christians at his university. He was aware of the differences between "extremely conservative and the more progressive Christians" (his words). We had a long visit and he genuinely seemed interested in my teaching, writing, and our ministry in Portland.

"I do have a question I am wanting to ask you," he said. "Since you would be considered a biblical scholar [his words], what are your thoughts on the virgin birth? I mean, most scholars reject that view, don't they?" His question was honest and I appreciated his thoughts. He continued, "It seems to me that this is too incredible to believe. Not only is it not repeatable, but it just seems odd for something like that to happen." I agreed and responded, "You're right. It is odd, unbelievable, and not repeatable. There are plenty of scholars who do believe in the virgin birth, but not all do." I shared with him that it fits completely within the "humiliation of God" theme throughout the Bible. He looked surprised so I began to talk about

God's humiliation and rejection throughout the prophets, in the crucifixion of Jesus, and the quenching of the Spirit. He nodded his head as I talked, as if he was hearing a different spin on Bible stories. "For me, the virgin birth is the ultimate humiliation of God. To enter this world in such a scandalous fashion seems typical of a God who gets close to people, even at the cost of being rejected, hurt, or other times loved and honored," I said. "It is the very driving force of what we believe. Even more, because of this he was able to live among those like him, who had a reputation, and who were seen as unworthy."

He smiled and said, "That makes sense. That's why Jesus hung out with outcasts, right?" I nodded my head and smiled. "So, then what is your take on Islam, don't they embrace Christ?" he asked. I mentioned to him that the Quran states that it would be shameful for Allah (God) to have a son and for that son to literally die on a cross. This is one major distinction between Christianity and Islam. Christians are willing to embrace the humiliation that is reflected in the incarnation, love, and mercy of God. "I hadn't heard that one before, but it makes sense," he said.

We had a great conversation about many things but one thing that stuck with me was that this was the first time I had verbally made the connection between the humiliation of God through the incarnation, and the driving force of the Spirit. The gospel of Jesus, Empire of God, and power of the Spirit were not manifested in large, glorious, dynamic displays of power and prestige. *They were manifested* in the birth of a baby to a young woman who quickly married her fiancé. *They were manifested* by a God of marginalized people exiled to Babylon or remaining in the ruins of what once was Jerusalem (the Holy City). *They were manifested* by a Lord who hung out with vulnerable people, suffered the most shameful physical torture, and died surrounded by criminals. *They were manifested* by a small group of uneducated people who were led by the Spirit to boldly speak of the resurrection. *They were manifested* in a small room with a traumatized Pharisee who was blind for three days, completely helpless. *They were manifested* among a people who continually faced resistance, physical violence, and threats but formed small congregations led by common people. *They were manifested* by a small band of these common people who traveled throughout the world running errands, delivering letters and reports, and praying for churches that their leader Paul had begun. *They were manifested* in a small apartment in Rome by a Pharisee who invited people into his place for a message and meal; through this even the soldiers heard the message of Jesus.

Because they were manifested in this manner, it was easy to resist, reject, and criticize the gospel of Jesus and the early Christian movement.

Luke was proud of this movement and wanted Theophilus and his readers to embrace it. How would Luke feel about the movement and how it is manifested today? Are we willing to have Jesus' Spirit unleashed on the church today and experience the results that Luke described?

13

THE SPIRIT UNLEASHED IN THE CHURCH TODAY

The Messiah will suffer and rise from the dead on the third day, and repentance and forgiveness of sins will be preached in his name to all Gentiles beginning at Jerusalem. (Luke 24:46–47)

SURELY THE CHALLENGE FOR *the church today is to be taken captive by the agenda of Jesus rather than seeking to mold him to fit our agenda.*[1]

LUKE'S SECOND VOLUME COMPLETED the two book series concerning the establishment, growth, and victories of a new empire. He, like many ancient authors, compared the founding of this new empire to the literary heroes of Greece and Rome. Jesus was the hero who founded, led, and restored this empire to the Jewish nation and throughout the world. While other stories of the life of Jesus were circulated among the early Christians he felt that he could deliver a better literary product and deliver it into the hands of Theophilus and his community. This was not a reflection of the other accounts, but an enhancement of their information as it was retold using the current techniques of rhetoricians and scribes. Luke rewrote the account as an epic story of a hero leading humans to establish what God always wanted, a nation of people who would influence their world.

1. Frost and Hirsch, *ReJesus*, 10.

Luke used a backdrop of the restoration of Judah from captivity and exile, although this captivity was social. Yahweh had led the captives home from captivity and through the prophets challenged the people to rebuild their lives, have a new vision of their future, and experience an alternate reality—what could be, rather than what was. It was not the elite returning from Babylon who had the final word in the documents, it was those who were labeled "sinners" and "outcasts" whom Jesus drew into the story of restoration and hope. God did not come to call the healthy, but the sick. This new empire was unique in that those who the hero on a journey typically destroyed (monsters and marginalized people) were now included in the empire, and offered healing, forgiveness, and salvation. For Luke the themes of repentance, forgiveness, comfort, shalom/peace, covenant, hospitality, and reconciliation were prevalent throughout the life and ministry of Jesus, the hero and son of God. His heroic journey ended at Jerusalem with rejection, punishment, and death. The Savior became the scapegoat and received the wrath of the people who, knowingly or unknowingly, rejected their Lord. He rose from the grave and spent time with his disciples, preparing them for the next phase of the story. The Gospel of Luke ended where it began, in the temple of Yahweh.

Acts continued the theme of restoration of a new empire, only this time through the Spirit of God and the appointed followers of Jesus. The disciples of Jesus brought the news of his resurrection throughout the world beginning at the center of resistance. The apostles proclaimed their message in the city where Jesus was murdered and yet overcame resistance from the local leaders. For Luke, the themes of the empire of mercy, compassion, reaching those on the margins, peace/shalom, repentance, and reconciliation thrived during times of persecution and resistance. Throughout Acts the message of Jesus as well as the messengers were opposed. While good leaders in their community were open to the story and even encouraged caution against resisting the Gospel, those who were corrupted and hardened in their hearts tried to overpower the early followers of Christ. The resistance continued wherever the message was proclaimed, coming from community leaders, rogue followers, and the Christians themselves. However, the Holy Spirit continued to empower the believers to boldly and courageously preach the message of the resurrection and endure the resistance. Leaders were appointed to lead the new congregations with the understanding that "we must suffer much for God's Empire."

Luke's audience, Theophilus and his community, would have come from the elite classes of society. While the Gospel challenged them to become friends of sinners and outcasts, Acts challenged them to endure and withstand the resistance to this empire. There was to be no comfortable church existence in this resurrected community. There would be resistance and the Spirit would empower the church to resist, proclaim boldly, and endure. However, in times of persecution and resistance there were those who offered hospitality, acceptance, and became strong leaders in this new empire. They quickly overshadowed the resistance as they continued to endure and proclaimed Jesus throughout their world.

Today the modern church not only struggles with accepting the book of Acts, but Luke's themes as well. While his Gospel narrative called us to focus on the marginalized, Acts calls us to be a people who thrive during resistance, endure rejection of an unbelievable (to some) message, and boldly proclaim that the Empire of Jesus involves practicing love, compassion, mercy, repentance, and reconciliation. In a time when much of our world, and Christianity, has tended to focus on safety, security, comfort, and convenience, Acts finds little place for these concerns. "Jesus is still calling us to come and join him in a far more reckless and exciting adventure than that of mere church attendance."[2]

When we began planting churches there was tremendous emphasis on what those who had exited Christian congregations said about us. We openly listened and admitted that we had been judgmental, arrogant, unforgiving, unloving, hypocritical, intolerant, and controlling. Many clergy have openly repented of this and many churches continue to work hard to reach those who have been driven away from our assemblies. We have worked to listen to and even offer a voice to those on the margins, as well as including those not in churches into our communities. There has been much work done to hear the cries of the vulnerable and make amends.

However, during this time I have also noticed that there are those who left the church because they did not want to conform to the life of Jesus. Jesus needed to be molded in their image. He needed to be "nonjudgmental" and "an overfunctioner" when it came to offering grace for our sins. This Jesus was not the Lord of the Gospels nor of Acts, where those who followed him were men and women who risked their lives for God's justice in a world that marginalized others. I was surprised at how many young people we worked with who were in love with the idea of a Jesus with justice, but unwilling to do the difficult work of Jesus and justice. It became easier to write about him and his policies than to actually sit down on the

2. Ibid., 11.

hard concrete next to a homeless person and try to find a solution to their struggles. It became easier to talk about women's rights than to actually hold a female victim's hands and walk with her in the journey for safety, justice, and empowerment. It became easier to present a talk on how men should treat women than it was to stand up to a group of men and explore with them how their current conversation was misogynistic. Somehow Christianity became a philosophy, rather than a way of life.

Even more, those who were devoted to the cause of Christ were viewed as either judgmental, radical, or out of touch with current issues. Paul was considered a misogynist, intolerant, judgmental, and controlling in the Christian faith. Yet reading Acts and observing his life suggests the opposite. Paul stood up for what he and others believed and even suffered PTSD because he felt compelled to take a beating for the Gentiles. In addition to this Luke indicated that Paul was the model of the Christian life. Paul followed the journey of Jesus to Jerusalem and suffered as he had. In the end Paul proved that his love for God's vision was stronger than his own will. For Luke, Paul should be considered a model of commitment, love, loyalty, and honor.

Luke wrote very little about the people who fell away from the faith during this movement. Other than Mark, little is known of those who did not endure the resistance, or who returned to their former lives. Luke briefly mentions those such as Ananias, Sapphira, Simon the Magician, Bar Jesus, and Felix who fail the test of the Christian life. Luke instead devoted time to those who succeeded, endured the resistance, and brought glory to God. For Luke, those who quit had little voice, while those who endured needed their stories told.

Is Luke's message the same today? In Luke 8:11–15, Jesus shared the parable of the Sower and indicated that one in three will actually bear fruit as disciples. Two in three will fall away. Whether those plants acknowledge that they fell or were just taking a hiatus, Jesus only spoke of the ones who endured to the end. In a culture that emphasizes convenience, shallow commitments, and self-centeredness, does Acts have a message for us? In our journey to find out what is wrong with the church, have we given voice to those like Ananias and Sapphira who only wanted personal gain from the faith community? Have we given voice to those like Simon the Magician who wanted financial gain in the Empire of Jesus, and left disappointed? Have we given voice to people who quit their faith because it called for a sacrifice, and were challenged by others? Have we spent time trying to alter a movement led by vision and thriving in resistance and suffering to one that invites people to relax in the sweet graces of God? Even more, have we tried to adapt a movement led by the Spirit and empowered by boldness and courage to reach those who are dominated by fear, anxiety, and weakness?

What is the hope for our future? I believe that Luke has shared that our future can once again be as bright as it was on the day of Pentecost. First, *the Empire of Jesus reflects courage, boldness, love, faith, and loyalty.* Jesus' people can once again recapture that joy and endurance found among Christians in other countries and that exists today as the empire flourishes among the marginalized. It is these qualities that will be important in our future leaders and as we seek to disciple others. While there were those that resisted there were others such as Lydia, the prison guard, Sosthenese, Timothy, Silas, Barnabas, Aristarchus, Gaius, Priscilla, Aquila, Cornelius, who embraced the unbelievable message of a resurrected Lord and opened their homes, hearts, and wallets to further the ministries of those who were tortured for the vision of the empire. The Spirit found these men and women and led or drove the missionaries to them. God so desired them to be saved that heaven and earth was moved so that common people could speak their language, eat their food, and share their homes.

Second, *we focus on those who endure, not on those who quit.* We are not judging others but encouraging those who believe and populate our churches. They are the ones who are less vocal and need guidance. Those who have left can be encouraged to return but those who have stayed have stayed for a reason. They are the ones the Spirit leads to proclaim their faith with boldness and courage. We as leaders must continue to call them to courage, faith, loyalty, and empower them to lead. Even though they must go through much suffering for the empire, they will be faithful.

Finally, *we band together as a people, united by the Spirit and encourage each other that our faith was born in suffering, resistance, and persecution.* When we endure together we experience the power and glory of Jesus, his empire, and the Spirit. Our movement is one born in adversity. We have a God who was pierced and still offered relationship, love, mercy, justice, and forgiveness. We have a Savior who was executed and overcame through the resurrection. We have a history of leaders who also suffered for a vision, which continued to grow through the next generation. The resurrection offers hope that in the midst of suffering is victory.

A movement born in adversity has risen. Can we continue to lead with that vision, mission, and boldness?

BIBLIOGRAPHY

Adams, Dwayne H. *The Sinner in Luke*. Eugene, OR: Pickwick, 2008.
Adewuya, J. Ayodegi. "The Sacrificial-Missiological Function of Paul's Sufferings in the Context of 2 Corinthians." In *Paul as Missionary: Identity, Activity, Theology, and Practice*, edited by Trevor J. Burke and Brian S. Rosner, 88–98. New York: Bloomsbury T & T Clark, 2012.
Anderson, Kevin L. *"But God Raised Him From the Dead": The Theology of Jesus' Resurrection in Luke-Acts*. Waynesboro, GA: Paternoster, 2006.
Apollinarius. *The Fragments of Papias. The Apostolic Fathers*. Edited by J. B. Lightfoot and J. R. Harner. Grand Rapids: Baker, 1984.
Aune, David E. *The New Testament in Its Literary Environment*. Philadelphia: Westminster, 1989.
Avalos, Hector. *Health Care and the Rise of Christianity*. Peabody, MA: Hendrickson, 1999.
Aviam, Mordecai. "People, Land, Economy, and Belief in First-Century Galilee and Its Origins: A Comprehensive Archaeological Synthesis." In *The Galilean Economy in the Time of Jesus*, edited by David A. Fiensy and Ralph K. Hawkins, 5–48. Atlanta: SBL, 2013.
Bachmann, Michael. "Jerusalem and Rome in Luke-Acts: Observations on the Structure and the Intended Message." In *Luke-Acts and Empire: Essays in Honor of Robert L. Brawley*, edited by David Rhoads, David Esterline, and Jae Won Lee, 60–83. Eugene, OR: Pickwick, 2011.
Biblia Hebraica Stuttgartensia. Edited by Karl Ellinger and Wilhelm Rudooph. Stuttgart: Deutsche Biblestiftung, 1977.
Bolger, Ryan K. "Introduction." In *The Gospel after Christendom: New Voices, New Cultures, New Expressions*, edited by Ryan K. Bolger, xxviii–xliv. Grand Rapids: Baker, 2012.
Bonz, Marianne Palmer. *The Past as Legacy: Luke-Acts and Ancient Epic*. Philadelphia: Fortress, 2000.
Borgman, Paul. *The Way According to Luke: Hearing the Whole Story of Luke-Acts*. Grand Rapids: Eerdmans, 2006.
Bouma-Prediger, Steven, and Brian J. Walsh. *Beyond Homelessness: Christian Faith in a Culture of Displacement*. Grand Rapids: Eerdmans, 2008.
Brawley, Robert L. *Luke-Acts and the Jews: Conflict, Apology, and Conciliation*. Atlanta: Scholars, 1987.
Brueggemann, Walter. *The Prophetic Imagination*. 2nd edition. Philadelphia: Fortress, 2001.

———. *The Practice of Prophetic Imagination: Preaching an Emancipating Word.* Minneapolis: Fortress, 2012.

Burke, Trevor J. "The Holy Spirit as the Controlling Dynamic in Paul's Role as Missionary to the Thessalonians." In *Paul as Missionary: Identity, Activity, Theology, and Practice*, edited by Trevor J. Burke and Brian S. Rosner, 142–57. New York: Bloomsbury T & T Clark, 2012.

Cancik, Hubert. "The History of Culture, Religion, and Institutions in Ancient Historiography: Philological Considerations Concerning Luke's History." *Journal of Biblical Literature* 116:4 (1997) 673–95.

Cassidy, Richard J. "Paul's Proclamation of *Lord* Jesus as a Chained Prisoner in Rome: Luke's Ending Is in His Beginning." In *Luke-Acts and Empire: Essays in Honor of Robert L. Brawley*, edited by David Rhoads, David Esterline, and Jae Won Lee, 142–53. Eugene, OR: Pickwick, 2011.

Chilton, Bruce. "Festivals and Holy Days: Jewish." In *Dictionary of New Testament Background*, edited by Craig A. Evans and Stanley E. Porter, 371–78. Downer's Grove, IL: InterVarsity, 2000.

Clark, Gillian. *Christianity and Roman Society.* New York: Cambridge University Press, 2004.

Clark, Ron. *Am I Sleeping with the Enemy? Males and Females in the Image of God.* Eugene, OR: Cascade, 2010.

———. *The Better Way: The Church of Agape in Emerging Corinth.* Eugene, OR: Pickwick, 2010.

———. *Emerging Elders.* Abilene, TX: ACU Press, 2005.

———. *The God of Second Chances: Finding Hope in the Prophets of Exile.* Eugene, OR: Cascade, 2012.

———. *Jesus Unleashed: Luke's Gospel for Emerging Christians.* Eugene, OR: Cascade, 2013.

Clegg, Tom, and Warren Bird. *Lost in America.* Loveland, CO: Group, 2001.

Collie, Robert, and Annelie Collie. *The Apostle Paul and Post-Traumatic Stress: From Woundedness to Wholeness.* Lima, OH: Fairway, 2011.

Conn, Harvie M., and Manuel Ortiz. *Urban Ministry: The Kingdom, the City, and the People of God.* Downer's Grove, IL: InterVarsity, 2001.

Conway, Colleen M. *Behold the Man: Jesus and Greco-Roman Masculinity.* New York: Oxford University Press, 2008.

Corley, Kathleen E. *Private Women Public Meals: Social Conflict in the Synoptic Tradition.* Peabody, MA: Hendrickson, 1993.

Crossan, John Dominic. *God and Empire: Jesus Against Rome Then and Now.* New York: Harper Collins, 2007.

Dawsey, James. *Peter's Last Sermon: Identity and Discipleship in the Gospel of Mark.* Macon, GA: Mercer University Press, 2010.

DeSilva, David. *Honor, Patronage, Kinship, and Purity: Unlocking New Testament Culture.* Downer's Grove, IL: InterVarsity, 2000.

———. "'Let the One Who Claims Honor Establish That Claim in the Lord': Honor Discourse in the Corinthian Correspondence." *BTB* 28:2 (Summer 1998) 61-74.

Dunn, Richard R., and Jana L. Sundene. *Shaping the Journey of Emerging Adults.* Downers Grove, IL: InterVarsity, 2012.

BIBLIOGRAPHY

Elliott, John H. "Temple Versus Household in Luke-Acts: A Contrast in Social Institutions." In *The Social World of Luke-Acts: Models for Interpretation*, edited by Jerome H. Neyrey, 211-240. Peabody, MA: Hendrickson, 1991.

Faix, Tobias. "Toward a Holistic Process of Transformational Mission." In *The Gospel after Christendom: New Voices, New Cultures, New Expressions*, edited by Ryan K. Bolger, 206-18. Grand Rapids: Baker, 2012.

Fant, Clyde E., and Mitchell G. Reddish. *A Guide to Biblical Sites in Greece and Turkey.* New York: Oxford, 2003.

Faulkner, Liam A. *Ancient Medicine: Sickness and Health in Greece and Rome.* Oxted, England: Collca, ebook, n.d.

Ferguson, Everett. *Baptism in the Early Church: History, Theology, and Liturgy in the First Five Centuries.* Grand Rapids: Eerdmans, 2009.

Fiensy, David A. "Assessing the Economy of Galilee in the Late Second Temple Period: Five Considerations." In *The Galilean Economy in the Time of Jesus*, edited by David A. Fiensy and Ralph K. Hawkins, 165-86. Atlanta: SBL, 2013.

Friesen, Steven J. "Prospects for a Demography of the Pauline Mission: Corinth Among the Churches." In *Urban Religion in Roman Corinth*, edited by Daniel N. Schowalter and Steven J. Friesen, 351-70. Cambridge, MA: Harvard University Press, 2005.

Frost, Michael. *The Road to Missional: Journey to the Center of the Church.* Grand Rapids: Baker, 2011.

Frost, Michael, and Alan Hirsch. *ReJesus: A Wild Messiah for a Missional Church.* Peabody, MA: Hendrickson, 2009.

———. *The Shaping of Things to Come: Innovation and Mission for the 21st-Century Church.* Peabody, MA: Hendrickson, 2003.

Garcia-Johnson, Oscar. "Mission within Hybrid Cultures: Transnationality and the Glocal Church." In *Paul as Missionary: Identity, Activity, Theology, and Practice*, edited by Trevor J. Burke and Brian S. Rosner, 113-26. New York: Bloomsbury T & T Clark, 2012.

Gehring, Roger W. *House Church and Mission: The Importance of Household Structures in Early Christianity.* Peabody, MA: Hendrickson, 2004.

Gibbs, Eddie. *Churchmorph: How Megatrends are Reshaping Christian Communities.* Grand Rapids: Baker, 2009.

Gibbs, Eddie, and Ryan K. Bolger. *Emerging Churches: Creating Christian Community in Postmodern Cultures.* Grand Rapids: Baker, 2005.

Gill, David W. J. "Achaia." In *The Book of Acts in Its First Century Setting: Volume 2: Graeco-Roman Setting*, edited by David W. J. Gill and Conrad Gempf, 433-54. Grand Rapids: Eerdmans, 1994.

———. "Macedonia." In *The Book of Acts in Its First Century Setting: Volume 2: Graeco-Roman Setting*, edited by David W. J. Gill and Conrad Gempf, 397-418. Grand Rapids: Eerdmans, 1994.

Gill, David W. J., and Bruce W. Winter. "Acts and Roman Religion." In *The Book of Acts in Its First Century Setting: Volume 2: Graeco-Roman Setting*, edited by David W. J. Gill and Conrad Gempf, 79-92. Grand Rapids: Eerdmans, 1994.

Grottanelli, Cristiano. *Kings and Prophets: Monarchic Power, Inspired Leadership, and Sacred Text in Biblical Narrative.* New York: Oxford University Press, 1999.

Guder, Darrell L., ed. *Missional Church: Vision for the Sending of the Church in North America.* Grand Rapids: Eerdmans, 1998.

Hall, Douglas John. *The Cross in Our Context: Jesus and the Suffering World*. Minneapolis: Fortress, 2003.

Hansen, G. Walter. "Galatia." In *The Book of Acts in Its First Century Setting: Volume 2: Graeco-Roman Setting*, edited by David W. J. Gill and Conrad Gempf, 377–96. Grand Rapids: Eerdmans, 1994.

Harland, Philip A. *Associations, Synagogues, and Congregations: Claiming a Place in Ancient Mediterranean Society*. Minneapolis: Fortress, 2003.

Haya-Prats, Gonzalo. *Empowered Believers: The Holy Spirit in the Book of Acts*. Edited by Paul Elbert. Translated by Scott A. Ellington. Eugene, OR: Cascade, 2011.

Hayes, J. Daniel. "Paul and the Multi-Ethnic First-Century World: Ethnicity and Christian Identity." In *Paul as Missionary: Identity, Activity, Theology, and Practice*, edited by Trevor J. Burke and Brian S. Rosner, 76–87. New York: Bloomsbury T & T Clark, 2012.

Hellerman, Joseph H. *The Ancient Church as Family*. Minneapolis: Fortress, 2001.

———. *Reconstructing Honor in Roman Philippi: Carmen Christi as Cursus Pudorum*. Cambridge: Cambridge University Press, 2005.

Hippocrates. *Works: On the Sacred Diseases*. Translated Francis Adams. The Perfect Library: Kindle edition, n.d.

Hirsch, Alan. *The Forgotten Ways: Reactivating the Missional Church*. Grand Rapids: Brazos, 2006.

Hoppe, Leslie J. *The Synagogues and Churches of Ancient Palestine*. Collegeville, MN: Liturgical, 1994.

Johnson, Luke Timothy. *The Acts of the Apostles*. Collegeville, MN: Liturgical, 1992.

———. *Messianic Exegesis*. Fortress, 1988.

———. *Prophetic Jesus, Prophetic Church*. Grand Rapids: Eerdmans, 2011.

Josephus. *Antiquities of the Jews. The Works of Josephus*. Translated by William Whiston. Peabody, MA: Hendrickson, 1985.

Juel, Donald. *Luke-Acts: The Promise of History*. Atlanta: John Knox, 1983.

Kim, Seyoon. "Paul as Eschatological Herald." In *Paul as Missionary: Identity, Activity, Theology, and Practice*, edited by Trevor J. Burke and Brian S. Rosner, 9–24. New York: Bloomsbury T & T Clark, 2012.

Kimball, Dan. *They Like Jesus But Not the Church*. Grand Rapids: Zondervan, 2007.

King, Martin Luther, Jr. *Why We Can't Wait*. New York: Mentor, 1964.

Kinnaman, David. *You Lost Me: Why Young Christians Are Leaving the Church . . . and Rethinking Faith*. Grand Rapids: Baker, 2011.

Kinnaman, David, and Gabe Lyons. *UnChristian: What a New Generation Really Thinks About Christianity . . . And Why It Matters*. Grand Rapids: Baker, 2009.

Klauck, Hans-Josef. *The Religious Context of Early Christianity: A Guide to Graeco-Roman Religions*. Minneapolis: Fortress, 2003.

Kuhn, Karl Allen. *The Kingdom According to Luke and Acts: A Social, Literary, and Theological Introduction*. Grand Rapids: Baker, 2015.

Lee, Jae Won. "Pilate and the Crucifixion of Jesus in Luke-Acts." In *Luke-Acts and Empire: Essays in Honor of Robert L. Brawley*, edited by David Rhoads, David Esterline, and Jae Won Lee, 84–106. Eugene, OR: Pickwick, 2011.

Levine, Amy-Jill. *The Misunderstood Jew: The Church and the Scandal of the Jewish Jesus*. New York: Harper Collins, 2006.

Lewis, Robert, and Rob Wilkins. *The Church of Irresistible Influence*. Grand Rapids: Zondervan, 2001.

BIBLIOGRAPHY

Longenecker, Bruce W. *Jesus on the Edge and God in the Gap: Luke 4 in Narrative Perspective*. Eugene, OR: Cascade, 2012.

MacDonald, Dennis R. *The Homeric Epics and the Gospel of Mark*. New Haven, CT: Yale University Press, 2000.

Malina, Bruce J. *The New Testament World*. Rev. ed. Louisville: Westminster John Knox, 1993.

———. "Reading Theory Perspective: Reading Luke-Acts." In *The Social World of Luke-Acts: Models for Interpretation,* edited by Jerome H. Neyrey, 3–23. Peabody, MA: Hendrickson, 1991.

Malina, Bruce J., and Jerome H. Neyrey. "Conflict in Luke-Acts: Labeling and Deviance Theory." In *The Social World of Luke-Acts: Models for Interpretation*, edited by Jerome H. Neyrey, 97–122. Peabody, MA: Hendrickson, 1991.

Malina, Bruce J., and John J. Pilch. *Social-Science Commentary on the Book of Acts*. Minneapolis: Fortress, 2008.

Marshall, I. Howard. *Luke: Historian and Theologian*. Grand Rapids: Zondervan, 1971.

McCarroll, Pamela R. *The End of Hope—The Beginning: Narratives of Hope in the Face of Death and Trauma*. Minneapolis: Fortress, 2014.

McCullough, C. Thomas. "City and Village in Lower Galilee: The Import of the Archaeological Excavations at Sepphoris and Khirbet Qana (Cana) for Framing the Economic Context of Jesus." In *The Galilean Economy in the Time of Jesus*, edited by David A. Fiensy and Ralph K. Hawkins, 49–74. Atlanta: SBL, 2013.

Miller, James C. "Paul and His Ethnicity: Reframing the Categories." In *Paul as Missionary: Identity, Activity, Theology, and Practice*, edited by Trevor J. Burke and Brian S. Rosner, 37–50. New York: Bloomsbury T & T Clark, 2012.

Mitchell, Don. *The Right to the City: Social Justice and the Fight for Public Space*. New York: Guilford, 2003.

Morgan, James M. *Encountering Images of Spiritual Transformation: The Thoroughfare Motif within the Plot of Luke-Acts*. Eugene, OR: Wipf and Stock, 2013.

Moxnes, Halvor. "Patron-Client Relations and the New Community in Luke-Acts." In *The Social World of Luke-Acts: Models for Interpretation,* edited by Jerome H. Neyrey, 241–68. Peabody, MA: Hendrickson, 1991.

Nanos, Mark. "The Question of Conceptualization: Qualifying Paul's Position on Circumcision in Dialogue with Josephus's Advisors to King Izates." In *Paul Within Judaism: Restoring the First-Century Context to the Apostle*, edited by Mark D. Nanos and Magnus Zetterholm, 105–52. Minneapolis: Fortress, 2015.

Nobbs, Alanna. "Cyprus." In *The Book of Acts in Its First Century Setting: Volume 2: Graeco-Roman Setting*, edited by David W. J. Gill and Conrad Gempf, 217–90. Grand Rapids: Eerdmans, 1994.

Novum Testamentum Graeca. 27th ed. Edited by Eberhard Nestle, Erwin Nestle, Barbara Aland, Kurt Aland, Johannes Karavidopoulos, Carlo M. Martini, and Bruce Metzger. Stuttgart: Deutsche Bibelgesellschaft, 1993.

Oden, Thomas. *The African Memory of Mark: Reassessing Early Church Tradition*. Downer's Grove, IL: InterVarsity, 2011.

Ovid. *Metamorphoses*. In *The Metamorphoses of Ovid: A New Verse Translation*, translated by Allen Mandelbaum. New York: Harvest, 1993.

Palmer, Darryl W. "Acts and the Ancient Historical Monograph." In *The Book of Acts in Its First Century Setting: Volume 1: Ancient Literary Setting*, edited by Bruce W. Winter and Andrew D. Clarke, 1–30. Grand Rapids: Eerdmans, 1993.

Parsons, Mikeal C. *Body and Character in Luke and Acts: The Subversion of Physiognomy in Early Christianity*. Waco, TX: Baylor University Press, 2011.

———. "Luke and the Progymnasmata: A Preliminary Investigation into the Preliminary Exercises." In *Contextualizing Acts: Lukan Narrative and Greco-Roman Discourse*, edited by Todd Penner and Caroline Vander Stichele, 43–63. Atlanta: SBL, 2003.

———. *Luke: Storyteller, Interpreter, Evangelist*. Peabody, MA: Hendrickson, 2007.

Penner, Todd. *In Praise of Christian Origins*. New York: T & T Clark. 2004.

Pickett, Raymond. "Luke and Empire: An Introduction." In *Luke-Acts and Empire: Essays in Honor of Robert L. Brawley*, edited by David Rhoads, David Esterline, and Jae Won Lee, 84–106. Eugene, OR: Pickwick, 2011.

Pilch, John J. *Visions and Healing in the Acts of the Apostles: How the Early Believers Experienced God*. Collegeville, MN: Liturgical, 2004.

Plato. *The Symposium*. Edited and translated by Christopher Gill. London: Penguin, 2003.

Puskas, Charles B. *The Conclusion of Luke-Acts: The Significance of Acts 28:16–31*. Eugene, OR: Pickwick, 2009.

Rainer, Thom S. *The Book of Church Growth: History, Theology, and Principles*. Nashville: Broadman, 1993.

———. *Breakout Churches: Discover How to Make the Leap*. Grand Rapids: Zondervan, 2005.

———. *Effective Evangelistic Churches: Successful Churches Reveal What Works and What Doesn't*. Nashville: Broadman and Holman, 1996.

———. *The Unchurched Next Door*. Grand Rapids: Zondervan, 2003.

Rambo, Shelly. *Spirit and Trauma: A Theology of Remaining*. Louisville: Westminster John Knox, 2010.

Rapske, Brian M. "Acts, Travel, and Shipwreck." In *The Book of Acts in Its First Century Setting: Volume 2: Graeco-Roman Setting*, edited by David W. J. Gill and Conrad Gempf, 1–47. Grand Rapids: Eerdmans, 1994.

———. *The Book of Acts and Paul in Roman Custody*. Grand Rapids: Eerdmans, 1994.

Reid, Barbara, E . "The Power of the Widows and How to Suppress It (Acts 6:1–7)." In *A Feminist Companion to the Acts of the Apostles*, edited by Amy-Jill Levine with Marianne Blickenstaff, 71–88. Edinburgh: T & T Clark, 2004.

———. "Women Prophets of God's Alternative Reign." In *Luke-Acts and Empire: Essays in Honor of Robert L. Brawley*, edited by David Rhoads, David Esterline, and Jae Won Lee, 45–59. Eugene, OR: Pickwick, 2011.

Revive, Hanoch. *The Elders in Ancient Israel*. Jerusalem: Magnes, 1989.

Robinson, Anthony B., and Robert W. Wall. *Called to Be Church: The Book of Acts for a New Day*. Grand Rapids: Eerdmans, 2006.

Rosner, Brian S. "The Glory of God in Paul's Missionary Theology and Practice." In *Paul as Missionary: Identity, Activity, Theology, and Practice*, edited by Trevor J. Burke and Brian S. Rosner, 158–68. New York: Bloomsbury T & T Clark, 2012.

Runesson, Anders. "The Question of Terminology: The Architecture of Contemporary Discussions of Paul." In *Paul Within Judaism: Restoring the First-Century Context to the Apostle*, edited by Mark D. Nanos and Magnus Zetterholm, 53–78. Minneapolis: Fortress, 2015.

Saldarini, Anthony J. *Pharisees, Scribes, and Sadducees in Palestinian Society: A Sociological Approach*. Grand Rapids: Eerdmans, 2001.

Schwartz, Saundra. "The Trial Scene in the Greek Novels and in Acts." In *Contextualizing Acts: Lukan Narrative and Greco-Roman Discourse*, edited by Todd Penner and Coroline Vander Stichele, 105-38. Atlanta: SBL, 2003.

Seccombe, David Peter. *Possessions and the Poor in Luke-Acts*. Linz: Studien zum Neuen Testament und Seiner Umwelt, 1982.

Shaw, Perry W. H. "Vulnerable Authority: A Theological Approach to Leadership and Teamwork." *Christian Education Journal* Series 3, 3:1 (2006) 119-33.

Shepherd, William H., Jr. *The Narrative Function of the Holy Spirit as a Character in Luke-Acts*. Atlanta: Scholars, 1994.

Simon, George K., Jr. *The Judas Syndrome: Why Good People Do Awful Things*. Nashville: Abingdon, 2013.

Smith, Dennis E., and Joseph B. Tyson. *Acts and Christian Beginnings: The Acts Seminar Report*. Salem, OR: Polebridge, 2013.

Spencer, F. Scott. *Journeying Through Acts: A Literary-Cultural Reading*. Peabody, MA: Hendrickson, 2004.

Stark, Rodney. *What Americans Really Believe*. Waco, TX: Baylor University Press, 2008.

Stetzer, Ed. *Planting New Churches in a Postmodern Age*. Nashville: Broadman and Holman, 2003.

Stronstad, Roger. *The Charismatic Theology of St. Luke*. Hendrickson: Peabody, 1984.

Thompson, Alan J. *The Acts of the Risen Lord Jesus*. Downers Grove, IL: InterVarsity, 2011.

Tickle, Phyllis. *The Great Emergence: How Christianity is Changing and Why*. 2nd ed. Grand Rapids: Baker, 2012.

Tracey, Robyn. "Syria." In *The Book of Acts in Its First Century Setting: Volume 2: Graeco-Roman Setting*, edited by David W. J. Gill and Conrad Gempf, 223-78. Grand Rapids: Eerdmans, 1994.

Treblico, Paul. "Asia." In *The Book of Acts in Its Greco-Roman Setting*, edited by D. W. J. Gill and C. Gempf, 291-362. Grand Rapids: Eerdmans, 1994.

Tyson, Joseph B. "From History to Rhetoric and Back: Assessing New Trends in Acts Studies." In *Contextualizing Acts: Lucan Narrative and Greco-Roman Discourse*, edited by Todd Penner and Caroline Vander Stichele, 23-42. Atlanta: SBL, 2003.

Wallace-Hadrill, Andrew. *Houses and Society in Pompeii and Herculaneum*. Princeton, NJ: Princeton University Press, 1994.

Walters, Patricia. *The Assumed Authorial Unity of Luke and Acts: A Reassessment of the Evidence*. New York: Cambridge University Press, 2009.

Walton, Steve. "Trying Paul or Trying Rome? Judges and Accused in the Roman Trials of Paul in Acts." In *Luke-Acts and Empire: Essays in Honor of Robert L. Brawley*, edited by David Rhoads, David Esterline, and Jae Won Lee, 122-41. Eugene, OR: Pickwick, 2011.

Willis, Timothy M. *The Elders of the City: A Study of the Elders-Laws in Deuteronomy*. Atlanta: SBL, 2001.

Wilson, Brittany E. *Unmanly Men: Refigurations of Masculinity in Luke-Acts*. New York: Oxford University Press, 2005.

Witherington, Ben, III. *The Acts of the Apostles: A Socio-Rhetorical Commentary*. Grand Rapids: Eerdmans, 1998.

Woodward, J. R. *Creating a Missional Culture: Equipping the Church for the Sake of the World*. Downer's Grove, IL: InterVarsity, 2012.

BIBLIOGRAPHY

Xenophon. *Ephesian Tale of Anthia and Habrocomes* 1.2. In *Women's Religions in the Greco-Roman World: A Sourcebook,* edited by Ross Shephard Kraemer, 58–59. New York: Oxford University Press, 2004.

Yamasaki-Ransom, Kazuhiko. "Paul, Agrippa I, and Antiochus IV: Two Persecutors in Acts in Light of 2 Maccabees 9." In *Luke-Acts and Empire: Essays in Honor of Robert L. Brawley,* edited by David Rhoads, David Esterline, and Jae Won Lee, 107–21. Eugene, OR: Pickwick, 2011.

Zetterholm, Karin Hedner. "The Question of Assumptions: Torah Observance in the First Century." In *Paul Within Judaism: Restoring the First-Century Context to the Apostle,* edited by Mark D. Nanos and Magnus Zetterholm, 76–103. Minneapolis: Fortress, 2015.

SUBJECT INDEX

Anxiety, 40, 57, 60, 74, 86, 90, 104, 131, 132, 180
Baptism/Baptized, 25, 30, 36, 37, 38, 58, 69, 70, 73, 79, 81, 103, 107, 122, 123, 124, 126, 134, 141, 142, 144, 147, 167, 170, 171
Boldness, 51, 56, 58, 65, 83, 93, 95, 97, 98, 103, 107, 171, 174, 176, 180
Captivity/Exile, 6, 9, 10, 13, 19, 20, 21, 25, 34, 35, 37, 70, 71, 72, 95, 111, 176, 177
Community, 7, 8, 13, 14, 15, 21, 23, 24, 28, 30, 33, 34, 36, 38–41, 43–45, 48–56, 58–65, 67, 69, 70, 71, 72, 73, 75, 79, 81, 83, 94–99, 101, 107–8, 110, 111, 116, 117, 119, 122, 127, 128, 129, 133, 135–38, 141, 145, 146, 147, 149, 150–52, 157, 162–64, 170, 176–79
Day of Yahweh, 9, 34, 35
Decline of the Church, 11, 40, 54, 108, 115, 116, 117, 138, 142, 151
Discipleship, 39, 44, 58, 99, 100, 102, 117, 179
Empire, 9–11, 13, 19, 20–26, 28, 29, 30–34, 36, 38–39, 47, 52, 58, 62, 64, 69–74, 76, 77, 79, 82 84, 87, 89, 90, 92, 94, 95, 96, 100–103, 107, 110–15, 118, 121, 126, 128, 129, 130, 132, 135, 136, 142, 146, 153, 158, 160, 165, 168, 170, 172–80
Forgiveness, 4, 5–7, 20, 21, 28, 29, 35–37, 44, 46, 47–48, 55, 65, 66, 70, 95, 95, 113, 129, 141, 150, 158, 162, 165, 166, 168, 170, 176, 177, 177, 180
Hospitality, 25, 39, 74, 75, 78, 84, 85, 96, 98, 117, 123, 128, 129, 138, 158, 161, 165, 170, 172, 177, 178
Journey, 9, 12, 15, 20, 25, 32, 39, 40, 45, 46, 78, 80, 96, 103, 118, 121, 128, 134, 144, 145, 146, 155, 160, 168–70, 177, 179
Leadership/Elders, 13, 15, 49, 50, 52, 61, 62, 63, 64, 67, 92, 100–101, 107, 110, 114, 115, 118, 129, 130, 145–49, 150, 151, 152, 155, 156, 164, 172, 173
Marginalized, 8, 9, 13–14, 21, 22, 23, 32, 44–46, 74, 76, 94, 103, 110, 172, 174, 177–80
Ministry/Minister, 4, 9, 14–16, 22, 25, 28, 29, 32, 33, 39, 40–46, 53–57, 61–66, 70–77, 81, 84, 91, 94, 95, 96, 99–104, 111, 114–20, 129–130, 135–52, 156, 161–66, 173, 177, 180
Peace/Shalom, 7–8, 25, 32, 44, 47, 49, 50, 52, 57, 62, 67, 74, 76, 83, 104, 112–17, 128–38, 145, 158, 166, 169, 177
Pentecost, 32–35, 39, 80, 180
Prophets, 4–14, 20–22, 34, 42, 46, 48, 52, 65, 66, 72–76, 91–94, 96, 103, 111, 114, 129, 158, 161, 166–76

SUBJECT INDEX

Reconciliation, 3, 7, 30, 34–41, 44–48, 52, 96, 109, 114, 136–38, 166, 177–78

Repentance, 5–7, 20, 30, 36–40, 43–48, 55, 70, 71, 85, 86, 103, 109, 110, 129, 142, 146, 158, 176–78

Resistance/Rejection, 7–9, 12, 14, 25, 29, 32, 36, 37, 43, 47, 49, 50, 54, 57–66, 69, 73–78, 80–84, 89–117, 120, 123–30, 133–36, 138, 141, 143, 146, 149, 153, 155–63, 165, 165, 166, 171–80

Resurrection, 10, 11, 14, 21–28, 32–34, 37, 38, 47, 50, 52, 55, 58, 69, 70, 71, 76, 77, 80–82, 89, 90, 94, 98, 101, 106, 131–133, 150, 159, 160–65, 172, 174, 177–80

Restoration, 7, 10–13, 20–23, 25–40, 44, 46, 47, 72, 96, 103, 106, 111, 129, 142, 145, 147, 176–77

Social Justice, 12, 21, 32, 39, 44, 45, 52, 53, 66, 103, 108, 116, 160, 161, 165, 178

Spirit, 2, 3, 4, 6, 10–16, 20–26, 28–29, 31-36, 39-45, 51–58, 60–61, 64–67, 69–71, 73–78, 81–85, 87, 89, 91–93, 95, 98–99, 103, 106, 110–12, 119–21, 123–24, 128, 130–32, 136–137, 140–44, 146–48, 162, 163, 165, 167, 168, 171–72, 174–80

Synagogues, 13, 14, 36–38, 64, 68, 72, 73, 77, 79, 90–97, 101, 112, 122, 128, 131–36, 140, 141, 143, 157, 158,

Trauma, 58, 62, 66–68, 75, 99–100, 114, 121, 124, 125, 138, 174, 180

Waiting for the Spirit, 1–4, 6–7, 10–14, 25–26, 30, 31, 32, 69, 75, 76, 80, 136

Witness, 4, 5, 10–11, 13–14, 20, 24–29, 33, 34, 35, 39, 42, 46, 51–55, 58, 58, 61, 63, 64, 66–71, 75, 76, 77, 81–83, 89, 91, 95, 97, 98, 99, 106, 115, 118, 127, 138, 146, 150, 152, 159, 161, 171, 172

SCRIPTURE INDEX

HEBREW BIBLE

Genesis
1:28	68
8:1	68
8:17	68
9:1	68
9:7	68
11	68
11:1–9	68
11:4	68
11:8	68
11:19	68
17:1–8	107
17:3–8	107

Exodus
32:4	38

Deuteronomy
9:18	131

Joshua
5:2–8	107

2 Kings
17:7–40	5

Isaiah
40–55	21, 96
40–66	71
40:3	6
40:31	1, 6
42:1	10, 20
49:6	21, 96
54:7	5
56:4–5	60
60	25
60:1–2	106
60:1–3	140
65:3	131
65:9 -21	81
65:17–25	16

Jeremiah
3:6–10	5
7:22–23	5
7:24–26	5–6
29:5–8	6
31:6	10
31:26	20
31:31	16
32:38	19
33:38	16

Ezekiel
2:5	76
37:1–14	21
37:14	21

SCRIPTURE INDEX

Hosea

8:5	131
12:7	6

Joel

2:28–32	10, 20, 21, 29, 34, 34

Amos

9:11	21
9:11–12	105, 111

Micah

3:8	10, 20
7:7	6

Nahum

1:7–8	118

Zephaniah

3:9	89

Haggai

2:19	7

Zechariah

1:1–6	129
12	43
1:7–6:8	129
3:9	7
11:10–11	5
11:8	9
12:10	9, 10, 20

Malachi

3:1	17

Psalms

16:7	125
69:25	29
77:2	125
77:6	125
106:29	131

119:55	125

Nehemiah

4:1–3	69

2 Chronicles

36:15–21	5
36:23	25

CHRISTIAN SCRIPTURES

Matthew

7:1	116
7:18	116
7:20	116
17:22–23	100
20:17–19	100

Mark

1:16–17	31
1:19–20	31
8:31–33	100
9:31	100
10:33–34	100

Luke

1–2	39
1:1–4	22, 24
1:3	23
1:4–11	26
1:5–8	49
1:10	26
1:12	82
1:16–71	26
1:32–33	26
1:35	20
1:41	20
1:67	20
2:25	26
2:26–27	20

SCRIPTURE INDEX

2:35	100	22:66–71	51
2:38	26	23:1–2	107
3:1–5	37	23:51	49
3:3	20	24:20	100
3:4-6	17	24:44–49	106
3:16	20	24:45–49	25, 142
3:21–22	20	24:46–47	176
3:41	20		
4:16–19	21, 25, 45, 77, 92	John	
5:3	31		
5:17–26	23	3:1–3	49
5:18–19	45	3:5	38
5:29–31	21, 45	4:8	69
7:27	17	12:6	27
7:34	21	13:2	27
8:11-15	179	13:27	27
8:40–56	77	21:15–19	80
9:13	62		
9:23–27	100, 102	Acts	
9:44	25, 101	1	136
9:51	144, 167	1–2	39
9:51–53	32	1:1–4	22
9:57	32	1:2	20
10:1–3	145	1:4	3
10:2	68	1:4–5	20
10:25–37	69	1:6	11, 39
10:38	32	1:6–8	91, 106
11:13	20, 21	1:8	4, 20, 71
11:14–28	56	1:12	113
11:23	155	1:12–15	91
13:18–19	143	1:15	20
13:31–33	32	1:15–22	28
13:32	101	1:25	71
14	20	2	11, 21, 34, 45
16:19–31	45	2:1–4	32
17:11	32	1:12–13	32
18	20	2:1–20	21
19:28	32	2:2–4	20
19:30	145	2:13	35, 35, 62
19:45-48	17	2:14–16	34
19:46	17	2:17	20
20:9–19	17	2:18	20
22–23	90	2:33	20
22:8	145	2:36–47	36-37
22:12	28, 113	2:38	20
22:18	26	2:41	38
22:53	17	3	45, 77

193

SCRIPTURE INDEX

3:2	45	9:32–38	76–77
3:13–18	46	9:34	77
3:19	20	9:38	79
3:25–26	46	10–11	157
3:26	47	10:9–23	78
4:1	50	10:19	20
4:4	49	10:23–24	80
4:8–17	50	10:28	80
4:12–16	54	10:38	20
4:13–14	34	10:44–47	20
4:25	20	11:1–3	78
4:25–31	91	11:12	20
4:31	20	11:15	20
4:32–37	51	11:17	80
5	111	11:19–26	82
5:3	20	11:24	20
5:9	20	11:26	90
5:12–16	54	11:28	20
5:29–42	56	12	27, 89
5:32	20	12:6–11	125
5:34	56	12:12	28
6:1–7	60–61	12:12–14	91, 113
6:5	20	12:20–25	83
6:7	49	12:24	83
6:7–9	64	13:1	20
6:8–15	64–65	13:1–2	91
6:9–10	39	13:1–3	91
6:10	20	13:1–4	91
6:14	107	13:4	20
7:51	20	13:5–12	91–92
7:54	20	13:9	93
7:54–8:1	66	13:13	113
8:1–8	68	13:14–16	94
8:15–19	20	13:26–32	94–95
8:20–25	70–71	13:38–39	95
8:26–36	21	13:46–48	95–96
8:29	20	13:47–48	21
8:32–35	73	13:52	20
8:34	73	14:1–7	97
8:39	20	14:11–20	98
9	62, 113, 157	14:21–25	100
9:1	67	14:28	101
9:1–6	68	15:1–4	107
9:1–19	49	15:5	110
9:4	68	15:6	56
9:15–16	99, 157	15:10	111
9:17	20	15:16–18	21

15:19–21	111	22:3	56
15:22–29	157	22:5	167
15:36–41	113	22:17–20	158, 160
16:1–5	118	22:17–22	157
16:6–7	121	22:22–29	159
16:9	23	22:24	56
16:11	23	22:28	94
16:11–15	122	22:29	167
16:12	24	23:1	159
16:18	124	23:2	160
16:25–34	124	23:11	159, 168
17:4–9	127	23:12–22	160
17:10–14	128	23:17–35	159
17:16–20	131	23:26	23
17:30	20	23:27	160
17:32–34	131	24:6–10	160
18:9–11	134	24:21	160
18:10	135	24:22	160
18:12–17	135	24:25	56
18:18–23	140	24:27	167
19	141	25:1–12	160
19–20	150	25:12	159
19:1–7	141–42, 142	26:1–32	160
19:10	143	26:11–15	168
19:11–20	143–44	26:19–23	158
19:20	143	26:28	160
19:26	143	26:29	167
19:35	143	26:30–31	56
20:1–21:28	144	26:32	167
20:2–5	145	27:10	169
20:7–12	145	27:21–26	169
20:17–35	101	27:25	20
20:19–21	146	27:31–38	169
20:22	20, 167	28:21	94
20:22–23	160	28:21–29	171
20:22–24	167	28:30–31	172
20:23	20		
20:28	20, 146	**Romans**	
20:36–38	147	1:18–32	112
21:11	20, 160, 167	6:1–6	37
21:12–14	147	8:6–11	11
21:13	167	14:16–18	53
21:17–25	156		
21:21	160	**1 Corinthians**	
21:27–36	160	1:1–2	134
21:33	167	1:26	136
22–23	90		

SCRIPTURE INDEX

2:3	134
6:11	37
6:12–20	112
8–10	120
8:1–13	112
9:20–22	141
16:2	141

2 Corinthians

5:10–11	137
5:20	137
11:25–32	144

Galatians

2:11–16	81
3:25–27	37

Philippians

1:13	161
2:20–22	119
4:22	161

Colossians

2:11–12	37
4:10	114
4:14	23
4:16	143

1 Timothy   129, 130

3:1–7	101

2 Timothy   129, 130

1:5	119

Titus   129, 130

3:5	37

1 Peter

3:21	37
5:1–4	101
5:13	114

Revelation

2–3	143

OTHER SOURCES

Apocrypha

2 Maccabees

1:11–12	83
1:17	83
7:31–36	83
9:4–6	83
9:11	83
9:18	83

JEWISH

Jubilees

1:1–26	33

Dead Sea Scrolls

CD 14:8–10	33
1 QS 1:20–21	33

Mishnah

Peach 2:6	56
Orlah 2:12	56
Shekinah 3:3	56
Yebamoth 16:7	56
Sotah 9:15	56
Gittin 4:2–3	56
Aboth 1:16	56